Enjoy your journey!
Heart Hugs
♡
Pamela Edwards

My
KALEIDOSCOPE
EYES

A JOURNAL JOURNEY WITH
RETINITIS PIGMENTOSA

PAMELA EDWARDS

BRONZEWOOD
BOOKS
EDEN PRAIRIE, MN

My Kaleidoscope Eyes

A Journal Journey with Retinitis Pigmentosa

Published by
Bronzewood Books
14920 Ironwood Ct.
Eden Prairie, MN 55346

Cover & Interior Design: Bronzewood Books

Edited by: Susan Stradiotto

Library of Congress Control Number: _____

Paperback ISBN-13: 978-1-949357-32-5

eBook ISBN-13: 978-1-949357-31-8

Printed in the USA

DEDICATION

I dedicate this book to my children Sarah Jane Moore, Tim Moore, and Alice Slaikeu. You are always my love energy force that illuminates my life. I am honored to be a part of your beautiful lives. You help me to grow. Heart hugs, always.

To my cherished husband, Donny. You allowed me to have time to find out who I really am. By doing that, we also discovered who we are. I love you. Heart hugs and joy.

Mostly I dedicate this book to ME. By going back and daring to peek at who I was going through this journey, I have brought the past me and now me, into one being. I am one with who I am and give myself a lifelong heart embrace.

IV

EPIGRAPH

THE PEACE OF WILD THINGS

by Wendell Berry

When despair for the world grows in me
and I wake in the night at the least sound
in fear of what my life and my children's lives may be,
I go and lie down where the wood drake
rests in his beauty on the water, and the great heron feeds.
I come into the peace of wild things
who do not tax their lives with forethought
of grief. I come into the presence of still water.
And I feel above me the day-blind stars
waiting with their light. For a time
I rest in the grace of the world, and am free. [1]

---

1   Wendell Berry, New and Collected Poems (Berkeley: Counter Point, 2012)

PREFACE

THIS IS GOING TO be one of the hardest things I've ever done. I'm going to travel through my emotions and let them show raw and frail as I go back for the very first time and expose my journey of going blind with retinitis pigmentosa (RP) starting in 1991. I have ten years of journals before this, but my focus is on this story.

This journey is going to be a selfish one.

I need to do this to somehow show myself that I am worth it, that I am not going day to day just being punished and made to go through my tragedies. There must be a reason for everything I've endured. Yes, I've gotten strong with every step, but I must remind myself of the great joys that have also come.

This passage brought me to massage, which I am very thankful for. I don't think of it as a job and never have. It's an opportunity to focus on the unconditional positive regard I feel and see in all my clients. And in the process, if I help someone, it is an extra delight to me.

I have started and stopped writing this book several times throughout the years. I first wanted to write so no one else would feel as lonely as I did the first several years after diagnosis, but it never felt completely right. The desire grew again during the past couple months, so much so, that it kept getting stronger until last week when I had a major epiphany, an idea that just felt so comfortably right.

I can't stop the flow of thoughts. It is 1:54 A.M. and I'm up writing because my mind won't hold anymore thoughts. I need to write them down knowing some of this will probably get edited out in the end, but that's okay. I'm writing this in the style I've become accustomed to through my 33 years of journaling. And so, with one deep breath and searching for my inner strength, I will start my kaleidoscope journey.

ACKNOWLEDGEMENTS

I WANT TO THANK my quiet angels who lifted and carried me through this journey. When I thought I couldn't continue, you were my wings. I appreciate you deeply.

Alphabetically: Barbara Anderson; Alicia Burgers; Joan Cassellius and her grandsons Eli and Jordy Cassellius; Kathy Duval; Shana Farrell; Rhende Hagemeister; LuAnn Scharmer; Kim Underdahl; and Nichole Wegner. Heart hugs to all.

To Angela Foster who read through and critiqued my earlier manuscript with helpful insights and encouragement. Heart hug.

Thank you isn't enough to say to my dear niece, Jessica Hooppaw, who transformed my writings into gems viewing my kaleidoscope world. You brought fresh eyes into every facet of each chapter. It was a delight and pleasure to have your thoughtful brainstorms. You also motivated me through those rough chapters encouraging and empowering me to go on. Heart hugs forever.

To Barbara Anderson for doing an edit, read-through, and writing the "About the Author" section. Heart hug.

To Susan Stradiotto who transitioned my thoughts into reality and captured my author photo. I am now a published author thanks to you. Heart hug.

FOREWORD

by Kim Underdahl

WITH THE ARTISTRY OF a memoirist, Pamela Edwards draws her personal extraordinary journey after learning she had been diagnosed with retinitis pigmentosa. She was told by doctors there was no cure and that she would eventually go totally blind.

My Kaleidoscope Eyes is a declaration of intent, a map into the longing of the soul and the desire to live passionately when coming face to face with a life changing sensory impairment.

As she spiraled down into the depths of the darkness where RP kept her captive, pain, self-defeating and negative hate surrounded her. She fought desperately to tweeze out the fragments of some positive ray of hope that kept her going.

"Don't give up! Your goal of sharing your story, the RP part of your story, is there." She heard, and was encouraged, and so she did.

You are holding in your hands a profound journal journey written by this amazing woman who found strength, wisdom, and courage to prevail through her transforming experiences. She is an inspiration for what she has done with her life considering her different ability.

She ran her own massage business for 22 years and found healing through massaging others. Healing and giving comfort to others showed her she was worth something and realized what a gift she had through massage.

Today, she functions as a normal person within her environment with her kaleidoscope life shining brighter than ever before. The dance with RP she has chosen to share with us will leave you with soul food for the mind and heart.

Joy is now her word for her journey.

Chapter One

Broken Bits and Pieces

March 1991

Howl, yip, yip, yip, howl!

I awaken from my slumber to the cries of nature, from calm and relaxed to . . .

Where am I?

"Yip, yip, yip, Hooooowl!"

Again, I hear yelps and realize the coyotes are gathering in packs as a family unit, serenading the night sky, creating a bond that dates back centuries. Living five miles from the nearest neighbor, I've become accustomed to the coyotes' midnight gatherings and know this is life in northern Minnesota. They are harmless, their yips and howls are comforting until they fade off into the distance.

A flood of memories suddenly drowns me, and tears begin flowing down my cheeks as I remember where I am and the direction my life has recently turned. Not wanting to face the glare of those scenes, of their reality, of their numbing pain, I decide to see if I can relax with a cup of tea.

As I wander down the hall toward the kitchen, I am grateful I recently added night-lights to all the outlets in the house. I chuckle as I realize it looks as though I'm a plane being guided on a runway toward my destination. They help even though I wasn't aware of the slow fading of my surroundings.

You're clear for a landing, Pamela, a voice in my mind says as if over a loudspeaker. My approach toward the kitchen is a slow quiet descent and arrival. I add water to my green ivy print teakettle and turn on the stove.

Waiting for the water to boil, I visualize a scene from years ago on a hot humid night while living on Lake Wabedo in Minnesota. I sat on my deck, listening to the small wren like Veery Thrush singing its evening song, the last bird I heard each night. Its words of encouragement encompassed my heart with the warmth of love.

"Trill-trill, trill-trill, trill-trill, trill," it sings, and my heart hears these words: "Life is good. There is joy in every moment, and you can feel it in your heart if you listen, listen, listen, hold on."

Its song was a series of trills that started on a higher pitch then gradually lowered. With each note I breathed deep, letting out fear that had enveloped me throughout the day. It would be okay; everything had always worked out for me—I could go on.

The whine of the teakettle brings me back to the kitchen where I prepare a delicious chamomile blend, wafting in its fragrance while wiping away a stray tear. I move to sit at the 1950s style red and white kitchen table with silver legs, taking deep breaths while sipping my tea.

Another delight enters my thoughts: my four-year-old daughter, Alice, running exuberantly around the table. She's dragging a long string of yarn behind her, squealing at each attempt made by Rex, our gray striped kitten, to attack her. He ran after the string and would sometimes take a shortcut under the table to surprise and amuse her.

I finish my tea and feel the urge to seek out my daughter's room. Following my lit path down the hall, I approach her doorway. Leaning upon its open frame, I'm paralyzed, unable to breathe or even enter. The night-light glows softly around her single bed. She is curled in a ball surrounding Rex in an embrace of total warmth. Her golden hair is spread in every direction on her pillow, across her face, and a few strands are covering Rex. Can I describe her face, its delicate features? Will I remember her soft four-year-old appearance?

I want the world to stop, to push the pause button so I won't forget.

At the end of her bed, against the wall, is a two-story playhouse; the entire front opens, showing a variety of rooms. I bought it years ago in hopes that I would someday have a daughter. Now, I love how she spends time creating adventures in her make-believe world.

Cautiously, I step into the room, hoping not to make a sound. Reaching forward to trace a curl on her forehead, I kiss her gently, a kiss that I will always hold dear and remember with continual love energy.

Rex stretches and looks up at me as if to say, "It's going to be okay."

Slowly, I retrace my steps and continue on—I have two more children I need to memorize.

My son, Timmy, is seven years old and sleeps in a bedroom near the front door. The lit hallway guides me to where I see him snuggled under his sheets. His sweet face has a gentle, soft smile as he exists in his dream world full of his joys. In the dim light, I can barely make out a line of trucks and cars along the wall, ready for tomorrow's adventures. I know it is also an attempt to make things safe for me, so I won't trip on them.

"Sleep well my dear little man," I say, gently kissing his forehead with a 'love you forever' kiss.

I'm reminded of his escapade from yesterday. I heard Rex continually meowing but couldn't find him. The sound eventually led me to Alice's room where Timmy had trapped Rex within the playhouse! It was rather amusing, seeing the desperate look of a kitten face pressed against the tiny window, showing mournful help me eyes—Rex and Alice didn't think so.

This past month has handed Timmy a new awareness of this changed life. As the only boy in the family, his thoughts took on the feeling he should be able to help take care of me. He's always had such a caring heart, and I love him deeply for this. I wish something could be done, but we don't have all the answers yet.

Then there is Sarah, my growing up too fast, oldest daughter, who is ten years old. Once again, I follow the runway lights that bring me to her room. Her shadowed silhouette is spread across her bed, as if not knowing which placement she would like, so she's trying them all at once. I reach for a wayward hand and replace it on the bed, giving it a tender, deep 'love you' kiss.

Today, I enjoyed our afternoon as she helped me rearrange the living room. The piano found a position where we created a joyful scene: she played her trumpet and I played the piano while Timmy and Alice danced around.

Sarah fills me with joy as she deciphers solutions for every segment of the day, but there isn't a resolution for today's problem. How will I care for her now?

I had the answers. Well, at least I thought I did, and then the world tipped me out, tossing me aside as a useless fall leaf drifting toward the unknown.

Will I be able to memorize her zest for life? What about her love of assisting anyone who needs her help, or that giving is more precious to her than receiving?

I cannot let go of these thoughts, of feeling unable to hold their cherished preservation. It's like grabbing at a cloud of smoke and watching my fingers slide through, empty . . . as empty as my heart feels. I must try no matter how painful. The pictures will fade away and I will lose again.

Try.

Keep trying.

Listen, listen, listen . . .

Chapter Two

THE PLUSES AND PERILS OF PAMELA

I am a hole in a flute that the Christ's breath moves through—Listen to this music. I am the concert from the mouth of every creature singing with the myriad chords.[1]

—Hafiz

REFLECTION, PRESENT DAY

As I OPENED MY journal written in 1991, the first thing to catch my attention was that I had named it "The Pluses and Perils of Pamela." I must have felt a real struggle already in my life and knew I had to go on.

It had been 25 years since I penned the words. Reading them for the first time brought back feelings of sorrow for the younger version of myself who did not yet know that retinitis pigmentosa was about to storm into my beingness and upend

---

1   Daniel Ladinsky, trans. *The Gift: Poems by Hafiz the Great Sufi Master*, 1999. New York: Penguin Compass, 2014.

my life in ways I could never have imagined.

Life had already changed dramatically two years earlier in 1989. Our family was living in the country on Lake Wabedo, eight miles from Longville, Minnesota, a small town with a population of 130 located in the center of the state about level with Duluth. Tim, my then husband, was a realtor in town and I was working as secretary at Town and Country Flooring, trying to add income to our family.

Tim was eleven when his mother died, and his father remarried soon after her death. I always felt he treated women as less than equal. We never discussed decisions, and I only learned about some major financial decisions after the fact. I attempted to learn more about these things, but he denied me.

A glowing ember lay deep inside me, exploding, like a burning spark in the bottom of an abyss. I felt I could no longer stay married. With each day's contrast, I felt fuel being added to that hunger. Was there more to life, to me, and for my children than what we were living? Could I extinguish the flame before it roared into unbearable agony and snubbed me out? It was one of the hardest decisions I ever made.

After the divorce, I started dating Donny Edwards, a man who was helping with carpet installation where I worked during the winter months while he was laid off. Otherwise, he worked out of town, doing heavy equipment operations in varying locations and coming home to the family farm on weekends where he lived with his youngest brother, David.

Donny was eleven years older than me, seemed to have a gentle heart, and took interest in me. He lived his whole life seven miles from Longville on a farm in Lake Inguadona and was eleventh of thirteen children, having seven sisters and five brothers. At the time, Donny was also divorced with a fifteen-year-old daughter, Ann, who lived in International Falls, Minnesota with her mother.

As I read the entries from 1991, I was living in the country about ten miles from Backus, Minnesota, a small town with a population of 250. Previously, we lived in Longville, Minnesota, which is nineteen miles to the northeast with an even smaller population of 150. As the welcome sign at the city limits says, "Longville is a destination vacation." A quaint quiet town with two roads that form a T. Busy summer days are filled with tourist shops, ice cream stands, and realtors, all trying to make the best living possible during the few short summer months. My rental property, the house I'd moved into after the divorce, had been sold. Due to lack of rental housing in Longville, the situation forced me to look elsewhere for my children and me to live.

In my mind's eye, I pictured the scene of the mile long, snow covered driveway with embankments reminiscent of snow mountains lining the wooded path toward our new home. The chimney billowed puffs of smoke from the basement wood-burning stove. The sky was a beautiful shade of blue giving me a new word, blue-tiful.

Inside, I kept the comforts of home to try to maintain a sameness in our new lives while we were seeking a familiar path. The Christmas tree leaned toward the wall in the living room, making everyone feel as if they had to tilt their heads to correct the distortion. Donny had used a rope and nail to secure the tree to the wall. We decorated the rope with strands of tinsel, uniformly outlining its direction.

The children and I had chuckled when Donny arrived with the tree. He and his brother were out cutting trees, and Donny was on the look out for the perfect tree to surprise me. Finding none, they spotted the top of a spruce. Donny pulled out his rifle, and after four shots, it came crashing down.

Any tree would have been a treat that year, as I had decided to forgo one.

✐ANUARY 1, 1991

I SPENT A CRISP ten-degree New Year's Eve with the kids at Donny's. A few minutes before midnight, David and Donny had to assist a cow giving birth by pulling a calf. The kids and I saw the curled wet form lying next to its mother when it was about ten minutes old.

Alice said it was gross.

✐ANUARY 2, 1991

The kids are at their dad's for a stay until Monday. I'm not used to having them gone. I went to choir practice at church. I'm directing. There are only five to ten people in the small choir, but I really like it.

ℛEFLECTION, PRESENT DAY

MUSIC HAS BEEN A big part of my life ever since I can remember.

As a child, I sang in church choirs. Piano lessons started when I was in second grade. Flute came in the fifth grade. In high school, I decided to go into a music career to be a teacher directing either a choir or a band, while sharing my love for the moments that music can transition your life. I went to college to pursue a career in music, but in my secod year, I dropped out to get married, thinking that was what women were supposed to do. Two weeks before the wedding, my fiancé backed out. Shattered, I didn't return to college and I met my first husband in Minneapolis, MN. Still, my arms had a sensation, a passion to move and feel the vibrations of music's graceful rhythm as it passed through every fiber of my being.

Directing the Salem Lutheran Church Choir from 1989-1991, and the Longville Community Choir in 1989, were very memorable moments for me.

Maybe my journey would one day include directing again, but music would always be in me, flowing out to calm and enhance my way, no matter what.

After the divorce, I wanted to play an instrument that I could sing along with. The guitar seemed too ordinary, so I chose the mandolin. Along with the piano I brought from my parents' house, I have a keyboard that Donny gave me as a birthday gift. A Native American flute is another gem that I dearly love to play. Its mellow tones soothe and satisfy with haunting rhythms flowing out to nurture my soul.

JANUARY 5, 1991

DAVID, DONNY, AND I went downhill skiing for the first time of the season. The snow was good, so it was easy gliding down the slopes. I love the freedom of meandering from side to side toward the bottom with such grace, ease, and feeling carefree. I fell a couple times, but not as bad as last year when I tried a more difficult hill.

REFLECTION, PRESENT DAY

During our early years of dating, Donny and I skied a lot. We even had our own sets of skis.

I miss the sensation of gliding on top of the world, gradually making a path to the valley, riding the lift back to the top, then repeating another journey.

Life takes changes and requires adjustments. I haven't adjusted or come up with a comfortable solution for this change—my diagnosis—yet. But today, I'm sure I could manage recapturing those sensations of skiing if the opportunity and desire arose.

January 6, 1991

I went to church, directed the choir, and taught Sunday school grades 3-4.

At 4:00 p.m., I went to a Cursillo Ultreya, the Lutheran church in Hackensack, Minnesota, and played my mandolin. A lot of people were there, but I was the only one from my church.

The Cursillo community, through our church, is a nationwide group that gets together to uplift people through their faith. I discovered it after my divorce two years earlier and have found it very comforting.

January 7, 1991

I worked in the Hackensack office today. The kids came home from their dad's at 6:00 p.m. Now the house doesn't feel so empty. It's so good to have them home. I'm trying so hard to start my new life on my own, raising my kids. I am working for Cass Company Insurance spread out through their three offices. Living here, in the country, near The Long Pine Store on Minnesota Highway 84, does have the benefit of heading approximately fifteen miles to each of the towns: west to Hackensack, south to Pine River, or north to the Longville office.

JANUARY 12, 1991

ALICIA IS SIX WEEKS older than me and has been my best friend since we were introduced to each other in 1980. Our lives are so similar that we usually are thinking the same thoughts. We have children close in ages, too. Today, we went shopping in Brainerd, saw the movie *Home Alone*, ate at the First Street Café, and had a slumber party at her house. Her husband Doug was at the Bemidji Hospital for an EMT class. We really had a great time. I cherish her friendship and support as we continually come up with solutions to problems or share a belly laugh when it seems most needed.

REFLECTION, PRESENT DAY

ALICIA AND I HAVE been dear friends since 1980, almost forty years now. We were both new in town; she moved here from Iowa and I, from Minneapolis, Minnesota.

"There's a new lady in town that I think you might like to meet," Dottie, a neighbor, told me one day. "She has a daughter about the same age as yours."

It's been a cherished friendship ever since. We held each other up during those early years and still do. Crafts became a way of connecting throughout time as we shared ideas for entertaining our children. We created a bond that is life essential.

True friends in every way.

Two peas in a pod.

JANUARY 18, 1991

MOM AND DAD CAME to visit from my hometown in

Wisconsin, Glenwood City, a small farming community with a population of about 800 people. Dad owns an electric business and Mom is a secretary at Holy Cross Lutheran Church. Their visits are rare with such a distance to travel, 235 miles. I didn't tell the kids they were coming, so they were really surprised.

Dad made bookshelves for each of the kids. It really organized their rooms.

I made a photo album for their fortieth wedding anniversary and gave it to them. Dad said it was the best gift.

JANUARY 21, 1991

MARTIN LUTHER KING, JR. Day and I didn't have to work.

Dad was supposed to have exploratory surgery on his prostate, but they decided to do a scope instead. They didn't find anything, so they sent him home. He sounds very frustrated. He's been taking medicine since last Thanksgiving.

I took Sarah to Dr. Marvin in Pine River for an annual eye exam today. Everything is okay. Since my glasses are incredibly old and worn, and it seems very hard to read through the scratches, I made an appointment for myself for next month.

JANUARY 29, 1991

SARAH AND TIMMY GOT on the school bus.

I worked in Longville, but because Alice was scheduled for early childhood screening, I had to take her to Sue, her daycare lady in Backus, instead of Darlene in Longville.

Alice had to hop on one leg, whistle, arrange blocks, say

her ABCs, and count to 100, which was very easy for her as she loves to count everything. They checked her eyes and hearing. She said they wanted her to pee in a cup, and she didn't want to because it was gross: I think that's her new word of the year. They also tested her blood.

January 31, 1991

I worked in Longville and took Alice to Darlene's daycare. It finally worked out for her to spend the night with Kylee, Darlene's daughter, who is the same age as Alice. I miss her so much. It's her first time staying without Sarah or Timmy—I'll pick her up tomorrow night.

I got a movie for Sarah, Timmy, and me to watch, *My Side of the Mountain*. I saw it when I used to work at the theatre in Glenwood City when I was sixteen. That was my first job ever, besides babysitting.

I called Mom and Dad. Dad wanted to talk to Timmy. He told Timmy he's feeling better because of his prayers. Timmy felt very proud of that and said he was going to pray harder tonight.

February 1, 1991

I worked in Hackensack. There was a big board meeting during my shift.

Later, I was given a bonus check from working in 1990. I wasn't sure why. Then they told me they want me to cover the office in Longville on Wednesday and Thursday until spring. I don't understand that either . . .

Then it became clear.

"Next fall we will only need you to work four days a week."

I was upset. Now I need to find a way to bring in more money. A reduction in my income is going to make it harder for ends to meet. Should I look into going to school in the fall, but for what?

I pray for strength and peace.

REFLECTION, PRESENT DAY

THIS ENTRY MARKED ANOTHER confusing event in my new journey that I didn't understand. I felt I was doing all the right things and trying to build a solid, stable life for my children after a disruption, but roadblocks seemed to always be thrown at me.

FEBRUARY 3, 1991

I'M THINKING MORE ABOUT what schooling I need to go to. I'm leaving it in God's hands.

FEBRUARY 5, 1991

I HAD MY ANNUAL eye appointment in Pine River today with Dr. Marvin. He said I needed a new prescription and also there was a pigment build up in my right eye. He wants to dilate and take pictures. I'll go in for that on the 18th, though I'm not sure why I have to go back.

"Something just isn't right," he said. "When I dilate them, I'll be able to get a better look."

It's hard enough having to drive all over the place from town to town working and paying for gas. I don't know that I have time either. Dr. Marvin says I must bring a driver because I won't be able to drive after my eyes are dilated. I hope my friend, Jan, can help. She's such a good friend and is my sponsor for Cursillo.

FEBRUARY 9, 1991

I WENT TO DONNY's while the kids were at their dad's. We ate at Patrick's Supper Club in Longville with David. We stayed and danced as the band *Mixed Emotions* played. I used to be one of their members.

REFLECTION, PRESENT DAY

MY MIND FONDLY RETURNED to loving the friendship and the enjoyment I received from playing music with that group. We played rock from the 60s and 70s. I played bass, keyboard, sometimes my flute, and sang harmonies. My only solo song was "The Lion Sleeps Tonight" by the Tokens, which they had me sing that night.

I still get requests to sing that when I go to karaoke.

FEBRUARY 12, 1991

I'VE BEEN GIVING PIANO lessons again. I had eleven piano students at one time. I love sharing the joy of playing, but it's so difficult when all I hear are excuses why they didn't practice. If I could only get through to them the joys of a lifetime when you discover music and the sense of peacefulness it brings as you sink into its depths of soothing tranquility, escaping into another dimension, a world that is yours to make into any desire you have. It will surround you, lift your wings, and help you to soar through each beat in your journey.

Reflection, Present day

All was well.

That past was dim and distant, a single muted-tone facet in my kaleidoscope spiral and ever-changing path. Each moment created a new segment. I looked forward to my horizon where I could experience joy in my now and eagerness for what was to come.

I paused, sitting in that moment and appreciating all that had been, all that was, and all that the future held.

Chapter Three

IN THE BLINK OF AN EYE

Dost doubt? Art racked with difficulties? To excess?
Have patience. "Patience is the key of all success!"
Be abstinent. Let not thy crowding thoughts run wild.[2]

—Rumi

MONDAY, FEBRUARY 18, 1991; PRESIDENT'S DAY

AT NOON, JAN CAME to take Timmy, Alice, and me to the eye doctor in Pine River. Because there wasn't school, Sarah had stayed at a friend's the night before.

I was listening to the radio station WJJY, and it said there could be a bad blizzard, one of the worst of the season. The snow had already started by the time Jan arrived.

While at the eye clinic, Jan kept Timmy and Alice busy in the waiting room.

---

2   Jalal al-Din Rumi, *The Mesnevi: Trübner's oriental series*, trans. James W. Redhouse, Release Date March 31, 2020: 667–669, https://www.gutenberg.org/files/61724/61724-h/61724-h.htm

Dr. Marvin's assistant dilated my eyes and gave me a visual field exam to test the peripheral vision. I then waited in a small room with a machine sitting on a table that looked like a big white box. I placed a patch over one eye, rested my chin on a ledge, and stared at a spot at the back of the box with the uncovered eye. A flashing spot was to appear frequently inside the box in all directions.

She said, "Keep looking at the center spot at the back and press this button each time you see a flashing light."

She handed me a device that looked like a small tube. It was attached to the machine by a chord and had a button on one end. I did as instructed. It seemed like a waste of time because I barely saw the light and only pushed the button a few times.

Afterward, I waited alone in a cold room so small I felt slightly claustrophobic. I constantly thought about how Jan was doing with my children. They seemed interested in the books in the lobby, so surely they were fine. But the snow must have started accumulating; I wondered how much had fallen. I hoped it wasn't too bad yet. Ten minutes later, I was told that the machine printout didn't come out correct, so the doctor wanted the test to be redone. I wasn't looking forward to that because it was a hard strain on my eyes.

The second test showed the same results; I was whisked across the hall to Dr. Marvin's office. He came in and looked into my eyes with a bright shocking white light.

"I think you have retinitis pigmentosa," he said.

"I have what-osa?" I said, confused.

"Retinitis pigmentosa, it's a hereditary blinding disease that takes the peripheral vision away first, leading to a tunnel vision before total blindness," he replied.

He showed me a book and talked on and on about tunnel

vision. Legally blind. No cure or prevention. Fifteen degrees of vision remain. Depression . . . Specialist . . .

It was all a blur!

He wrote down the spelling of this new diagnosis—this new entity that was creeping into the room. I felt a coldness numbing me from deep within, a sensation very unfamiliar, but I also knew it was here to stay. The words had been spoken never to be taken away again.

Time could not rewind and change this story.

He handed me the number of a retinal specialist in Minneapolis, told me to make an appointment there, and said to call him if I had any questions.

Hand trembling, I took the paper. My words were stuck behind the lump in my throat and my eyes stung, so I blinked at him helplessly. *What questions? What could I ask? He wasn't talking to me, was he?*

Am I dreaming?

The first flood of tears came as I went to the waiting room and saw Jan reading to the children.

"I'm going blind!" I exclaimed. "I have retinitis pig-something."

She was also in disbelief as we quickly bundled up the kids for the journey through the ever-deepening snow.

"Oh my, how horrible!" she said as she quickly swiped her arm over her side of the windshield, brushing off her side of the now six inches of snow. It was coming down in sheets of white, so thick that you couldn't distinguish any flakes. There were only a few tracks in the road from courageous vehicles that had recently ventured through town.

After we were all settled in the car, I tried to see out my side, the passenger's side, the side that hadn't been swept off, but I couldn't.

I looked quizzically at Jan before saying, "That's okay, I'm going blind anyway."

We stared at each other, not really knowing how to react. I tried to laugh, but instead, more tears rolled.

Timmy asked, "Mommy, what's the matter?"

I said, through more tears, "The doctor just told me that I'm going blind!"

Without hesitation he shouted, "Oh goodie! We get a dog!"

REFLECTION, PRESENT DAY

DIAGNOSIS DAY FOR MY eyes, a day that I will never forget. Those first few words from my precious son have kept me going through all these years. Timmy's words helped me come out of the depths of despair that overwhelmed me. They helped me through the times I let the ocean of tears flow through my heart as waterfalls out of my soul to cleanse and refresh. His words held great joy, like the song of the Veery Thrush. They have redirected my path when I was ready, or even when I was not ready, to look toward my blessings.

MONDAY, FEBRUARY 18, 1991; CONTINUED

I WAS SCARED, BUT I held that thought tightly in until Sarah had returned home from her friend's house and all three were in bed. I called Mom, and at first, she thought I was joking until she could hear the tears in my voice.

"How do you spell that?" she asked

"R-e-t-i-n-i-t-i-s p-i-g-m-e-n-t-o-s-a," I spelled, then

pronounced, "Retinitis pigmentosa."

"I'll talk to the eye clinic in town tomorrow and find out more about it," she said. "I'm so sorry to hear this."

I heard Dad pick up the extension phone. Telling them about my day and what the doctor had said made the reality of it sink in. I cried, feeling their supportive words of concern and love. I felt a sense of calm knowing they would be there throughout this new journey, lifting me up, helping with solutions, and giving comfort.

Donny came to see me as soon as I called him, regardless of the blizzard that had dumped thirteen inches of snow and was now drifting with the gusting winds. He held me tight as I cried.

"Make it go away," I blurted. "I need to see, to be there for my children."

My world went silent. Donny could only hold me tight and listen.

*F*EBRUARY 19, 1991

I COULDN'T SLEEP LAST night. I was afraid to close my eyes; to wake in the morning, to open my eyes and see only dark. Not able to see ever again. I can't believe I'm going blind. It explains a lot though. It's always been hard for me to see when it's dark.

I called Dr. Marvin and had him make an appointment for me in Minneapolis for next week. Donny said he would take me. Mom and Dad want to be there with me too.

Dear Lord, please help me.

Sarah talked with her teacher about it. I'm trying not to excite the kids. A lot of people are praying for me.

Chapter Four

HIT REWIND

FEBRUARY 19, 1991

I WASN'T ABLE TO get much done at work today. I was at the Hackensack office and shared my news with friend and co-worker, Cheryl. She was concentrating on a list of numbers on the adding machine. Her right-hand fingers speedily flew as if all of them are waving at the same time while simultaneously staring at the list before her. Not once did she have to look at the accuracy of the numbers. The ribbon of rolled paper whirled with a steady rhythm.

I'm always mesmerized by the speed and calm surrounding her as she conducts her office task.

"I had an eye appointment yesterday and was told I'm going blind," I said to her while I filed papers in her office.

"Really, so you think I'll do all the paperwork from now on?" she said with an unbelieving chuckle.

"Dr. Marvin says it's retinitis pigmentosa, and there isn't

a cure. He's made an appointment for me to see a specialist in Minneapolis next week, so I'm going to need Monday off," I replied.

She started to realize then that I wasn't joking.

A flurry of questions my mind couldn't contain anymore, came blurting out: "Will I remember what my children look like?" I asked. "How am I going to get around without driving? What job is going to hire me? How am I going to support the kids and myself? How am I going to tell if I have my period?"

"Well," Cheryl said as if she had the answer for the last question. "Your dog will tell you."

We laughed and cried at the same time as we tried to embrace the pain away.

FEBRUARY 20, 1991

ALICE IS FIVE YEARS old today! Sarah, Timmy, and I woke her with traditional songs and gifts. Dad once told me little girls should always get dolls for presents and she had such excitement in her face. After opening the gift of the new doll, she wanted breakfast in my bed: scrambled eggs, grape jelly on toast, and orange juice.

I worked in Pine River today and mistakenly left my car lights on; the battery was dead when I was done with work. I calmly prayed for quick help and got it. A man was walking by and I asked him for help.

"I just bought jumper cables," he said as he pulled them out of the bag he was carrying and helped me get my car going.

Wow! Thank you, God, for always watching over me. I needed to be reminded of that.

*F*EBRUARY 21, 1991

THE WORD OF MY diagnosis had gotten out, and as I worked today in Longville, a lot of people stopped by to tell me they were praying for me. There was an ache with each time the door opened, and another face entered. Each one entering made my hurt sink deeper into knowing it was for real, it wasn't going away, it was here to stay and do its damage.

I met with Pastor Monson at noon for a private healing service. That refreshed me a little.

Darlene's daycare had a birthday party for Alice. She was so thrilled. I'm glad this hasn't disrupted her little world.

*F*EBRUARY 22, 1991

I DROPPED THE KIDS off at their dad's in the morning. I really hated to see them go today. They help me forget about my problems.

When I got home, I noticed my front door was open three inches with snow drifting in. The basement door was also open. A disturbing realization came to me; someone had been in my house. I had to get keys for the kids and keep the house locked from now on. It was so unsettling to know I had an intruder. I didn't see any evidence, though, so maybe it was just the wind.

*F*EBRUARY 24, 1991

MY EARLIEST INTEREST IN music came to me as a young girl singing in the children's church choir. I loved the happy tunes that seemed to keep the world shining. Then one Sunday, the congregation sang "What Wondrous Love Is This," a hymn that sounded haunting. It caught my attention, and I wanted to know why it was different. I later discovered that it was in a minor key, whatever that was. A new facet to my world entered with intrigue and delight. The spiral of desire to know different textures of music increased throughout the years. Like a magnet, music drew my focus into a lifelong world.

My racing mind remembered that day long ago. It seemed fitting and comforting to have the Salem Lutheran Church choir sing that song today. As I directed the small group, I felt embraced and uplifted. My arms flowed to the gentle rhythm. A sense of peaceful calm settled into my heart for a brief moment.

I'm nervous about tomorrow's eye exam in Minneapolis. My mind has so many questions, and yet, I really have no clue what I should be asking. I'm so glad that I have people who will be there to support me.

FEBRUARY 25, 1991

DONNY AND I LEFT at three o'clock in the morning, heading south to the Cities[3] for the over three-hour journey to my appointment. Mom and Dad arrived shortly after we did, and I was surprised that my sister, Joan, was also with them. I couldn't believe she came.

She said, "I want to support you through this in any way that I can."

I was so thankful to be embraced by that surrounding love. It was a buffer cushioning me from the pain and terror that had started to dwell deep within.

---

3   Publisher's note: This is short for Twin Cities, also known as Minneapolis and St. Paul, Minnesota and the surrounding suburbs.

While waiting to be called, I saw a lady with a white blind cane—Is that going to be me soon? I can't stand to think about that right now. I'm so scared.

It took six hours at Park Avenue Medical Building to complete all the tests.

They dilated my eyes, which made them sore. The pain intensified when they told me to open them as wide and as long as I could while they shined a bright light into them. The lady doing it wasn't very nice at all and kept getting mad at me but I was trying the best I could.

I only saw Dr. Gilbert briefly when I was finished with all the tests. He handed me a brochure about blindness.

"Yes, you have retinitis pigmentosa," he said. "Go home; learn Braille. Don't have any kids because it's hereditary. And find a job doing something without sight—preferably, an occupation where you can help others, because there is nothing we can do for you. Helping others will keep you from getting depressed."

That was it.

Nothing compassionate about it at all.

It was like he was proud to tell me, and that was his job. Have a nice day!

Retinitis pigmentosa—no cure . . . no treatment . . . no transplant . . . no surgery . . . no nothing. They didn't know how far it would progress or how fast. It could have been a month, a year, or thirty years. If I wasn't already numb from shock, his words would have devastated me, but I didn't think I could feel any worse.

Mom and Dad were heartsick and blamed themselves for passing this on to me. I tried to reassure them it wasn't anything they did, and I would be fine. Saying goodbye to them was so hard. I didn't want to let go. I wanted them to take me back home again, to the day when this wasn't part of my life. Like, maybe if I could rewind time and replay the visit to the doctor, the diagnosis wouldn't be real.

But it was real.

After long hugs, we parted and went our separate ways. They headed east while we ventured north.

Donny sat in silence on the ride home. He didn't know what to say. What was there to say? I tried to grasp it all, all the tests, what they meant. What was I going to do? I was going blind and was still a single mom with three young children.

Braille, hereditary, no cure, no hope, depression, darkness, disease . . . something unwanted, taking over my body, my world, my life. How did I let it in? I wasn't in charge anymore and never would be again.

I'm not normal.

I'm different now, and everyone will know.

My eyes flowed rivers of tears on that journey home. I was unable to read the brochure that I had been given.

The next week, I received a report of findings from the exam: "The periphery shows bone spicule pigmentations of moderate degree with pigment epithelial irregularities that would be fairly typical of retinitis pigmentosa. No treatment, of course, exists at the present time. Follow-up every two years is recommended."

FEBRUARY 26, 1991

MY EYES DIDN'T WANT to open this morning. They were so sore. I had to work in Pine River and pick up the kids from their dad's afterward. The phone rang steady all night. Donny called me; my friend LuAnn from high school called; my Aunt Barb from California called; Sarah's teacher called. So many friends were praying for me.

I had a dream the kids couldn't live with me anymore because I was blind. I also dreamt they were grown, but they didn't have any faces.

REFLECTION, PRESENT DAY

I HAVE ALWAYS HAD very colorful and vivid dreams. There were many of these in those first few days that I think I repressed. But when I woke each morning, I had feelings of sinking deeper and deeper, of being smothered—covered by the darkness and loneliness rolling in like a low fog consuming me. Slowly, it flowed in, surrounding my feet, ankles, getting deeper, thicker, with an all-encompassing intrusion.

My nightmares haunted me—dreams of never seeing my precious children again and only hearing them call my name in darkness, dreams where I couldn't see my girls dressed up for prom or Timmy in tux, or dreams of being at their weddings but only envisioning the splendor in my imagination.

Chapter Five

WATERFALL TEARS

I wish I could show you,
When you are lonely or in the darkness,
The Astonishing Light
Of your own Being.[4]

—Hafiz

FEBRUARY 27, 1991

I WORKED IN HACKENSACK and spent most of the day writing
to different foundations for retinitis pigmentosa information.
That was hard. I actually felt that if I could ignore this new
declaration, maybe it didn't happen and it would disappear,
just vanish back to where it came from.

Sarah and Timmy had problems with their house keys,
so they took an ax and chopped open the wood shoot door
in the back of the house. I told them they should've gone to
the neighbors, but oh, how wonderful of them to take the

---

4   Daniel Ladinsky and Hafiz, *I heard God Laughing: Poems of Hope and Joy,*
(United States: Hampton Roads), 1.

problem and come up with a solution. Besides, it's winter and the closest neighbor lived a mile away.

*F*EBRUARY 28, 1991

I WORKED IN LONGVILLE today.

I find it depressing when well-meaning people stop by to give me a hug and say they're praying for me. Stop it! With each person knowing, it becomes more real. How can it go away if you keep giving it attention? But I can't ignore it and find myself testing my vision in different ways to see if it's true.

I held my arms straight out, palms facing away from me, fingers spread and thumbs touching. As I looked at where they touched, it became real. I panicked when I couldn't see my fingers! Even wiggling them I couldn't.

How can this be? How did I not see this coming? Okay, yup, I had to put that pun in there to lighten my mood or I'll go crazy.

I had too many questions with no answers. Dr. Marvin called to see how I was doing. He wanted the truth, so I told him.

"I'm scared," I said. "I want the diagnosis to go away. I'm having nightmares and don't know where to turn anymore."

He was sympathetic and explained again about what was happening with my eyes. This time I wasn't as traumatized and was able to grasp some of what he said. Evidently, the pigment cells of the retina were dying, and the debris formed bone spurs. This happened with the peripheral, outer vision first, leaving the center and causing a central tunnel field of view.

Dr. Marvin continued. "The retina has two types of cells,

rod and cone cells. The rod cells affect the lightness and without them, it's harder to see at night. They also control glare from bright lights, so as they diminish, a halo-type glow is seen around objects. The cone cells of the retina affect the colors and how you see them."

This would explain why I have always adjusted to situations of colors and brightness without having a clue that I had a vision problem. I assumed everyone saw like that and I needed to pay better attention. As I walked, I always looked down at the ground and scanned for where my foot is landing. Whenever I played games with the kids, I couldn't tell between the colors blue-green, pink-orange, or brown-purple. I usually sat where the light was the brightest but not glaring.

For years, while I was driving, I told the children to tell me if they see a deer, not by pointing, but by telling me where it was. We almost made a game out of the travel to see who can see the most wildlife.

"I see a deer on Mom's side in the ditch," Sarah would say.

March 1, 1991

Timmy talked with his teacher about my eyes. He's afraid I will lose my sight overnight and it will hurt. I talked to him too and tried reassuring him that it wouldn't go that fast, maybe not at all, and it wouldn't be painful.

Oh, my poor precious children. What are you going through with this? It's so very hard for me to grasp even a shred of what it means, what the future holds for us. How can I possibly explain it to them without having them be afraid? I'm still trying to adjust to the divorce two years ago and now this.

Dear God, why? How will I go on? *Can* I go on? I can't

take this burden. I want to listen to your direction. Where do you need me to go? I'll try to listen, but I know you'll understand that, at the moment, I'm numb.

I can't hear the trill-trill, trill-trill, trill-trill, trill of my Veery Thrush.

*M*ARCH 2, 1991, AFTERNOON

IT WAS A DAY for housework. I made a list for everyone to choose their chores. We worked hard all day.

Now, I think, we'll go to dinner and a movie. I'm feeling now like there's so much to do before there's no sight.

*M*ARCH 2, 1991, EVENING

DONNY CAME AND TOOK us all to see the movie, *White Fang*. Timmy really liked it.

My oldest sister, Rita, who also lived in Wisconsin, called this morning. That was the first time I'd talked to her since my diagnosis. Mom also called to just check in. She said that her parents, Grandma and Grandpa Allram, are concerned and are praying for me. I still hadn't heard from my brother, Steve.

I miss my family now more than ever.

*M*ARCH 3, 1991

WE WENT TO CHURCH, and I had the choir sing, "Within the Shadow of the Cross." Sarah sang with us too. I received many comments on how it was the best the choir had ever sounded.

I love to direct.

We ate pizza at Donny's. I suspected he was having problems dealing with me losing my sight, but he didn't talk about it. I tried to understand his silence.

I went to a Cursillo event in Brainerd with members from church. I played my mandolin. The church was packed. I talked with a lady about my retinitis pigmentosa. She had just had surgery for a different eye disease and regained sight in one eye. Maybe, eventually, there would be a cure for me.

On the ride home, a friend told me of someone he knew in St. Paul who had worked with the blind for seven years.

I'll call her.

REFLECTION, PRESENT DAY

TODAY WAS FILLED WITH emotion as I traveled back in my journals—for the first time ever—to the early moments of my diagnosis. I secluded myself in my studio to relive each painful moment while trying to tell you my journey. I cried waterfall tears a moment earlier, but I felt refreshed and ready to continue sharing. I just needed more tissue.

I knew that I had become a vibrant, strong, and joyful woman. These journals were shining a light, showing me just how far I had come. With each past entry, I felt an uplifting surge of clarity in my desires to press through the pain toward a brighter future.

MARCH 4, 1991

I DIDN'T WANT TO work today, but I did. Alice wanted me to stay home with her. I really wanted to. She must have felt lost and lonely too, even though I tried ridiculously hard not to show my pain.

Tomorrow will be better for her, because I work in Longville and she will go to Darlene's daycare. She loves it so much more there. I'm running constantly and missing my children as they grow.

I called the lady from St. Paul. Her name is Deanne, and she will be visiting in two weeks with items to share about Braille.

*M*ARCH 12, 1991

WHILE I WORKED IN Pine River, I stopped at Dr. Marvin's office. He showed me the pictures he had taken of my eyes. He acted like I'm not supposed to worry, but then Dr. Gilbert said to learn Braille because there isn't a cure or prevention.

I cry a lot, but not in front of the kids. I'm so scared. I wish I knew more.

I gave a piano lesson to Jake. He came to the house with his mother, Vicki. She shared that she goes to massage school in the Cities and gave me a foot massage. That felt amazing.

"You should go to massage school," she said. "That would be perfect for you if you're going blind."

I don't know if I want to do that. I don't want to turn away from my passion for music. There must be something I could do in a music career . . . The only thing that comes to mind is a blind piano tuner.

*R*EFLECTION, PRESENT DAY

AND SO, THE DELICATE seed planted by Vicki, the notioof being a masseuse, was rejected, but still found a space within me to lay dormant until it would be noticed and be fertilized. All in God's timing.

Oh, my, here come the waterfall tears again.

Chapter Six

IN THE DEPTHS OF DESPAIR, A SEED IS PLANTED

MARCH 16, 1991

I MET WITH DEANNE this afternoon about her Braille classes in the Cities. She had some Braille books and other information. Looking at those huge books, even touching them, brought a huge feeling of despair as I felt my inner being retreating, collapsing down, and curling into indescribable gloom.

This was it, an acknowledgment of the beginning of the end of my world as I know it. Our first twenty minutes consisted of her holding me as I let the floodgates open and released the past months' unspent fears in unstoppable cascades. Yes, tears had fallen throughout those weeks, but nothing compared to that spiral of emotions. I believed the breakdown was because she knew my future.

Deanne was very tender-hearted as she showed the items she brought, objects to aid in my new journey toward blindness. As she presented each piece, I felt my world crumbling. Till now, I had been able to pretend this was happening to someone else. It really wasn't me, and I was watching a movie where I wasn't the main character.

First, she showed me four large books, thickly padded 12" x 10" x 1 ½". They looked like scrapbooks to put photos in, but they were Braille books full of raised bumps—no words, no pictures, just raised bumps lining only the pages on the right. The covers had the only words. As I reached for them, I felt as if I was reaching for a coiled snake, ready to attack and devour me.

She also gave me a manila envelope, which contained an eye mask, a slate, a stylus, and a Braille eraser. They were foreign objects to me that I didn't *want* to know anything about. Maybe at a later date, when I had to use them, I would.

I hope.

ℳARCH 20, 1991

DR. MARVIN TOLD ME of a lady in Texas who also had retinitis pigmentosa. Dorothy Stiefel lived in Texas, was sixty, and still had some central sight. She called me to share information about her support group, a newsletter she published, and a book she had written: *The Business of LIVING with Retinitis Pigmentosa.* She wanted to send me a copy, sounded very positive about life, and casually called it RP.

This feels like a ray of hope.

ℳARCH 24, 1991

LUANN, MY DEAREST FRIEND since I was in grade school, came from Wisconsin to visit for the weekend. Before she left, she started crying.

"Stop," I said. "It was so good to just be happy for the

weekend. Thank you so much for visiting."

I probably should have had a good cry session, but it felt normal not to. LuAnn had an uncle who also had RP and was mostly blind.

It's heart wrenching to know somebody who has a relative with it. It makes it more real. It isn't just a dream. It's a glaring reality I have to face it and do something about, because it is here to stay. I want to go back to before I was diagnosed and change the script, undo the pain.

ℳarch 26, 1991

THE GUSTAVUS ADOLPHUS SYMPHONY Orchestra played at St. Andrew's Episcopal Church in Grand Rapids tonight. I really wanted to go but couldn't find anyone else to go with. I avoided driving at night. I would have been devastated if I hurt someone because of my loss of night vision. Donny had a mud day off work, so he took me. He didn't enjoy it at all, but I think he enjoyed that I loved it.

At least that's what I want to believe.

ℛeflection, Present day

DARK PLACES SURROUNDED ME as I sank into an abyss that gripped me. My world as I knew it was gone, drifting off without noticing or caring that I wasn't along. This was new, unfamiliar, lonely, desolate, and oh-so-frightening.

Braille, in its existence, was to me an act of giving up, of allowing the murky, gloomy reality to slap into my face . . . this new face that didn't have eyes. In a blink, I wasn't whole anymore. Where was the hope in that? All that I knew, all that I embraced as my now, all my adjusting to single parenthood had been snatched out from under me. I couldn't stop the fall. I couldn't try. I just couldn't.

Somehow, in my depths of despair, I saw new facets in my kaleidoscope, bringing a subtle glimmer, yet they drew me toward a sustaining light that I had never seen or felt before. Those facets were built from the help and comfort offered by my friends and through allowing them to know my true self.

Focus on music reappeared, wrapping itself around my hurting heart as it always had throughout my life. I could escape as its melody lulled my mind toward relaxation, allowing me to forget about the dark. Healing me where I was with a persistent energy.

Chapter Seven

COME SOAR WITH ME

THE KITE

by Michael Driscoll

I often sit and wish that I
Could be a kite up in the sky,
And ride upon the breeze and go
Whichever way I chanced to blow.[5]

*M*ARCH 30, 1991

IT WAS EASTER, AND Mom and Dad came to spend the whole
weekend with us. We had a great time trying to fly kites in
a nearby field—a day to let go, gather laughs, memories,
and escape. March breezes were gusting, blowing all cares
away, perfect for launching the bright red kite my parents
brought. Wind and sun had previously melted the winter's
snow, letting the nearby field with stubbed corn stalks greet
us as we arrived.

---

5   Michael Driscoll, *A Child's Introduction to Poetry (Revised and Updated):
Listen While You Learn About the Magic Words That Have Moved Mountains, Won Battles,
and Made us Laugh and Cry.* (United States: Running Press, 2020), 11

Excitement was in every word as the children positioned themselves, listening to instructions from Grandpa Lee on how to accomplish lift-off.

"Sarah, hold the ball of string letting it ease out when the kite rises," he said, "Timmy, you take the kite and run as fast as you can, careful not to step on the tail."

Timmy was thrilled to show his expert running skills, one of his most favorite things to do.

Alice giggled with Grandma Lee while we watched Timmy's attempts and determination to launch the kite into the air. It didn't take long for him to finally get the right speed, let go, and watch it rise up, up, up while Sarah carefully let out more string as needed. She held tight against the tug on the string and soon gave her siblings their turns.

I watched the carefree wavering of the kite letting go, scripting a message to me of starting fresh and forgetting the darkness, rising up where nothing mattered.

The sky was greeting the arrival of spring with robin egg blue as the vibrant red kite was followed by a meandering tail repeating the kite's every single whim. Rising cotton-candy clouds gazed on, seeming to smile, which gave me a sense of beauty and uplifted my soul. In the distant woods I could hear the song of my Veery Thrush. I delighted in the sound entering my heart, creating a crescendo of the scene.

"Come soar with me," the kite beckoned. "Release all sorrow, all pain, and replace them with joy and memories of happy times. Gather yourself and flow whichever way you chance to."

✳ ✳ ✳

MOM HAD READ THROUGH all my RP information and found that I might be able to apply for the State Services for the Blind rehab program. Dad shared with me how deep his faith was and how I could rely on God's love to help me through everything. I'm so glad they were there to assist me through the heartache and struggle. I couldn't do it alone; I felt worthless and wanted to give up.

The flyer that was given to me in the Cities had addresses of different organizations for the blind. I had sent letters to all of them, asking for help weeks before and only received one reply. It was asking me for a donation. Not one word of encouragement or what I could do for help.

I've noticed that not many people want to be around me anymore. All I see on their faces is, *"Poor Pamela,"* or *"Boy, I'm so glad this isn't happening to me."* How can I presume to know how other people are feeling?

REFLECTION, PRESENT DAY

THANK YOU, MOM, FOR picking me up at this point and realizing I needed help to move one foot forward, to take a step toward not allowing myself to go deeper into self-pity and despair.

I was wasting away into seclusion from my own choices. I didn't call or visit friends after seeing their reactions. I felt nobody wanted to be with me anymore because all I could do was cry. They didn't know how to help.

This was the beginnings of depression enveloping me, covering me, allowing me to take comfort only in my disability. I would let the world go on without me. I felt too exhausted to find a way out of my ever-deepening tunnel.

*A*PRIL 5, 1991

MOM'S GENTLE GUIDANCE LED me to Ralston DuBois from State Services for the Blind[6] in Brainerd, Minnesota, about fifty miles south. He called, but didn't have too long to talk, so he said he'd send release forms for my records in Minneapolis to review.

I'm not sure what kind of services he offers, but I'm sure God is watching over me like Dad said.

I bought three pairs of amber sunglasses today. Dorothy, the lady with RP from Texas, told me they would help, and they really do. Right away, I noticed the glare isn't as bad and for that, I'm so grateful.

I was told at work today that part-time will start on May 1st.

I hope I hear from SSB rehab soon. I'm so glad that I can feel a small ray of God's comfort at times like this. I know His plan for me is good.

Trying to accept these changes is overwhelming.

*A*PRIL 11, 1991

MOM CALLED BECAUSE I wrote her about my part-time work. Her positivity sure is a boost for me. She's going to call for a hearing test for me. It's a side effect of RP called Usher's Syndrome—I can't take much more!

---

6   Publisher's note: State Services for the Blind of Minnesota is abbreviated SSB. Website as of this printing: https://mn.gov/deed/ssb/.

REFLECTION, PRESENT DAY

YES, THAT'S RIGHT. USHER'S Syndrome is another disease associated with retinitis pigmentosa. It causes hearing loss. So, not only would I be blind, but I wouldn't be able to hear either! I'd be another Helen Keller.

I thought, *Dear God, are you serious? I'm not that strong, and I don't want to be! That is just too much to face. I didn't think I could hurt worse, but the brick walls keep coming and I slam into them.*

Oh my, I was getting too sad again. I needed to change my focus and one of my favorite jokes came to mind . . . *What did the fish say when he swam into the brick wall?*

Dam!

I snorted with laughter to myself.

Chapter Eight

The Dream

But those who trust in the Lord, they will find new strength. They will soar high on wings like eagles. They will run and not grow weary. They will walk and not faint.

—*Isiah 40:31*[7]

*A*PRIL 13, 1991

I HAD A DREAM I was on an eagle's back flying through the sky. Later I told Thea, my pastor's wife, about my dream because she studies them. She told me the eagle has the sharpest eyes of all creatures and that my life's journey is going to soar like the eagle in my dream.

"Rely and put your trust in Him," she said. "He loves and cares for you deeply as He lifts you up and holds you in His hands."

I was soaring, flying, to where? I didn't know, but I sensed

---

7   Thomas Nelson Inc., *The Holy Bible: Revised Standard Version* (New York, 1972)

everything would be fine . . . just like it's supposed to be.

I sat on the back of a great eagle, taking in deep breaths of exhilarating joy and releasing all tension. I saw elegant details of white feathers on His head. I felt secure with my legs wrapped around His neck. He was completely in charge of my journey as long as I allowed Him to be. He became the source of my comfort as I relaxed on His back, breathing in an experience of pure exuberance.

A feeling of peace enveloped me as He carried me, soaring effortlessly. A beautiful, fluffy cloud surrounded us as we glided through it, soaring with an ever-present ease of momentum.

I was safe from harm. I was secure. I was loved.

We were one, traveling on a wonderful adventure. The eagle would use its powerful vision to guide me toward a voyage free from my world's limitations. I could do anything with the new knowledge deep within.

I am never alone, even in the shadows. We are one, a spiritual team seeking joy.

REFLECTION, PRESENT DAY

THIS WAS ONE OF my favorite dreams that recurred several times in the first year after diagnosis. "Let go and let God inside" was the message that came to me through this imagery.

I would love to experience it again, but all I need to remind myself of the peaceful soaring is to think of an eagle.

April 14, 1991

I AM UPSET ABOUT everything—work, RP, Usher's Syndrome. Mostly though, I don't want to have my ears tested. I can't deal with the RP yet to even think about losing my hearing too!

April 16, 1991

I DREAMED LAST NIGHT that there was a cure for RP. I remembered being able to see the stars. Now, when I looked at the night sky to see stars, I couldn't. When had they disappeared? I must have noticed they weren't there and realized something was wrong.

No cure. Those words dwell in me.

I wanted to change them and someone to tell me that what I had lost already would come back soon. How could I not have known I was having vision problems?

As a little girl, I remember sitting on the porch of Grandpa Lee's country home. The evening sky danced its dance as we watched for shooting stars. My cousins, brother, and sisters joined the search. The sky was so bright and full of billions and billions of stars.

I'm not sure when the decrease started as I aged, but now, I can't see the stars at all. I can see the planets though because they are brighter.

Reflection, Present day

THERE WAS A NASA space station in orbit, and I received emails telling me when it would travel over our home. It sent me the time, location in the night sky, and how long its journey would be over us. I was thrilled to still be able to see this.

Even through the pain in my heart over not seeing the stars anymore, I had to focus on the joy.

*A*PRIL 16, 1991, CONTINUED

MY MOODS ARE HARD to handle. There's so much happening to me. I don't have the time to just sit and grieve, so I do it a little at a time, all day long. I hurt so much! I keep praying and feel God has a plan for me. I have faith in what He's doing.

A story on KTIG, a Christian radio station that I listened to, told of a lady who had been blind since birth.

"I don't know anything different than to be blind," she said. "A so-called Christian friend once suggested that I wouldn't be blind if I had more faith."

The announcer said, "You should hit that person with your cane and tell her it wouldn't hurt if she had more faith."

That was great advice and a little humorous, but I didn't think I could do that. Well, okay . . . maybe if I had a cane.

But I'd probably miss.

*R*EFLECTION, PRESENT DAY

HUMOR IS SUCH AN odd way to hide shocking emotions. Throughout the years, I've heard many well-meaning people use it as a knee-jerk reaction when they're stumped at what else to say. Now that I do have a cane and have adjusted to these encounters, I know that I will never use it as a weapon.

April 18, 1991

TIMMY TURNED EIGHT YEARS old today. Sarah, Alice, and I woke him with gifts and birthday songs. He was so excited.

In the afternoon, I arranged a plane ride for us in Longville. The small plane had room for four people, so Timmy and Sarah went for the first ride. Timmy even got the opportunity to fly the plane. Alice, Donny, and I went next. Alice giggled the whole time. We flew over our house and I took pictures. And yes, I was a little surprised I could find it.

I'm never really sure what to expect with my eyes anymore.

Later that afternoon, Donny took us to his neighbor's farm, where we saw twenty newborn sheep.

"This was the best birthday ever!" Timmy exclaimed as I tucked him into bed that night.

It's so important to keep the happy times surrounding us, to direct our focus toward the positive. It reminds me of what Mom would tell me to do when the kids were having their fits.

"Change the subject," she would say. "Have them look out the window at the pink rabbit that just hopped by. Run with them to go find it."

It worked—every time. They forgot why they were so upset, even though they knew there was no such thing as a pink rabbit. Or was there? They had to find out.

May 8, 1991

I HAD AN APPOINTMENT in Brainerd for my ears. Everything was fine! I no longer had to worry about Usher's Syndrome. Oh my! What exciting news, but the joy wasn't as full as I thought it would be.

I want to be told the same thing about RP.

I want to wake from this nightmare.

May 9, 1991

Alice had kindergarten day in Backus, a town between Hackensack and Pine River. She got to ride a school bus for the first time. I went with her.

Later in the day, I played my mandolin for Timmy's second grade class and Sarah's fifth grade class. What enjoyment! Sarah's teacher gave me great words of encouragement to go back to school.

I went to the University in Eau Claire, Wisconsin after high school in hopes of being an elementary music teacher, but I let distractions take me away.

Could I really go back to school and become the music teacher I wanted to be since the second grade?

Reflection, Present day

Music was always going to be a huge part of me and had taken different forms, always evolving and changing, singing to my inner being.

Or could it be that my inner being sings to me?

May 16, 1991

I didn't sleep much last night. I was worried about meeting with Ralston from Social Services for the Blind.

But . . . it went very well. I qualified for their services. First, they would do an evaluation of my interests. He also provided information for similar services in Wisconsin and gave me a name of his client, Barbara, who gave him permission to share her number so we could contact each other.

She also has RP.

*M*AY 17, 1991

WHILE I WAS MOWING the lawn and close to the house, I ran over a baseball. It hit the house, ricocheted back and . . . SMACK! It hit me in the head above my right ear. The kids came running. Sarah got an ice pack, Timmy thought I should quit, and Alice got me a lawn chair.

*R*EFLECTION, PRESENT DAY

A FLASH OF A cartoon scene enters my thoughts; Tom and Jerry. Chasing around the house they go, and Tom steps on a rake that Jerry places in his path. POW! Stars and birds circling his head as he slumps to the ground.

That incident was the first of many, which made me pause and realize that I was indeed going blind. I remember how upset I was because I didn't see the ball. Before I started mowing, the kids had helped scour the yard picking up debris. I was shocked at the sudden jolt and pain of the intrusion into my world.

My children were so good and caring. My diagnosis was also theirs. They adjusted their lives also during this journey and have since grown into compassionate adulthood.

I can laugh about that incident now. I guess it's a blessing in disguise not to have to mow the lawn again.

May 22, 1991

I'm getting depressed, again, still.

I talked with a lady that represents the Wisconsin Office for the Blind and Visually Impaired[8]; she didn't have anything for me unless I moved there.

I talked with Barbara for the first time today. She gave me such strength, but just like with Dorothy, it was another depressing acknowledgment of what was happening to me.

Still, I feel so relieved to know someone that knows exactly what I'm feeling.

June 14, 1991

My friends, Cheryl and Alicia, came over to practice for the June Docks Jamboree, an anual music celebration in Longville. We developed our trio musical group over the past few years. They both played guitar while I joined in with keyboard, mandolin, or flute. Cheryl sang lead and Alicia accompanied with alto. I joined in as descant. We played a wide variety of songs, but mostly contemporary Christian music. Of all the music I've ever played, this was my favorite. Our harmony blended so well.

I feel guilty about having our practices at my house because I don't drive at night anymore. It sure is an awakening experience, being handicapped. I can notice change already. When I look at one person, I don't see the person to either

---

8   Wisconsin Office for the Blind and Visually Impaired, abbreviated OBVI. Website link as of the time of this publication: https://www.dhs.wisconsin.gov/blind/index. htm.

side of them.

$\mathcal{R}$EFLECTION, PRESENT DAY

I GUESS I REALLY didn't write much about my emotions. Looking back, I felt numb and like I was slowly becoming aware of my vision loss.

$\mathcal{J}$UNE 22, 1991

JUNE DOCKS JAMBOREE WAS today. We had a great time performing for the small crowd gathered in the warmth of the summer day. I was grateful for the canopy shading us from the sun and the gentle breeze coming from the lake: Alicia remembered clothes pins to secure our music from flying off the stands.

As we played, friends tapped their feet, clapped their hands, and moved to our offered rhythms. Joy was on all the faces supporting us.

Twelve other musical groups joined in the festivities during their designated time slots. All the names were placed in a bucket for three, $100, prizes. This was our third year playing and not winning, but we did it because we enjoyed it so much.

$\mathcal{J}$UNE 26, 1991

MOM CALLED TO SUPPORT me for tomorrow's testing with State Services for the Blind in Brainerd. She was worried about me because I was nervous. I lived so far away from her ... about a five-hour drive to see them. I loved driving and couldn't bear the thought that I wouldn't be able to anymore.

This test was another acknowledgment of going blind; I think that's what bothered me the most.

I feel so alone. Though, I know God is with me and that is a comfort.

I called my sister, Rita, and talked with her. I felt better after that.

June 27, 1991

The evaluation test at SSB took ninety minutes: math, spelling, memorizing numbers, job choices, and many other questions. I had been very nervous.

I panicked when I left to go to the SSB office at Brainerd Technical College for a financial aid packet. It was noon and people were everywhere. I was so afraid that I wasn't going to see someone or something.

Why didn't this ever bother me before? I've always been a very good driver without any tickets my whole life.

July 2, 1991

I made an appointment at the University of Minnesota and then canceled it when Mom said I didn't need it for two years. She told me to go to Dr. Marvin in Pine River for now for check-ups, if needed.

I cried most of the day.

I miss the kids when they're gone to their dad's—I hate being alone.

REFLECTION, PRESENT DAY

I CAN SEE JUST how much my parents and children were involved in this journey with me. They were walking with me, supporting me, and helping me. I couldn't see and they were my eyes. It reminded me of the poem, called "Footprints."

When, during the hard times of life, there was only one set of footprints in the sand, God said, "It was me that carried you."

In my case, I can look back and see all of their footprints too.

Chapter Nine

SPINNING SPIRAL

I HAVE A TERRIBLE headache and I usually don't like to take aspirin, but today, I did. Surely, it's just tension from waiting to hear results from SSB.

I still can't get used to not driving at night. It's my own decision, but I feel it's necessary. I don't want to hurt anyone, and I've realized I really can't see well in the dark. At night, the glare of the upcoming cars hurts my eyes and causes a halo around everything. I'm losing my freedom already. What will I do when I can't drive at all? I'm writing in my journal now, but what will I do when I'm blind? I've written my journals for my children as a way to preserve the cute things they were doing in their young lives. Maybe they will be interested in reading them to me or I could record them. But the longer I journal, the more I know that the words are meant for me. They give me a sense of ownership—of who I am—as I put pen to paper.

I want to grow a flower garden with flowers of every shape and color, something now to see, to remember for when I can't. Sunsets too, I want to see every one of them. And sunrises. They are so lovely.

Last night, while lying in bed, I tried to focus on a reflection on my ceiling light when it was off, and the room was dark. It was coming from my runway night-light. I couldn't see it when I looked directly at it, only when I looked just above it. That seemed so odd. I never noticed my vision like that before.

Who is controlling my vision?! Stop pushing the wrong buttons! Let me get back to me, the person who can handle life's journeys! You're spinning things into a spiral.

I'm dizzy and don't like this ride.

*J*ULY 23, 1991

MOM TOLD ME TO remember God's will, that in His time, things will be done.

Ralston visited today, and we talked about a course in Red Wing, Minnesota for Band Instrument Repair. They had openings in the fall I could take while waiting for their piano tuning and repair program to begin the following year. These were suggestions leaning toward my music interests.

Pastor Monson visited for two-and-a-half hours today. He was such a comfort.

My Aunt Barb, my godmother who lives in California, wrote a letter to me, urging me to make my moves thoughtfully, prayerfully: *Once you have decided, don't wonder about it. Know you made the best decision you could, based on your experience and present information. Also, find a smile and joy each day and write it down,* her letter read.

Donny called. He was home, haying at the farm. He goes back to road construction early in the morning and will be gone all week. We talked a long time; I slept much better after that.

July 25, 1991

Today was time for my six-month eye appointment already. Jan drove me to Pine River, where Dr. Marvin dilated my eyes. He had me take another field vision test. The inner, central vision was the same, but the peripheral was darker, showing more loss.

I talked to Mom and Dad in the evening. They weren't happy about me possibly going 225 miles south to school in Red Wing for Band Instrument Repair. They think I've disrupted my children's lives enough with the divorce and moving so much.

Sarah told me to do what I would be happy doing—at least she approves.

Reflection, Present day

Somewhere in the past few months of this journal, I made the decision to go to Red Wing. The reason why doesn't show in my writing, but I was adamant that I go into a field that had something to do with music. Piano tuning, it seemed, would be my best option without sight. That's all I could visualize when I combined blindness and music. Red Wing Technical College offered a Piano Repair and Tuning course starting in the fall of 1992; the state had given me a grant to go and take their Band Instrument Repair course in the meantime.

*J*ULY 25, 1991, CONTINUED

MY PARENTS WERE VERY concerned about uprooting the children and disrupting their lives, again, so soon after the divorce. For my part, I only felt the need to find some way of supporting them.

*J*ULY 28, 1991

AT CHURCH, THE CHOIR had seventeen members who sang at both services. It was probably my last time directing, so I chose a hymn that held deep meaning for me, "I'm But a Stranger Here, Heaven Is My Home." It's my Dad's favorite, and he was touched when I told him.

I love directing more than anything.

After church, Donny and I rode his cycle, a Honda Goldwing, to see the movie *City Slickers*. It was so good to laugh and forget my worries.

*J*ULY 29, 1991

SARAH IS MAKING A list of school items for sixth grade, Alice is doing a puzzle, and Timmy is spending the night with a friend. I feel confident that we will be going to Red Wing, Minnesota, about 225 miles and a four-hour drive south of here. I feel it's the right decision.

I'm anxious, which is a lot better than feeling depressed.

*A*UGUST 1, 1991

RALSTON CAME TODAY TO review the interest test. We

decided that Red Wing seemed the best decision. He called the counselor and made an appointment for me to meet her next week.

I have so much to do! I just need to take a deep breath, pray and jump. Actually, I need to fly on an eagle's wings. God will carry me through.

*R*EFLECTION, PRESENT DAY

I'M REMINDED OF THE message Dorothy Stiefel wrote in her book: *Out of all the pain, fear, doubt, guilt and self-deprecation came a renewed person.*[9]

The journey continued as I took a step forward, not sure really where I was going or what I would do, but it was something. I felt drawn in that direction. I couldn't just sit and let my world fall apart without trying.

But as I read my journal now for the first time since writing it, and think back to that time in my life, it still feels surreal.

---

9   Dorothy H. Stiefel, *Retinitis Pigmentosa: Dealing with the Threat of Loss.* United States: Business of Living Publications, 1988. Publisher's note: The book is out of print, so the message quoted is from Pamela's memory.

Chapter Ten

NEW BEGINNINGS

*People used to ask me what I wanted to be
when I grew up and I'd say "Happy!" That was
all I wanted to be.*[10]

—Goldie Hawn

AUGUST 18, 1991

IT'S MOVING TO RED Wing day.

Mom, Dad, and my sister, Rita, arrived yesterday.

This morning, we went to church. I played with the contemporary group during the service. I played my flute during "On Eagle's Wings." There was cake and an offering basket for me. I was overwhelmed by the love surrounding me as my church family wished me well on my new journey.

---

10   Lynn Hirschenberg, "Solid Goldie," Vanity Fair (March 1992): 220, https:// archive.vanityfair.com/article/1992/3/solid-goldie. Publisher's note: It is said that John Lennon made a similar quote, but there is no substantive evidence.

Later, there was a potluck picnic at a resort in my honor. They gave me a beautiful eagle statue because of my dream.

It was hard to say good-bye.

AUGUST 19, 1991

WE MOVED INTO OUR new home, an apartment across the street from the technical college. I was sick during the night, which must have been just a release of nerves.

REFLECTION, PRESENT DAY

A whirlwind of activities and emotions enveloped our lives as we made efforts to become part of that new world, that new being. If I continued on with the details and kept busy, I seemed to push the fear away . . . all the while wondering how long I could do that.

AUGUST 22, 1991

WE'RE STILL UNPACKING AND shopping for school supplies.

Twin Bluff Middle School gave us a tour of where Sarah will be going to sixth grade. Somehow, I feel comfortable driving during the day in this unfamiliar town. The financial aid office at school gave me a full grant.

Everything is running smoothly, so far.

Donny came to visit and seemed impressed with the apartment and town. He drove me around to get me accustomed to everything. We discovered Colvill Park and watched barges travel on the Mississippi River.

Memorial Park Bluff was another great find as we

traveled up, up, up to the top with a spectacular view of Red Wing as it smoothly touched the riverbanks of the majestic Mississippi flowing toward the south. A barge was docked along the opposite shore, waiting for its route to continue. Several fishing boats and sailboats enjoyed the pleasant day as they glided through the streaming waters. At the distance from the bluffs, cars were dots on the pavement while people walking the sidewalks looked like ants. A subtle breeze wafted up from the valley below, swirling gently, tousling our hair and bringing an aroma of the water below.

I close my eyes taking in a deep breath that calms my senses from all the new adventures of the past few weeks. As I open them an eagle soars below in the valley.

I have the sensation as if I could sit on its wings: ease, peace and tranquility enfold me. I am one with its energy, riding on its back, encompassed in its comforting strength. I let go of all worried thoughts, excited for our adventure toward our new horizon. I am eager, filled with an anticipation of joy, like I experience on Christmas mornings. I rest, assured knowing all is well, and can appreciate the relief in this vision momentum allowing my concerns to stay behind. I shiver in exhilaration as I reconnect with my purpose, with my zest for life and with myself.

Love is in the air. Love is everywhere.

All is well.

I am free.

All is well.

Trill, trill, trill . . . listen, listen, listen . . . hold on. I don't travel alone, and in my mind, I can hear my Veery Thrush.

As I breathed in and out, Donny brought a beautiful sight to my attention. Across the valley toward the south stood another bluff of equal height. Barn Bluff, that could only be ventured by climbing its zig-zagging path to the top. We would definitely have to do that someday.

And there I was, in a different part of a new world. I had to show my strength and confidence to my children, even though I felt like cowering in a corner somewhere, afraid to do anything. They would be on their own journeys, meeting new friends at yet another new school. I thought I had all the details laid out: Sarah was entering sixth grade at Twin Bluffs Middle School. Timmy was in the third grade and Alice was in kindergarten; both would be attending Sunnyside Elementary School. At noon, Alice would ride a bus to the daycare within the Red Wing Technical College where I'd be taking my Band Instrument Repair course.

Lord, help us to glide on eagles' wings.

SEPTEMBER 3, 1991

OUR FIRST DAY OF school went mostly well.

I learned a lot and have a lot to learn.

I was amazed that my twenty classmates came from around the world: Austria, Botswana, Canada, St. Thomas, Taiwan, and many areas of the United States. They were an interesting, eclectic group. Several of the men came from the service and would be stationed after they were done with school.

We met our instructors: Gene would teach woodwind repair and John would be our instructor for brass.

Alice was all smiles when I went to get her at the daycare.

"I love kindergarten, but I don't have any homework," she said, talking non-stop, everything spilling out of her with excitement about her new world.

Timmy liked everything too, except recess. "The boys swear too much and do naughty things."

Sarah had a tough, lonely, and scary day. She didn't have enough money at lunch and was embarrassed.

In celebration of our first day, and because I had never had the opportunity where we lived before, I ordered pizza to be delivered. Alice wanted to tell the delivery man, "Keep the change, you filthy animal!" like in the movie *Home Alone*.

SEPTEMBER 6, 1991

I LEARNED HOW TO do chemical flushing of trumpets today. I got nervous, but I knew I could do it. I had also been taught how to use the lathe to make parts for the trumpet. As long as I focused on what I was doing, I thought I'd be okay.

I really enjoy my class.

SEPTEMBER 16, 1991

THIS MORNING, AFTER BREAKFAST, Timmy wanted us to look out the window. There, we watched as Calvin, a classmate of mine who lives in our apartment building, walked to school. He was bundled from head to toe with a hat, mittens, coat, pants, and boots. Only his island brown nose was peeking out from under the scarf wrapped around his neck. He had never been out of his country island, St. Thomas, and was nervous to experience the cold of winter.

There was a light covering of frost on the ground—typical for a fall morning—which would disappear with the morning sun. We giggled at this odd character and wondered how he would manage when there really was cold and snow.

Today was my first quiz. I studied hard, but I misread one

question and misnamed a few parts on the nomenclature of the trumpet piston.

September 23, 1991

I HAD A DEPRESSING day at school. I worked on a lead pipe dent and, because of the dim light, I totally ruined it. I worked so hard.

I really have to watch my attitude and pray for patience.

September 27, 1991

JOHN, MY INSTRUCTOR, GOT me a lamp for my workbench. I could take it to any station. It really helped, and the others began calling me "the lamp lady." I think they were just tired of fixing my mistakes.

October 14, 1991

THE WATER PUMP WENT out on my car.

I saw Dr. Goeppinger today and he prescribed Prozac and referred me to a psychologist for depression. I feel embarrassed to be taking Prozac. But of course I'm depressed. I have too many things to try to control that are out of my control. Part of me thought the system wanted to make money off my demise.

A black cloud came rolling in but I wasn't even aware of it. It surrounded me as I had been focused on the daily care and loving of my children . . . of getting us through the day to day routines of school, homework, play, making ends meet, just living, and trying to be happy.

I ignored the darkness cloud of RP while it had been creeping up on me. I could feel it breathing on the back of my neck, reminding me that it was going to win. It may not have been that day, the next week, or in the next year, but it *was* too powerful to defeat. It had been declared the winner and I the victim.

"Give in," RP called, ringing in my head. "You aren't good enough to overcome anything else, so how do you think you can ever do this?"

I can't hear my Veery Thrush, even though I know it is always there. I'm deaf to its song and desperately want to hear it lift me from this despair.

October 20, 1991

I'M SPENDING THE WEEKEND in Longville with Donny while the kids are with their dad. It's good to be back.

Jan invited me to a Cursillo event to hear Mary, a frequent speaker, give a talk. Mary told of the renewed strength she had seen with my blindness—I cried. It was the first depression I felt during the weekend, but it was so refreshing to be there. I missed my friends. So many people were praying for me.

October 22, 1991

I STARTED WORKING ON a French horn today and learned how to restring rotary valves. I had no idea they even had strings in them. I spent a lot of the day at the lathe making a tool for it.

Later that day, Sarah asked me, "How much can you see, Mom?"

"Raise your arm over your head," I said. "Now, while I'm

looking at your face, wiggle your fingers."

"Mom, I am," she said with a concerned voice when she realized I hadn't seen them at all.

How thoughtful you are, Sarah, to want to know and experience what I'm going through. I don't praise you enough for all the help you do for me. You help me to keep taking steps and I thank you for being such a big part of my strength—I love you.

October 23, 1991

ALICE WAS UP MOST of the night with fever and earache. I stayed home with her. We played games and relaxed.

At 3:00 P.M., Sarah was home from school and stayed with Alice while I went to my first appointment with a psychologist. The room was extremely dark with a dim lamp in the corner.

"Sit there," she said.

I'm sure she must have pointed, but of course I couldn't see where. I felt overwhelmed and not good enough to request brighter lights. I thought I would cry a lot, but I didn't cry at all. I wasn't sure what to expect. I wanted to rid myself of the feeling that things are closing in on me, but I couldn't do anything about it.

October 24, 1991

ALICE RECOVERED AND WENT to school. Sarah came down with a cold but didn't want to miss school because of all the homework.

I worked on French horns again today. While I restrung

the keys, I broke the bridge during the stress test. Luckily, it was an old beater horn for practicing. I joked with John that I must be under a lot of stress.

I called my dear high school friend, LuAnn, to talk about my depression and being on drugs. She was glad I did something but cautioned me about side effects.

"If anything changes," she said, "get off of it."

Chapter Eleven

EPIC HALLOWEEN BLIZZARD

*Keep your face to the sunshine and you cannot
see the shadows. It's what the sunflowers do.*[11]

—*Helen Keller*

OCTOBER 30, 1991

MOM STAYED WITH THE kids while I traveled with my class
on a field trip to see how certain band instruments are made.

We are going to South Bend, Indiana first to tour Fox
Products. They make oboes and bassoons.

OCTOBER 31, 1991

THIS MORNING, WE PACKED up and left Elkhart, Indiana to

---

11   "Keep Your Face Always Towards the Sunshine, and the Shadows Will Fall Behind You," Quote Investigator, March 5, 2009, https://quoteinvestigator.com/2019/03/05/
sunshine/#note-21912-21

visit Ferree's Tools Inc. in Battle Creek, Michigan where they make tools for repairing instruments. It was interesting to see how all the parts for each instrument were made but disheartening to find out that none of the workers knew anything about the instrument that would be the final product.

I wonder how Mom is doing.

One of Sarah's friends was planning to have a Halloween party, and Sarah would spend the night afterward. Donny would be driving his daughter, Ann, to Missouri to start college.

My ears started a painful humming today.

I wonder if it's from the Prozac.

*N*OVEMBER 1, 1991

WE HAD THE YAMAHA Musical Products, Inc. tour today in Grand Rapids, Michigan. It was a very neat and clean workplace. They had lunch for us and took us out for supper. They really treated us the best out of all the plants we toured.

We watched the weather report from Michigan and heard about the biggest snowfall ever in Minnesota, twenty-four inches. Wouldn't you know, it was the only time in my life that I'd been out of the Midwest for winter, and I missed an epic blizzard.

I love when the snow blankets the earth in a deep comforter. I wonder how yesterday went for Mom while the kids had their scheduled parties and trick-or-treating. I sure wish I had the chance to call her but there isn't a way.

November 2, 1991

Sarah turned twelve years old today and I wasn't there to wake her with gifts and songs. I missed that but knew my mom was making the day very special for her as she always did when I was young.

I'll see her soon.

November 3, 1991

The field trip was over, and it was time to go back home to Minnesota. We saw the Sears Tower in Chicago, the tallest building in the world. By the time we got to Madison, Wisconsin, we started to see signs of sleet.

"Is this what snow looks like?" Calvin queried with his Jamaican style accent. "I imagined it to be whiter than this."

Several of us explained that we would be seeing flakes the further north we traveled, and we were right.

We had a chance to get off the bus while at a gas station. The faces of those experiencing the cold of winter for the first time were awestruck, like they'd just walked into a new world. Their knees were stiff as they tried to manage the grips of their shoes on the glare sheet of ice covering the parking lot. Unfortunately, most were unsuccessful. Slipping and sliding, feeling the snowflakes, grabbing each other to try to stand . . . all brought joy to the seasoned faces of those who had experienced the delight of winter. A snowball fight soon ensued before we assembled again to board the bus and continue the rest of the journey home.

*R*eflection, Present day

The Halloween Blizzard of 1991 with 24 inches of snow is a day that all Minnesotans remember exactly where they were and what they were trying to do.

Usually winter snows come a few inches at a time, making life's common tasks doable. In a typical winter, Minnesota can get two to three inches in a light storm or six to eight inches in a bigger event. These snows accumulate throughout the season because of the cold temperatures but are still manageable when they reach two feet. It's only considered a blizzard when a large amount is dumped on the area in a very short amount of time—like in one day. Usually, accompanying these storm systems are colder temperatures and high winds that blow the snow, producing white-out conditions and making it difficult to see further than a few feet. As these winds carry the snow, huge drifts occur surrounding objects in the storm's path.

The world stops.

Towns are crippled. Freeways have gates to close off traffic until plows are able to navigate after the storm passes. A hushed slumber-like eeriness encompasses all.

*N*ovember 3, 1991, Continued

Red Wing had turned into a winter wonderland—crisp, white, clean, but daunting—as if someone shook a snow globe but forgot to stop shaking it. Mountains of snowbanks were everywhere as the city tried to recover.

The bus was silent as it approached our school's parking lot. Eyes focused out the windows through circles cleared in the gathering frost. The glare of the bright sun reflecting off the white snow forced me to turn away, burning into my eyes and making them unable to see the winter scene.

The snow drifted through the unplowed lot. Not a car was in sight.

"Where's my car?" asked Shane. "How am I going to get home?"

Suddenly, someone spotted an antenna sticking out of one of the mounds of snow. All the cars had been buried.

I gathered my suitcase and walked the three blocks to my apartment. Thankfully, the road had been plowed.

Mom and the kids were glad to see me, and each had their story to tell of their blizzard experience. First, I wanted to give Sarah her birthday hug and kiss and find out about her Halloween Party. Mom hadn't trusted the weather and didn't let Sarah go. I was happy to hear she stayed safely at home.

After scraping the snow off Mom's car, she traveled back to her home in Wisconsin, about fifty miles away.

My ears were better in the afternoon. Mom wanted me to go to the emergency room, but I didn't.

NOVEMBER 4, 1991

BREAKDOWN!

I had a 2 ½ hour lecture at school on French horns. Then I got a terrible letter from financial aid, a form letter, not to allow me into class until the forms were filled out. I had told Larry, the financial aid person at the school, I would be gone for a week on the class field trip but would get the information to him as soon as I received it.

I ended up leaving class, going home, and finding relief when I found the necessary information in the mail.

I broke down anyway.

I also got a call from Joe, my new mobility training instructor. He said we would be starting next week, using a white cane.

I'm scared and keep hoping my RP is just a dream. Things like this bring me back to reality.

I pray for eagle wings again.

NOVEMBER 5, 1991

MY EARS ARE STILL ringing, but I feel a little better today.

Donny left for home after dropping me off at school.

I did a chemical flush on a French horn. I also soldered a new bridge to it. I really enjoy school, being able to prove to myself, that I can do things. It helps me to think of other thoughts, more positive, uplifting thoughts to help me through the tough times.

All of yesterday's problems returned, but they didn't seem as gloomy. I needed to keep a positive attitude, but some days, like the prior day, I couldn't.

I hate days like that.

NOVEMBER 6, 1991

MY EAR RINGING WOKE me during the night. I was scared but didn't call anyone. I already scheduled an appointment on Thursday to see the doctor.

At school, I worked on the French horn rotary valve and dents. I'm getting good at smoothing them out. It's such an accomplished feeling, to glide my hand over the smooth brass when I've perfected the technique.

*N*OVEMBER 7, 1991

I DID MORE FRENCH horn skills today at school. Making a back bearing plate holder out of steel on the lathe was a major triumph.

I feel so good about myself on days like today.

I saw the doctor and have a slight ear infection, which he gave me medication for. As I was on my ride home from the other side of town, I came close to running a lady over in the crosswalk! I didn't see her!

"Watch where you're going!" a voice screamed at me.

She was right next to me, at my driver side window, giving me a look of fierce scorn. That was the most frightening thing that had ever happened to me. I was concentrating on my surrounding points of focus. So many of them. Which ones should I choose? There was so much more traffic in this town.

I'm done, done . . . giving up . . . I feel like a failure because I can't drive anymore. I won't take that chance of hurting an innocent bystander ever again.

Independence is the freedom to go, be, or do anything you choose. Without my permission, RP has taken this away. Yes, it is my decision to be safe and to care for myself but I'm depleted, worn out, giving in.

Take it, RP! Take my freedom and take my sense of self-worth.

I let go as I plummet once again toward the hole . . . that dark hole with its wide-open mouth, anticipating the taste of me.

It swallows me.

Donny sent me a beautiful basket of flowers for the first time ever! He called too, which makes me feel so appreciated and loved.

The kids and I were invited to a delicious, authentic Taiwanese dinner with my classmate Kai-Ti and his wife Carole. They are from Taiwan. Shane and Ed went too and drove us there. I was extremely impressed at the quantity and quality of the meal with such simple ingredients and appliances. It was delicious.

The school gave me an application for a scholarship for the blind. Larry, from financial aid, apologized for the mishap on Monday. I also received a paper that said my financial aid was finished.

I'm confused but can hear the Veery Thrush singing once again . . . listen, listen, listen . . . hold on . . . let go, let God.

REFLECTION, PRESENT DAY

OH MY GOODNESS! I actually held my breath as I reread these journal entries. There were so many parts to what I was struggling with: being gone on a field trip and missing Sarah's birthday, an ear infection, missing Donny, financial aid being briefly rejected, and then facing the white cane, where everyone would know that I couldn't see. Oh, and the most hurtful decision of all, choosing not to drive. Ever. Again.

Reliving all of it overwhelmed me, but I also felt the power in knowing that someone really was watching over me.

And still is.

*N*OVEMBER 8, 1991

I MET WITH MY psychologist, Dr. Baldwin, again today. She made me realize a few things I wasn't aware of. I hadn't written about my blindness in this journal. I had been hiding my feelings, so when I had to actually face things, it devastated me! She wanted me to try to write more about RP and how I felt. I hid my feelings with the thought that if I acknowledged them, they became real.

There are, to me, similarities between blindness and helplessness and being . . . stupid.

*R*EFLECTION, PRESENT DAY

SOME SORROWS ARE TOO deep for crying.

Chapter Twelve

WHITE CANE

*There is nothing to writing. All you do is
sit at a typewriter and bleed.*[12]

*N*OVEMBER 11, 1991

WE CONTINUED WORKING ON the French horn at school.

Part of the day was a lecture on overhauls. It sounded like a lot to know, but taking each step, one at a time, made the improvement seem effortless.

Maybe I could start looking at life that way, to look at the problem as if there is always a solution.

Joe, my mobility instructor, came today for my first lesson. I was so glad that Donny was here for support, that he showed concern and interest.

---

12   "Writing Is Easy; You Just Open a Vein and Bleed," Quote Investigator, September 14, 2011, https://quoteinvestigator.com/2011/09/14/writing-bleed/. Publisher's note: There is controversy about the specific phrasing and origin of this quote. Among those credited are Ernest Hemingway, Friedrich Nietzche, and Thomas Wolfe.

I'm scared of the unknown but feel guided that this is what I need.

Joe would be working with me for six weeks now and six more weeks in the spring. We would start the following week with sighted guide training, which involved showing others how to assist me. The cane would come later.

The more accepting I could be of my RP, even though I didn't want to be, the easier it would get.

REFLECTION, PRESENT DAY

THAT EXCEEDINGLY DIFFICULT TRANSITION in my life was freeing in so many ways. Joe was very patient and kind as he guided me only as far as I was willing to go on any given day. I am greatly appreciative of his kindness and proud of myself for enduring throughout those lessons.

Today, sighted guide training is how I walk when I am in public with another person even while using my cane. As they are on my left side, I know where they are without having to look for them. I can easily, when necessary, reach forward and gently hold their elbow with my left hand as my right is busy taping—step, tap, step—as I follow one step behind the guide. This enables me to know if they have taken a step, stopped, or if we are going up/down stairs.

Cane travel helps me navigate when I'm alone but also alerts others that I may not see them and to take caution. Most people are comforted by my subtle needs in public to keep me and everyone safe. Many feelings implode on me at times when others stare and treat me unkindly, but mostly, I've learned their reaction is not as much about them as it is about me and my safety.

November 12, 1991

I was called from school today to get Timmy. He was running relay races and hit the wall with his wrist. Donny and I took him to the clinic where they took an x-ray and the doctor thought there was a hairline fracture, so the doctor put him in a brace. They instructed me to call the radiologist tomorrow to see if they thought he should have a cast.

Donny traveled back north, while the kids and I returned to school. Timmy wanted to show everyone his brace. Sarah had acolyte training at church and had to find a ride with a friend.

It really bothers me that I have to depend on others for rides for me and my children. I feel like a failure, unworthy because I can't drive anymore.

November 14, 1991

Today, each student was given a box that had trumpet parts. From that, we are to rebuild it to playing condition. I worked all day soldering on a trumpet, so intricate and precise. I thought I was doing a good job then found out I was doing it wrong . . .

"I can only do one moment at a time," I keep reminding myself. "Listen, listen, listen . . . hold on."

November 15, 1991

I worked so hard at school today, but still struggled. I dented a horn when I lost it on the buffer. That machine runs so fast it's hard for me to take enough caution with my vision.

I told Donny what kind of a day I had. He made me feel

so good. "Look at what you can do instead," he said.

I think the pressure of the quarter ending and not getting the instruments done is bothering me.

I've been concentrating on my RP. How do I accept it, this new entity that has taken root and made its home inside of me? It's so hard to think about it, because so many emotions come at once: fear, anger, denial, sadness, loneliness—like nobody could possibly know how I'm feeling. I hope it'll go away, pretend it's not true. Ignore it and it will leave?

There is a force. It's a dark, a black void in space . . . a nothing. It is wedging itself between me and the rest of the world. The distance is placing me into another category of being, of being a non-being, unworthy of privileges, delights, joys...

Unworthy of life itself.

November 17, 1991

I've considered trying to talk about one emotion at a time concerning my RP, like my therapist suggested—first is fear.

I dreamed that I had to move back to the house where we lived after I separated from my ex-husband and before my divorce. I felt like I had to go back because I wasn't doing well enough in Red Wing.

I *fear* that being blind is going to make me stupid and dependent again.

I *fear* failure.

I *fear* once again having to give in and crawl back to . . . nothingness.

November 18. 1991

JOE CAME AND WE worked on mobility training. He gave me a white cane that had red on the lower part. I didn't want to even touch the cane. I was afraid of it and felt like once I did touch it, it would never let me go. It would be glued to my hand for all to see my stupidity and mock me.

He taught me how to protect myself in unfamiliar areas, by holding it across my body. I was surprised to discover the cane actually had a golf grip. It was flat on one side, making it easier to maneuver.

"Hold the flat side of the grip in the palm of your hand while extending your pointer finger," he said. "This way, your finger tends to point the way you are going."

We started by walking down the hallway at my school. He showed me to tap the cane toward my left side, and then I could walk forward with my right foot. This meant the cane had checked for clearance already on my left, so I'd take the next step with my left foot and tap to my right.

Tap, step, tap, step, tap, step tap . . . swinging the cane in front of me as I walked down the hall, keenly aware of the echo from the taps. This new skill comforted me; I could easily tell when the echo altered because of a doorway or change in structure. I could walk without having to look down in fear of tripping over something.

I cried so hard after the kids went to bed. I cried over giving up and giving in to the inevitable.

I AM GOING BLIND!

"Oh, but dear child, you are loved!" a voice whispered from my core. "This is a priceless tool that will give you the freedom you so desire, that lifts your heart to the vibration of song. Your heart needs tender care. Your eyes have not given up. They are introducing you toward a new, spectacular you.

I can hear the song, and I will sing it to you. Listen, listen, listen . . . hold on."

November 22, 1991

I HAD MY FIRST quarter exam today. It took ninety minutes and my score was 8/6B. I was pretty pleased with that! I proved to myself that I'm not stupid; I can learn.

I am worth it.

December 12, 1991

DONNY HAD A JOB interview for another trucking company today. He said he'd be hauling waste out of state and gone for five days a week. We talked for a long time and he decided to take it.

He starts in four days.

December 16, 1991

I HAVEN'T WRITTEN AS much lately—I think it's because my therapist wants me to write about my eyes. It's so hard for me to do that. I realize now that I'm hiding my feelings. She suggests writing for 30 minutes only once a week with someone there to support me.

December 17, 1991

I CLEANED MY SISTER Rita's high school clarinet today. Tonight, Calvin, a fellow student from St. Thomas, stopped in. He wanted to know about my eyes, so I told him.

"Someone at school asked me about you," he said, "and I told them I didn't know what was wrong. They said they had waved at you, but you didn't see them."

"I hope they didn't think I was ignoring them," I replied.

Calvin was very sincere and concerned. It hurt me to know that people could tell. I shared with him what RP was and what it was doing to my eyes. Explaining that it was slowly decreasing what sight I had, but I didn't know how long it was going to take. I also told him I was taking white cane travel lessons and would start using that when I'm done.

December 18, 1991

I GOT MY REPORT card today and my grade point average was 3.688! I was very pleased about that.

I tried to finish Rita's clarinet, but I haven't learned how to do the cork on the tenons yet.

December 23, 1991

PEOPLE FROM TOWN STOPPED by with six bags of groceries and two huge garbage bags of Christmas presents. I cried!

Dear Lord, thank you for watching over us.

Recap, 1991

WHAT A YEAR! So much has happened. Most of all, my trust in God grew. By visualizing eagle's wings, I've been able to make it through all my events.

I learned this year about retinitis pigmentosa. I learned to adjust, or at least, I tried.

The children have blossomed.

My love for Donny grew.

I moved to Red Wing and started school.

Chapter Thirteen

He is Always Watching Me

January 5, 1992

Timmy had his first ski lesson through the school at Mt. Frontenac. He almost chickened out, but I'm glad he didn't. He had a great time and can't wait until the next lesson.

January 10, 1992

I got an award at school that puts me on the President's list! I've worked extremely hard to do the best I can. It's amazing that after all these years, I can still learn things. I guess I thought at some point, I wouldn't be able to.

It sure does boost my self-esteem.

January 20, 1992

I've been tossing and turning for an hour, so I thought I'd

do some journal catch up. It's been such a busy week.

I went to an appointment with my therapist even though I wanted to cancel it because I hadn't done the writing assignment about my eyes like she had requested. I still hadn't been able to take even a few minutes to write about them.

Timmy complained about his right testicle hurting before school one day. He still went, but afterward, it was so bad he could hardly walk. It was swollen and his side hurt too. I called the hospital and they said to bring him in. Calvin was glad to take us and stayed with us the whole time.

At first, they suspected appendix, hernia, or twisted testicle. A nurse put an IV in his hand so they could put in a dye to take x-rays to see if any veins were pinched.

"This might hurt a little," she cautioned, "but I only want to do this once. You can scream and cry if you want, but don't move." Then she turned to me and said, "And it would be no fair if Mom hit the floor."

Timmy was so good. He did scream a little but stayed very still. That's when I had to ask for a chair.

"Hey Mom," Timmy said, "I'm the one that's sick!"

Nothing was found in the x-rays, so they suspected just a virus. They sent us home with antibiotics and he stayed home the rest of the week.

I had a test on the clarinet and got one wrong. In the afternoon, I had an eye appointment. Timmy did too. I had a field vision test done. My vision showed a decrease. The doctor said I shouldn't be driving anymore, and I told him I decided that last November. He set up an appointment for me to see Dr. Knobloch in Minneapolis to have an ERG[13] test done.

"That will tell how your remaining cone cells are doing," he explained.

"I frequently see beams of light floating through my vision," I said. "What are those from?"

"They are a delayed reaction of changes of light," he answered. "Your brain is trying to adjust for the lack of retina cells."

I had many more questions but decided to save them for the next appointment.

January 23, 1992

DONNY LEFT FOR WORK this morning, but last night I cried about my eyes. I hate to do that in front of him, because I think that he will think I'm giving up. I'm not though. It's just all so overwhelming.

I left school at noon today because I couldn't concentrate on my work.

I'm very depressed about the eye exam. It's a lot to think about.

Mom and Dad came to visit us last Sunday, and I was so glad they did. They seemed so concerned about me and the children, as if they thought this was their fault entirely.

It's not. How could it be?

Alice read to me last night.

---

13   Corinna Underwood (healthline.com), "Electroretinography," updated April 20, 2020, https://www.healthline.com/health/electroretinography. This web article defines ERG as, "An Electroretinography (ERG) test, also known as an electroretinogram, measures the electrical response of the light-sensitive cells in your eyes."

She's doing so well. Now she wants to read everything. Does she think I can't see enough to read anymore? Fine, if that is the catalyst for her enjoying reading to me, so be it.

Sarah had her first speech meet last Saturday. I was so proud of her! She got a purple ribbon and has five more meets to go to.

Timmy's pain is completely gone.

I try to hide my feelings from the kids, but I'm sure they're aware of my hurt. They are going through so much, too, and I try to be very supportive in all of their lives.

"You knew this was coming," an inner voice said. "Get over it and get on with it. Face it, you are going blind! You won't be able to do many things. So, are you going to adjust and claim your independence in other ways or cower in a corner and whine for others to take care of you? You do have choices. Listen, listen, listen . . . hold on."

JANUARY 27, 1992

I GOT MY QUARTERLY report today, and I've done very well.

I repaired a flute today. It felt so familiar and easy since I've played one since I was ten. Maybe I could specialize in repairing them.

Sarah got a white ribbon at her speech meet—I'm very proud of her.

FEBRUARY 6, 1992

LAST TUESDAY, DONNY TOOK me to an eye appointment at the University of Minnesota with Dr. Knobloch. I had an ERG done to tell how the remaining cone cells are—not too good.

"You are legally blind with 12% central vision remaining," he said. "No more driving at all. You will only have ten years of central vision." He was as unsympathetic as the first retinal specialist I saw last year.

I'm so glad Donny was there for me. It's been two days since the appointment, and I'm emotionally drained. I feel like I just want to be alone and sleep.

Ten years, *only* ten years, keeps repeating in my brain.

On Monday, I met with my therapist and we talked a lot about my vision. We discussed ways I could adjust myself to each new obstacle I would face.

Until my next therapy session, I'm going to walk once a week with my cane. The first couple times will be difficult, but Joe has taught me a lot of techniques. I hope I can do it tonight.

Going up stairs is interesting as I hold the cane vertical in front of me. The cane taps the front of each step as I ascend. Tap, step, tap, step, tap, step, up, up, up . . . I go while holding the railing to my right. I'm still not emotionally ready to walk in public, but I'm hoping for the courage to start.

Last Saturday, Timmy, Donny, and I went to Mt. Frontenac to ski. Timmy wanted to show us his new skills. He really did well as I watched from the bottom of the hill. Donny described where he was at the top of the hill so I could locate his little frame. Timmy descended the slope, weaving and turning with ease, then swoosh, he slid to a halt in front of us with a huge smile of delight. I'm really proud of him going through the whole program.

REFLECTION, PRESENT DAY

TOO MANY TRAUMAS WERE affecting my inner soul that I couldn't endure. I couldn't put them in writing, but they are important to this story. In only a few days, several events occurred to change the rest of my life.

I learned that Red Wing had dropped their Piano Tuning/Repair course, which was the only reason I moved to Red Wing. Seriously, this was the only reason I jerked my family away from the known to start a new life—a life that pushed me into becoming a confident new me. I crushed my children's world with the intention of finding a new and better life.

And just like that, it was gone.

I was declared legally blind. Anything less than twenty degrees of central vision is considered blind. I'm less than that at twelve degrees, and I understood that my world would become entirely dark within ten years. That would have been 2002. What future did I have? How could I prepare for it financially and emotionally?

I had to start using my white cane. I took deep breaths of confidence and tried not to let it escape with each exhale.

I should be able to do this—I should be able to. I should be able to.

Joe took me downtown, left me at a corner, told me the number address of where I was. Then, he told me where he was going to be and that I had to find him.

All cities are made of grids with streets and avenues. Each block starts another sequence of numbers increasing as the distance becomes farther away from the center of town. The odd number buildings are on one side and even on the other. This should be easy enough.

He wanted me to wear a mask to simulate the total darkness, but I couldn't bear the thought of that and told him I would rather close my eyes.

I was pleased that I was able to find him and mostly not trip over anything. He was always watching me from a distance, especially at intersections, where I had to listen for the traffic before continuing. Every corner was different, and none are disability friendly.

That can be very aggravating.

I decided to take myself off Prozac.

Of course I was depressed; they told me I would be. But I didn't want to take drugs to numb that feeling. I needed to face whatever else wanted to hurt me. Besides, I didn't like the side effects.

I felt numb, and the medicine didn't allow me to hurt anymore. Without feelings, there was no pain. Where was I going? What was I doing? I felt the road being ripped from beneath my feet again, but I was falling instead of soaring, spiraling into the unknown. I didn't want to see what was going to happen next.

I wanted the darkness to come and have its way with me. To end the torture that haunted me every waking moment. If I gave in, maybe the pain wouldn't be so bad. Then I could possibly have tolerated it. I wouldn't have to be so strong. I wouldn't have to endure the suffering, the insane chaos of a life I had messed up. I felt unworthy, not good enough to have a normal and productive life.

I was never ever good enough. Always on the bottom looking up at happy faces, faces of people who had blessed lives.

But not me.

Reading the entries from 1992 and remembering made

my heart go out to my earlier self—a young woman who struggled through dark times. I wanted to wrap her in my arms, set her in my lap, hold her so she would know I cared about her.

I wished to say to myself the words I'd longed to hear back then, the words I needed to hear:

You are so worthy of every single one of your heart's desires. You are traveling through stages as a butterfly and learning so much. If your wings were given to you at this point, you would only fly with them straight into the flame and be burned.

Wait. Be patient. There is so much strength inside you, waiting to soar. It will blossom a little at a time. You have seeds that are being planted daily by you and by people you meet. Seeds, that will take root in their time and grow within you. There will be an enormous fragrant bouquet of flowers, of every shape, size, and color. You won't need to see them to appreciate them. Their aroma, growth, and joy will fill your deepest desires. You can't gather the seeds you planted today. They are being well nurtured and will blossom in full when it is harvest time.

Take heart my dear one; you are loved.

Chapter Fourteen

PLANTING SEEDS

FEBRUARY 18, 1992

I REALLY LOVE REPAIRING flutes because I'm so familiar with how they should sound.

I was home from school, watching a video from Powell Flute and feeling depressed again about my RP.

One year ago, I was diagnosed and the whole world as I knew it changed.

Today, while home alone, I cried and let my emotions flow. It should have made them dry up, but it drew more tears, more feelings that drown me in sorrows: I'm sinking in a whirlpool I've created, swirling, and tossing about. I'm dizzy and can't focus, but I feel waves building so immensely, it seems a tsunami of crushing proportions has become my life.

On Sunday, I made the challenging decision to start using my cane. My sister, Joan, came to get us to spend the day in

Glenwood City, Wisconsin. Her support strengthened me.

"You can do this!" she encouraged "You've been training for months and have told me how you're able to look up instead of at your feet."

That was true. I wasn't aware that I had transitioned slowly from looking down at the ground to scanning my surroundings so that I could see it better. I've been using my cane every day since and feel more comfortable. Amazingly, I can walk without looking down all the time.

The first day using my cane to go to school had been the biggest challenge. I had to walk three blocks down the road without a sidewalk, cross a busy road that didn't have crosswalks, enter the parking lot of the school, and head toward the entrance. I gathered all the courage I had and tried to pretend I had been doing it all along, that the routine was just another part of me . . . a new day with my new eyes.

Walking tall and proud, I entered the building. A classmate approached and put a coin in my coffee mug!

"Here's my donation," he said. "Spend it wisely."

I didn't realize that I looked like a beggar carrying a cup and wearing sunglasses. I had to laugh with him about it, even though I felt devastated inside. But the more I laughed, the more I relaxed.

What a sight I must have been.

My classmates were silent about my new device; I hadn't prepared them for the new development. They had been aware I suffered from a vision disease, but to them, I seemed normal. I could read, and most times, I didn't run into things. Today, they treated me with tender loving care, helping and guiding me in advance of my every move.

Returning home from school was another adventure. I chose to store my empty coffee mug in my backpack while using the cane and wearing sunglasses. Before crossing the busy road, I had to wait for a school bus to turn down the road I would be walking on. A young boy looked out the back window and gave me the middle finger. He sure was shocked when I returned the salutation!

I learned a big lesson today. If I'm upset, the whole world is too, but if I can relax, even just a little, maybe I can take another step, and the next, and the next . . .

*F*EBRUARY 23, 1992

I'M SO PROUD OF Sarah.

She had her final speech meet yesterday; Donny and I went to listen. She did a six-to-eight-minute prose reading from *Where the Red Fern Grows*. She didn't make the final round, but I really think she did better than some of those who went on. What a great experience for her.

I still use my cane wherever I go. The more I do, the more I accept my RP . . . I think.

*M*ARCH 9, 1992

I HAVEN'T STOPPED USING my cane since I started.

We spent last weekend in Longville. Donny and I stayed at the farm while the kids were with their dad.

I went to a Cursillo renewal with women who had become a strong support network. I was so inspired by their unconditional love I gave the closing prayer. One of the ladies suggested I do some writing.

I'll have to try. Maybe it will help me with my feelings of RP.

Listen, listen, listen . . . hold on.

$\mathcal{R}$EFLECTION, PRESENT DAY

ANOTHER DELICATE SEED HAD been planted, and it waited for its time as I gathered information.

With a sun shining bright, a wonderful bounty sprouted roots, anchoring my inner being toward the daylight, filling my soul with warmth. Nurturing soil cocoons this seedling as loving friends watered it daily, comforting the seed while it anchored my foundation. It made a path steady, strong, and true. It vibrated with delight at what was to come, what *I* was to become.

$\mathcal{M}$ARCH 10, 1992

MOM AND DAD PICKED us up to go to my nephew's birthday party.

I feel like such a burden, not being able to drive, but my parents want to do as much as they can for me and my family while we adjust to this new way of living.

My sisters had a good talk with me. They begged me to move back to Wisconsin to be closer to them and the rest of the family. "It would be easier for you," they said, but moving would also make it easier for them to assist me.

I tried planning the move last week and realized again that God has to lead me. I needed to evaluate all my options . . . jobs, housing, comfort for me and the children.

*C*MARCH 15, 1992

LAST WEEK, OUR CLASS started working on oboes. Now I understand why they said the instrument was a wooden tube covered with glue and rolled in keys. The oboe has an insane number of keys doing a lot of different things.

I had a conference with my instructors. I got six wrong on my exam, earning me an A-. They wrote letters on my behalf to a couple job prospects. On Thursday, I received a call from The Music Loft in Cedar Rapids, Iowa about a job. They expressed interest in me, but they only offered to pay on commission, didn't provide benefits, and seemed so far away.

I've been very moody and emotional. I didn't go to Lenten Services because I wouldn't call for a ride for fear of being disappointed. I know people would love to help, but when they have other commitments and feel bad they can't help, I feel worse. I'd rather not go through that rejection.

I'm angry. It hurts. I cry so easily.

God's timing . . . I happened to turn the TV to a sermon talking about bearing one another's burdens. I've had so many places to be at that I won't go because I hate to ask. He spoke to me through the minister on TV, and I felt more at ease in seeking transportation assistance from friends.

Yesterday, Donny, the kids, and I went to Glenwood City in the afternoon. Mom and I visited Grandma and Grandpa Allram at the Glenhaven nursing home where they share a room.

Grandma is ninety-one and has multiple sclerosis. She can't move without help.

They feel so sorry for me and my eyes.

"I'm praying for a miracle," Grandma said.

Grandpa cried about it.

I must have faith that God will provide for all our travels. We learn our lessons through our journeys.

March 25, 1992

I GOT MY REPORT card today and was very pleased. I also sent papers out for Legal Aid Services to represent me with Social Security Income.

Ouch! I just ran to see why Timmy was upset and ran into the corner of the half-open hallway door. It caused a huge egg on my forehead and one on my arm. Boy, did I cry hard, not because of the pain but over being shocked then angry at myself for not seeing it.

I hate going blind!

I couldn't help the tears and really didn't want the kids to see me like that. I'm sure they are as devastated by the accident as me. Timmy felt so bad, and my heart just broke.

How am I supposed to make the next incident easier? There will be many, I'm sure.

March 29, 1992

I SPENT THE DAY at home cleaning. It snowed last night, making the roads icy. We didn't go to church.

I still hate asking for rides.

April 2, 1992

I'M ALONE.

The kids are with their dad because they don't have

school tomorrow. Donny and I will be going to Longville for the weekend to bring them home.

My head still hurts from running into the door: Donny took me to the doctor, who said I have a concussion. He said I should rest and to take Tylenol for the pain. He wanted to take x-rays, but he wouldn't have been able to do anything, so I declined. He told me to return if I felt tingling anywhere.

I've been working on an oboe and started saxophone lessons.

Per the curriculum, students learn how to play each instrument we repair. I really enjoy that part of class.

* * *

RALSTON, FROM STATE SERVICES for the Blind, visited today. He sent my application to Shell Lake, Wisconsin for a three-week piano tuning course. State Services offered to pay for the course, tools, my dorm room, and food.

I love the idea of tuning and repairing pianos. I'm not sure how it translates into a living or an occupation, but it feels like a door opening. I don't know how being an instrument technician will work with the prediction of blindness.

APRIL 7, 1992

DONNY AND I WENT to Longville for the weekend while the kids were with their dad. Cheryl, Alicia, and I played our trio at church. So many people thanked us for playing and said we did a great job.

I really miss our trio.

I received a letter from school notifying me that I'd been chosen as a finalist for a scholarship from Northern States Power Company. It stated I'd been identified as a student who "exemplified the highest standards of student achievement" and notified me of an interview tomorrow.

God's timing . . . He surely shows me His love. Life is an adventure. I must pay attention to each moment and make the most of it, turn it into a joyful memory, something to bring a smile in the future.

REFLECTION, PRESENT DAY

AND I WAS FINDING joy. Though, I wanted to add a clarifying note—

My journey to Red Wing was for the purpose of becoming a piano repair/tuning technician. The Band Instrument Repair was something I had interest in doing while waiting for those classes to start. And, at the time, I thought I would have sight to continue in that field. Instead, the doctors told me my vision was decreasing at an accelerated rate and would maybe only last ten years.

APRIL 19, 1992

SARAH'S TALKING TO HER friend, Bambi. Alice and Timmy are watching *Home Improvement*. Donny is gone doing road work near Willow River, Minnesota for a job he started last week.

Aloneness is hard.

APRIL 30, 1992

I'M THIRTY-FIVE YEARS OLD today. I'm not sure what I expected from life, but this isn't it. The only part of my life that has meaning is that I have three wonderful children who are blessings to me every day. I'm so thankful for them.

I was surprised to find a gift on my bench at school. Agnus, a classmate from Austria, made a turning stick for me with my name and her initials on it. She was pleased that I knew it was used for making lefse, a tortilla-style Norwegian delight made from potatoes.

I shall cherish and use this gift for years to come.

May 8, 1992

There was a dinner party for my classmates and me. I played a short piccolo piece for the presenting of the beef. It was great fun to celebrate our upcoming graduation.

Soon, we all go our separate ways around the world.

I also had my last cane travel class with Joe. He has sensed my emotions as we traveled together through this part of my journey, and he said he could tell a big difference in how I depend on the cane, how it's become a part of me and my new world.

I appreciate his kind way of assisting me, and I grasp that it's part of me now. However, it's hard to find a comfort in its assistance while I hate it at the same time. It's still a snake to me. It teases and mocks me at my minimalist effort in taking control over RP.

Tap, step, sting, tap, step, sting. I'll continue this death march while wearing my happy face mask to show the world that I'm just fine . . . just fine . . . *tap, step, sting.*

I've been thinking more about starting Braille–yet another mocking tool of despair. It could be a useful tool in my future. It's probably better if I learn it while there is still sight left.

My eyes seem worse, especially my right one. I've been thinking about moving to Glenwood City to be closer to family. I hate the thought of going there and just doing nothing—it's another option I should pray about. I admit, it has been so nice being able to visit my family while living here instead of so far away in northern Minnesota.

*M*AY 28, 1992

I'VE SEARCHED FOR A house to rent in downtown Red Wing, but nothing is available. Maybe I can find someone to apprentice under for piano tuning. I don't think three weeks of class will give me enough knowledge.

Today was my last day of school, and I had so many emotions. I felt sad to see so many friends leave, knowing I'd probably never see them again. I was impatient about wanting to know where I would go from there. And then . . . a part of me was excited that this part of my journey would finally be over.

Red caps and gowns filled the classroom as we busily prepared for our exit down the hall toward the graduation ceremony. Hugs and well wishes were exchanged. The men in class from the armed services had been given their assignments. Greg received great applause and congratulations as he announced he would be stationed in Hawaii. Others would return to their homeland to create or join businesses: Ed to Canada, Kai-Ti to Taiwan, Calvin to the isle of St. Thomas, and Agnus to Austria. Instructors, John and Gene, made the rounds hugging, encouraging, and congratulating each of their students.

At the time to leave, we followed in a line toward our destination. Other classes from the college did the same. A slowing shuffle was the only progress as we neared the entrance. Tapping my cane in a slow rhythm, I navigated my way while playing follow-the-leader into the auditorium.

A glimpse told me the lighting was dim with lights only on the raised stage in the front where the teachers had gathered. A pile of diplomas waited on a table to one side.

As we snaked through a maze of chairs, I heard a loon call from the audience.

"Whoo, hoooo!" It echoed. "We're over here!"

I recognized the call as the one I taught my children to blow through their fisted hands. My eyes slowly adjusted to the change in lighting, and I turned left to find a beaming row of family members applauding and cheering me on. From the distance, I could barely make out their faces and noticed my dad wiping away a tear.

Besides my children, Donny, and my parents, I was delighted to see my sister, Rita, her daughter, Jessica, my sister, Joan, and her husband, John. Then there was my brother, Steve, my dad's brother, Uncle Orland, his wife, Aunt Carol, and my mobility instructor, Joe, and his wife, Kris.

Each one of them have been supporters and a part of my encouragement team, rooting me on to keep going. Throughout the past year I felt their warm embrace of unconditional love. To them, my limited vision didn't matter. They saw the true *me*, my abilities. Like a peacock with my plume of feathers spread, I strutted myself proudly, not afraid to display what I had done.

I have done it!

As soon as I found my seat, I placed my hands to my mouth and gave them a return loon whistle.

"Whoo, hoooo, whoo, hoooo, whoo, hoooo!" I called, representing each one of my children.

I've done it! I thought to myself. *I have taken a step forward and proved that I can learn. I can become something with who and what I am.*

Several speeches were delivered before diplomas were handed out. One row at a time stood and progressed toward the platform after each name was called.

Suddenly, it struck me that I would have to walk up those stairs. Six of them, I thought. I would cross in front of everyone, in front of thousands of people, accept my diploma, then go down the six stairs on the opposite side and return to where I *thought* my seat waited.

And before I could blink, it was done.

I graduated from Red Wing Technical College with a degree in Band Instrument Repair! My heart knew I probably wouldn't be able to build upon the accomplishment, but oh how proud I felt that I accepted the challenge. Fear of the unknown had been my predominant feeling, but I had also been afraid of being blind and feeling stupid.

Learning new tools brings satisfaction and knowledge that I can be independent and confident in my abilities. I can adjust to my new path. I now know that I am able to go forward, able to take on new challenges while seeking the solutions.

Challenge accepted, executed and . . . DONE!

Chapter Fifteen

She Climbed to the Top and Rejoiced

June 23, 1992

It's a beautiful summer morning. The kids are at summer school. They catch a bus at eight and come home at noon. Sarah is taking an aerospace course and building models. Timmy is in a sport spectacular. Alice is in kindergarten kaleidoscope going to Crystal Cave, the zoo, and doing other special things every day.

My mind has been on my next move. Where to live? What to do? I'm trying to be patient. I have a Social Security Income hearing on July 28 in Minneapolis. I'm hoping that will give me insight into which direction I should go.

Let go and let God . . . again.

July 1, 1992

I've been considering going to school for massage therapy

like Vicki suggested last year. She has her own business twenty miles from Longville in Walker, Minnesota and is doing very well. This would be something I could do in one place in almost any town and still do piano tuning part-time. It's another option to think about.

*R*EFLECTION, PRESENT DAY

THE SEED TOOK ANOTHER drink of nourishing blessed water, enabling another root to bury through the soil. It stretched like a cat after a long nap to bring life to each limb.

*J*ULY 12, 1992

SUNDAY, THE CHILDREN AND I went to Glenwood City because I couldn't stand to be in Red Wing anymore. Mom and Dad brought us back last night. While we were there, Mom and I looked at a few houses for sale. They were real fire hazards.

Monday night, Joan and I went to church for service. Mom had gone to the service Sunday and said we should sit in the crying section. The sermon was titled, *Take up your Cross.*

Tuesday, Mom gave me a Social Security phone number to call to find out how much money I could expect. They quoted a lower amount than what I had previously been told. That felt like another low kick since there's no way I can buy a house or get out of renting with that income. There must be another solution.

July 26, 1992

MOM BROUGHT ME TO Shell Lake, Wisconsin earlier this afternoon. I'm in a dorm room here for the three-week piano tuning course. The kids are with their dad. I miss them so much already, but I have their pictures next to my bed. I'm glad they have a chance to spend this time with him.

July 27, 1992

IT'S BEEN A LONG day of learning and Dot, my instructor, makes everything seem so simple. Dot is a small stout framed woman who loves wearing polka dot, knee-length, full skirted dresses to represent her name.

"My real name is Dorothy," she said, "but everyone calls me Dot."

My class only had four students and one of them was from Glenwood City. Her uncle was my doctor when I was young.

We used the tuning lever and mutes on the middle section of a piano. How interesting to be able to hear the wave vibrations in each beat. Each note produced a different pattern, some faster than others, and all needed to be accurate to be in tune with the other. Fascinating!

People look when I walk through town with my cane, but a few are courteous and ask me about it. I'm still uncomfortable, but I've discovered this feeling isn't about me using the cane, it's about how I feel when other people stare at me. So I find myself trying to act blind . . . whatever that is.

Dot said she can get some information on Blind Piano Tuners. Maybe that will be the direction to go in. I just need to take it easy and try not to overdo it.

JULY 29, 1992

YESTERDAY WE LEARNED MORE about the temperament of the piano and how to set it using a step-by-step formula. I'm sure it will be frustrating at first, but I won't give up.

My eyes feel very foggy this morning from reading all the specific details. I'm wondering how a totally blind person would tune a piano. They must trust their hearing and feeling to guide them. Maybe Dot's information will shed some light on that topic.

AUGUST 4, 1992

I WORKED A LOT on piano keys today. Yesterday, I replaced my first string.

AUGUST 5, 1992

I JUST CAME BACK from a walk through town. While I was on a street corner, I hesitated as a car roared at the stop sign then sped off.

"It's okay to cross now, ma'am," called a man's voice. He had gone to the middle of the intersection and held out his arms to stop the traffic.

I said, "thank you," and continued on.

As I walked, tears came to my eyes. People do care about me. This man was willing to be helpful without asking, even though he didn't know me. I said a blessing prayer for him.

I've been dreaming about houses. I can't stay in the apartment in Red Wing any longer with my feelings of isolation from my family. I feel more comforted living closer to them than I did in Longville after the diagnosis, but I want to be closer still.

* * *

Within a piano, each key has a hammer that strikes strings, either a group of two or three strings. A twangy sound can be heard if the strings aren't in tune, it's like hearing an old country song where the piano isn't smooth, giving the music its desired honky-tonk effect. There is also a formula of beat waves between each note which blew my mind when I discovered that facet of the piano. In itself, it is a kaleidoscope of sounds resonating with each other and creating perfect harmony.

I could really hear an improvement today in the tuning waves. I closed my eyes to listen for the oneness that two strings develop as I slowly tightened or loosened one peg. I pressed the piano key, setting off the note's vibration across the two strings the hammer had hit. With the slight twist of the lever on one peg string, the resonance increased or decreased until I understood which direction would bring the two strings' sounds into oneness. Slowly, the wave became less and less until . . . *ahhh*, they became one, in tune with each other, two strings, side by side, finding a mutual tone. The note A.

* * *

Knowing that piano tuning probably won't be enough, my mind is still racing to find other means of income. I'm looking at taking classes for massage therapy in addition to piano tuning.

August 11, 1992

Today I spliced a string clarifying a good temperament. I

love this! I wish I would have taken this class before. I have to keep at it and do it every day though. I wonder what a full year of piano tuning and repair would have been like if Red Wing Technical College would have started the course.

"By the time you tune your 2,000th piano," Dot said, "you'll know what you are doing."

How in the heck am I going to find that many pianos to tune and make a living doing it?

Last night, I couldn't sleep and wrote a song called, "Someday Soon." It's depressing, but optimistic.

REFLECTION, PRESENT DAY

I'M SORRY TO SAY that I have since lost this song.

AUGUST 16, 1992

I RETURNED HOME TO Red Wing and slept in my own bed last night. I was told that my local church needs its piano tuned. They also asked me to be Sunday School Superintendent.

I've thought and prayed about it. If I stay in Red Wing, I would like to accept. It will help me gain more exposure to the tuning business. I'll also need to move downtown where I can walk to do my own errands.

I feel empowered by the new knowledge I have obtained. A sense of pride envelopes me with requests for my services. Can I walk out of this gloom and brighten my life through doing for others? Momentum surges, saying that I can, but my overwhelming desire to just be with family squelches the flow. Something else will work out, won't it?

Thank you, dear Lord, for your guidance.

AUGUST 20, 1992

THIS MORNING MY SISTER, Rita, called. I told her about the townhouse information I had received for Eau Claire, Wisconsin, where she lives. She had the same ad. I called for an appointment and they have openings on Sunday. This feels comfortable, like a plan is waiting to embrace us.

Dear God, help me to help my family go in the direction you need us to go. It's in Your hands. I pray for the children to understand that I don't want to keep disrupting their lives. I hope this is the last move in a long time.

I tuned my piano and need so much more practice. Surely, it hadn't been tuned since before my parents sold it to me in 1984. They bought it when I was young to replace the old upright. It helped me escape, spiraling and uplifting my emotions while creating another musical world.

Peace envelopes me when I play.

Saturday, Rita came and picked us up to go to Eau Claire. We showed the kids the city. They seemed excited about maybe moving there. Even Sarah, but she didn't show it too much. Mom and Dad also came on Sunday while we were staying with Rita, so we all went to look at the townhouse. I decided to rent the one that will be ready in November.

My heart bleeds for so many things, but mostly for Sarah. How can I show her that this is the right thing to do when I am just as scared? We finally feel accustomed to our life here in Red Wing and now, another move. This was only temporary for my schooling, but I didn't convey that to her. I want to reassure her that we will be okay.

August 30, 1992

Timmy and Alice were watching *Willy Wonka and the Chocolate Factory* when Sarah came home. She had been at her friend's house for the afternoon but came home early because Heidi's kitten attacked her. I took her to the kitchen to clean up the scratches.

Since I last wrote, many things have happened.

Tuesday, I contacted Dave, a piano tuner in Red Wing. He came out and said he would help me develop my tuning skills by having me shadow his appointments—State Services for the Blind will pay for it.

My housing in Eau Claire almost fell through. I couldn't have the townhouse without rental assistance. I called Eau Claire housing to find out how far I was on the list. They said I could use a voucher, and after much confusion, I found out I have a voucher and can use it.

It bothers me that I can't get the right help sometimes.

September 2, 1992

School starts for the kids on Tuesday. I think we've got everything.

Mom came over to take me to an eye appointment. I've noticed a decrease in vision this summer and wanted to check to see if something else was happening. There was a slight change, but nothing else. The doctor gave me a referral for another eye doctor in Eau Claire and for State Services for the Blind in Wisconsin.

On the way back from the clinic, Mom and I were talking about the booster MMR shot the new state law required Sarah to have before going into the seventh grade. The kids were in the back seat.

"What does MMR stand for?" Timmy asked.

Sarah very seriously said, "Measles, mumps and rebellion."

We chuckled about that as it was supposed to be rubella.

SARAH'S FRIEND, HEIDI, CALLED to say we needed to call the clinic about having rabies shots. A week passed since the kitten attacked Sarah, and I've taken care of the scratches with peroxide. Apparently, the kitten was feral and has disappeared after attacking Sarah and several other children.

The clinic told me that because of the 1% chance of rabies, it was best to administer the series of six shots in her stomach.

I'm going to get her flowers, hopefully that will ease the pain.

* * *

I RECEIVED A CALL notifying me that I can get into a townhouse sooner than November. I made some calls to rental assistance to see if that would be a problem with the voucher.

We will be moving October 24. I've been busy phoning and doing all the things that need to get done. It was depressing yesterday, but today things have gone well.

SEPTEMBER 11, 1992

WHILE I WAS MAKING caramel apples for Sarah, I accidentally hit Alice in the head. I turned to put the glass measuring cup of caramels into the microwave and didn't see her.

"Now I know you're really going blind," Alice sobbed.

I felt so bad. She cried and I held her tight.

Later she asked, "What is it like going blind?"

It was hard to explain, but I thought it might be easier to show her. I took an empty cake mix box, cut it to make a rectangle, then poked two holes where her eyes would be. She held this mask up to her face and was amazed.

"Wow, you really can't see much of anything!" she exclaimed.

She spent the rest of the evening walking around, seeing a glimpse into my new world with the mask. This was a precious love energy moment.

SEPTEMBER 14, 1992

THE KIDS ARE AT school, and it's too quiet here.

Last Saturday morning, we packed a lunch and ventured off to climb Barn Bluff on the Mississippi River in Red Wing. We had a great time, enjoying the spectacular views of the city below. A few barges were chugging their way to their next destination. Sarah found beautiful rocks to add to her collection at home.

Timmy did a lot of climbing . . . up this way, he turned, climbed over a rock, followed the path, went around a huge boulder, and up another steep slope. Moving a branch out of the way, I looked for the kids scattered in all directions as they chose their own route. Giggles carried on the breeze, along with oohs, ahhs, and squeals of delight at each new discovery were some of the amazing journeys of the day.

The top of the bluff was a different world, one of carefree play. We selected a field of grass to lay our blanket down and enjoy our treats. It was the same lunch we always have: peanut butter and jelly sandwiches, carrot and celery sticks, a bag of chips, a juice box, and a cupcake for dessert. The fresh air and adventure made it taste so much more delicious. We drank in the beauty surrounding us before continuing.

The weather was perfect. Before heading back down, we asked someone to take a picture of us with the city below and the Mississippi as a backdrop. The trek down took us to the backside, the north shady side, then to the river side of the bluff. There were several groups of rock climbers selecting their various routes with a few conquering their destination. The bluff looked like an abacus with beads of climbers at different stages.

The children were mesmerized watching them with visions in their minds of wanting to try that someday. My mind chuckled as I hoped that they wouldn't, but if it made them happy . . .

Go for it.

REFLECTION, PRESENT DAY

THIS IS HOW MY journey went. I hadn't realized it until today as I remembered this day with fondness, this gem had been buried for over 25 years.

This journey through my journals amazed me, inspired me, and allowed me to relive my adventures. It hurt too much to even glimpse them before, but as I wrote, that there was a purpose that I hadn't understood—couldn't have hoped to understand—at that time. I simply had to write what was going on inside me so that someday I could reach back and hold the young woman who couldn't stand, who couldn't fly, who couldn't . . .

A vision slowly appeared to me out of my darkness.

Comforting her had been my heart's desire for a long time. The vision became crystal clear as I relaxed into the inspiring guidance from within. I needed to look back at my story so I could uncover the depths of guilt and grief that overwhelmed me. I even commented to Alice on her twenty-seventh birthday, that I had never felt good enough for anything, that I took my punishments because I didn't think I deserved anything decent in my life. I was shocked to learn then that she considered me one of the strongest women she knew.

I wanted to nurture that little girl inside, that me who curled in a corner, consumed by the darkness. I needed to show her the depths of her journey, to reveal to her how she walked around each boulder she encountered. She never sat in a pile of *poor me*. She stood up and went on, looking and searching for her purpose, her path of joy. She climbed this way, up a step, moved a branch, discovered another clarifying moment, rested, and continued on. She found her daily joy and her meaning, not only for her, but for her children. She had to provide for them. She couldn't give up. She climbed to the top.

And she rejoiced!

Chapter Sixteen

A MOMENT OF PEACE

SEPTEMBER 25, 1992

I STARTED MY FIRST Braille lesson. I have to study a little every day to get used to the texture of the raised dots.

REFLECTION, PRESENT DAY

I WASN'T SURPRISED THAT I only briefly mentioned I had started Braille lessons. At the time, the less I said about it and the more I did, the better I felt. Ignoring it helped me not get so depressed.

State Services for the Blind connected me with my classes through Hadley School for the Blind in Winnetka, Illinois. My instructor, Joan, was from Edina, Minnesota. She would send me a cassette tape telling me what my next lesson was in my workbook, *Step by Step Braille Reading Course*, the same book that Deanne had showed me in Longville.

I hated doing these lessons as much as I hated the cane travel course, but I forced myself the whole while, kicking and screaming on the inside, just to get through them. The same sensation came over me as my first introduction to the cane. Not as a snake, but larger . . . a lion ready to pounce and devour my hand as I reached for it.

I did learn a simple technique through Braille class that helps me even today when I read printed material. I place my left pointer finger at the beginning of the line, leave it there, read the line, then return my vision to my finger before I drop it down to the next line to read. My limited central vision doesn't allow me to see the whole line at once. Even as I write this, I can maybe see half the line, definitely not the whole page.

In Braille reading, the same technique applies to keep placement on the page. The left pointer finger stays at the beginning of the line while the right pointer finger glides gently over the raised dots, connecting letters forming the words like a secret code.

October 13, 1992

I went with Dave to the Sheldon Theatre to tune the Steinway grand piano. What a great experience. The resonance of sound encompassed the entire stage while outpouring to the seating area. It was such a rich feeling, much more so than inside a small room. My ears were ecstatic with themselves as if they devoured a delicious meal then finished it with a robust port wine in the crescendo of satisfaction.

I sent in my first Braille lesson today; I'll start the next one tomorrow. There is a pattern that repeats itself, for instance A and K are similar except K has a lower dot. Same with B and L and it continues through the alphabet. I do feel a bit of accomplishment, but still hate the idea of learning to live blind.

ℓⱯOVEMBER 4, 1992

WE FINALLY MOVED INTO our new townhouse in Eau Claire. Rita really helped to make us feel at home and get the kids familiar with their new schools.

Timmy and Alice started right away. Sarah started the following Monday on her thirteenth birthday. That was the beginning of the second quarter, and I thought it would be easier for her. We woke her with gifts and singing then sent her to school.

ℓⱯOVEMBER 18, 1992

TIMMY READ THE BOOK, *Stone Fox*. When he finished at 9:30 P.M., he came to me crying so hard. The main character had died. We sat and cuddled while he told me about it. He's such a caring boy, and I love him so much.

Last Thursday, Sarah and I walked four blocks to her school for an open house. I met her teachers. They all had high praise for her grades and acceptability.

I'm so proud of how she's adjusted and doing the best she can. I love her so much.

ⱭECEMBER 10, 1992

MOM WAS HERE TO go Christmas shopping with me. We stopped at the mall where Alice and Timmy went to see Santa. Later, Alice let us know that it wasn't the real Santa for three reasons.

"First, he yawned," she reported. "Then he didn't say, 'Ho! Ho! Ho!' And three, I slipped my hand up his sleeve and his arm was hairy!"

Mom and I held our chuckles in as she told us her observations.

Timmy's class had to write in their school journal about when they first found out that Santa wasn't real. Timmy questioned me that day about how it all works. He still believed . . . until then.

DECEMBER 23, 1992

IT'S TWO DAYS BEFORE Christmas. We've been wrapping and putting gifts to exchange under the tree. The kids are so excited. I love this magical time of season, the decorating, putting cards that we receive on the wall, and mostly the baking.

I enjoyed making lefse with my new turning stick from Agnus. Alice rolled and made the first one. We enjoyed the tradition of eating the last made sheets as a reward. The delicious taste of melted butter and sugar made us each smile. My sister, Rita, said it was almost as good as Grandma Lee's. Grandma Lee was my dad's mother, Alice Holte Lee. She was also Alice's namesake.

I love the candles on the Advent wreath, how their glow illuminates the room while creating shadows on the walls, the fresh smell from the different candles, and the weekly routine, sharing turns as we light a new candle each Sunday.

DECEMBER 26, 1992

WE HAD A WONDERFUL Christmas. Alice sang with her

church choir at one of the services. She was so cute in her red robe as she stood in front, squirming around in her too-long sleeves, blowing kisses, and waving at us. People all around giggled, enjoying her antics while all the other kids stood very still. When she sang, she really enunciated every word with thorough joy.

I'll cherish that memory forever.

After the Christmas service, Rita drove us around town to look at the lights on the houses. I had a neighbor lady put the gifts under the tree while we were gone. Alice was so excited that Santa had been there. Timmy knew that someone else had placed them there, but I could tell, he still wanted to believe.

My parents did this when I was young. After our Christmas dinner, we would all get into the car so that Dad could drive us around town to see the lights. I finally figured out the magic. Mom would always be the last one to get into the car as she would be placing the presents under the tree while we waited for her. It was great joy to see that, but once again, we missed Santa when we returned.

December 29, 1992

Today I'm at Donny's farm in Longville.

I felt a need to call Mom last night and am glad I did. She told me her mother, Grandma Ida Allram, passed away at age ninety-two. I had a dream about Grandma last night. She wanted me to rock her and sing to her while she died. Mom was always asking me to sing to Grandma and Grandpa when I visited.

December 30, 1992

Grandma Allram's funeral was today. Alice was very intrigued. She didn't understand what was going on. Her cousin, Michael, age 4, commented that Grandma can't talk anymore, and we won't see her again.

"But she'll always be in our hearts," Alice replied.

After the funeral, the families gathered at the Allram Farm near Ridgeland, Wisconsin. A group of cousins and kids went to the barn.

"Pew!" Alice said after her very brief visit to the barn while holding her nose.

My cousin, Jim, said, "Her comment in the barn was, 'I never want to be a cow!'"

Reflection, Present day

As 1992 came to a close, I reflected on its journey as a transition of a moment in time. A transition like the one that Grandma had taken. I felt her life with MS confined to a wheelchair ran parallel to my own, living with RP and my diminishing sight. Little by little, daily changes, always adjusting to the new present. Could I have taken lessons from her apparent confidence and never complaining? She seemed the strongest woman I knew, exuding happiness and smiling joy, excited about our visits, and waving good-bye from the window as we left. I wonder how she felt about herself.

The blank pages have been filled and a new chapter opens.

Chapter Seventeen

SETBACKS

DON'T QUIT

by John Greenleaf Whittier

When things go wrong as they sometimes will,
When the road you're trudging seems all uphill,
When the funds are low and the debts are high,
And you want to smile, but you have to sigh.
When care is pressing you down a bit,
Rest if you must, but don't you quit.

Success is failure turned inside out,
The silver tint of the clouds of doubt,
And you never can tell how close you are,
It may be near when it seems afar.
So, stick to the fight when you're hardest hit–
It's when things go wrong that you mustn't quit.[14]

---

14   Publisher's note: John Greenleaf Whittier's poem "Don't Quit" is in the public
domain.

*I*ntroduction 1993

When selecting 1993's journal, I thought the above poem on the front cover was appropriate. I needed inspiration to get through the upcoming year.

I also found a cartoon from *Dennis the Menace* to put on the inside cover. Dennis was looking out a window at the night sky with a friend.

"I wouldn't mind the dark if I could SEE in it better," Dennis said.

That's how I felt . . . or wanted to feel . . . that it wasn't going to be so bad.

*J*anuary 3, 1993

After church, Donny left to go back to Longville. He was with me for ten days and offered great support during the funeral.

I went to my nephew's birthday party. Rita drove her car with Sarah, my niece, Tammy, and me. My other niece, Jessica, drove my car with Timmy and Alice.

I still hate not driving. Out of everything that's been taken away, not being able to drive is the hardest. It's my main source of independence. Having to rely on others pisses me off. I was never late before and now I have to patiently wait on someone else's time schedule. If I dwell on that thought, it hurts too much. So, if I need to, I allow myself a brief moment to throw a temper tantrum, stomp my feet, give a loud scream of anguish, and then I get on with life.

Focusing on, why me, moments usually only makes it worse. Having to rely on others' time frames is honing my ability to organize all the details of our busy lives. I keep lists of items needed so that I'm ready at any moment's notice. I'm always prepared and proud of myself for developing that skill.

I was told recently that I'm not the only one that must depend on others.

"Just to get a glass of milk to your table, there's an extensive production process. And everyone involved depends on everyone else," the woman smugly said as if she had solved my life trauma.

Well, let me tell you, she was so proud of thinking up that little tidbit of information. I wanted to smack her. Well, not really, but it sure didn't make me feel any better.

"Oh my, yes, thank you!" she probably wanted me to say. "Now I can go on with my life and feel happy, happy, happy about everything, because everyone has to rely on others for everything!"

Bull crap! It made me feel worse as I crawled back into my place, the dark corner of my world where I wouldn't disturb other "normal" people.

*J*ANUARY 4, 1993

I TALKED TO FIVE of the seventh-grade science classes today, including Sarah's. I talked about retinitis pigmentosa and what it has done to my vision. Rita made some overhead slides to use for a demonstration. It was interesting to hear the questions in each class.

"Now how are you going to make money?" asked a student.

"What about a seeing eye dog?" asked another.

I answered the best I could. "I'm trying to develop an

occupation where I can make money," I said. "I've been told that having a seeing eye dog would require almost complete blindness so that I would totally rely on the dog's skills. I still have enough vision so that isn't necessary yet."

The Longville Lions Club generously offered to pay for one when the time comes.

I told the classes about my upcoming eye appointment. They wished me well, but I grew depressed on my walk home. I had talked about my RP over and over again telling the same gloom-filled future while putting a smile on my face.

"There isn't a cure or prevention," I said.

No recovery. I didn't know what I was going to do. No hope, no cure, no nothing. *Poor me . . .*

I felt even worse when I returned home and opened the mail. My Social Security amount wasn't even close to what I was told I would receive. I tried so hard for so long to get Social Security because I believed I would be able to get off assistance and provide a better life for the children.

Dear God, I know you watch over me and I must be patient, but I hurt so. I want to be able to provide for myself and my family, anything they need. Most of all, I was told that the back pay I've been waiting for isn't going to come. I called my attorney and he couldn't explain anything.

Listen, listen, listen . . . hold on.

REFLECTION, PRESENT DAY

THE SEED WAS BEING nudged to begin its journey, growing strong in the pain while sending out another root of courage.

*J*ANUARY 5, 1993

MY ANNUAL EYE APPOINTMENT is today. Uncle Morris took me to see Dr. Lee Hofer at the Chippewa Valley Eye Clinic. I had a visual field test taken, and they provided another printout. It was like looking through a kaleidoscope tunnel. The tiny central circle at the end was bright and mostly clear, but it looked like someone had taken a brush full of paint and splattered the sides, blocking out light and leaving clumps of darkness.

The darkness blocks my sight, blocks my hope, blocks my joy.

"Your central clear vision shows about ten degrees remaining," Dr. Hofer explained in a very caring and concerned tone. "Compared to your chart from last year, there is a decrease."

No, no, no that's not what I wanted to hear! I had been preparing myself for weeks, convincing myself that this was going to show an improvement, that the diagnosis had been wrong.

I was crushed as, once again, my world plummeted away from me. All facets within my kaleidoscope were glaring at me, mocking me as I slumped back into darkness, into the corner of nothingness where I could feel only numb. I was going blind and couldn't be expected to accomplish anything else. Would it be okay to just exist? Be a non-entity?

*J*ANUARY 12, 1993

SARAH IS HOME FROM school eating the freshly baked chocolate chip cookies and drinking chocolate milk. The other two will be home shortly. It has snowed about four inches so far today. I know Timmy will go sledding with his friends.

JANUARY 15, 1993

I HAD SUCH A depressing day. I finally wrote a letter to the judge who I saw last September for Social Security. I even called the Eau Claire office. Then, in the mail, I received a letter about the amount being changed again.

I'm so tired of the run-around and always different amounts. I can't plan a budget or pay all the bills.

Lord, please carry me through my pain. I know you are always with me. Today, I want to give up. I need more sunshine in my life. Today, I keep thinking of all the tragedies in my life, my failed marriage, the armed robbery in 1984, my RP, not having a career, and so much more. I must remember what sunshine I do have, like my beautiful children, a nice townhouse, a loving family that is close, and a friendly church and neighbors.

REFLECTION, PRESENT DAY

As I READ MY journal, I felt the defeat as I grouped my list of negatives, proving how unworthy I felt. These included my armed robbery of 1984. I'd never felt so helpless in all my life as I did in that moment, a moment that could have ended in so many different ways. I was so traumatized by the event that I didn't write about it in my journal until February 11, 1985. Before I shared this story, I wanted to set the scene of where I was.

In 1984, I was married to Tim and renting a house on Lake Wabedo eight miles from Longville, Minnesota. The population was 191. We had two children, Sarah, age five, and Timmy was fifteen months old.

Here's the story taken from my journal entry from February 1985.

*F*EBRUARY 5, 1985

ON DECEMBER 8, 1984, I was working at Pat's One Stop gas station and convenience store in Longville, Minnesota. I worked alone in the evenings before closing at 9 P.M. I really enjoyed working there and met a lot of interesting people.

At 8:46 P.M. the phone rang.

"Hello," I answered, "Pat's One Stop, how can I help you?"

"What time do you close?" a gruff voice asked.

I told him 9 o'clock, and he hung up. Four minutes later, he called again and said his friend was coming to get some bacon, but he wanted to know the prices. Like a trusting employee, I got the six prices he insisted I get for him. I had to walk to the back of the store for this. As I set the phone on the counter, I noticed headlights from across the street in the parking lot but thought nothing of them. I returned to the phone and started reading off the prices of bacon to him.

While I was talking to the man on the phone, a man stepped just inside the door. I didn't look up as I was reading off the bacon prices, so he had to get my attention.

"Put the phone down, bitch!" he said. "This is a stick up! Put it down!"

I was thinking, *How rude*, when I slowly gazed up, a motion that seemed paused in time as I realized what was on the other side of the counter. A small black handgun, not much bigger than the fist gripping it, with a short double barrel that was pointed right at my face.

At first, I thought it was a joke or that it was made of

licorice, then I looked up at his face and saw he wasn't kidding. He was wearing a ski cap to cover his hair, then a nylon stocking over his entire head. His face was squished flat and was a shiny white. No facial hair at all. His eyes squeezed into dark slits.

"Put the phone on the counter, bitch!" he repeated with more aggression.

I did as he said. He then told me to put all the money in a bag. I reached under the counter for a bag and noticed the crowbar there in case of robberies. Right, I wasn't about to take on a gun by using a crowbar. I opened the cash register and put all the paper money from the drawer into it. He mumbled something I couldn't understand. I couldn't hear it because my heart was beating so fast and loud.

"Give me the money under the counter!" he yelled at me.

He thought there was more money under the counter, but there wasn't.

"Hurry up or I'll shoot you, bitch!"

I shoved the bag across the countertop to him and told him that was all there was. He grabbed it and told me to go into the cooler at the back of the store.

I wasn't going fast enough, and he yelled again, "Run, bitch!"

So I ran. In a panic, I ran as fast as I could. When I got to the walk-in cooler, I tried to breathe. Slowly I crawled on the cold floor toward the shelving of bacon where I could see the front door. He was gone. I scooted right out because I was getting claustrophobic.

Slowly, I crawled against the back wall, listening for any noise. I needed to get to the phone and call for help. The man was still on the phone. Hysterically, I told him that I was robbed and to call the police. I hung up, but when I picked the receiver back up, he was still on the line. He did this four times. The last time, I could hear someone entering in the background on his end.

REFLECTION, PRESENT DAY

THIS WAS 1984, PRE-911 in Longville, pre-cell phone, and pre-video surveillance.

FEBRUARY 5, 1985, CONTINUED

WHEN I WAS ABLE to get through, I called Pat, the owner of the store, and told him what happened. A policeman came and got a description from me.

"This will be a great story to tell your grandchildren," was all I remember him saying to me.

That made me mad. That night, I didn't have the car, so Tim had to come and get me. I'm glad he didn't come when the robbery was happening. The kids, Sarah and Timmy, were asleep in the back seat and he always pulled up to the front door and waited for me to close the store. He could've trapped the robber while he was inside the store.

I knew he wasn't a local because I knew everyone by working there, but he must have been staying close enough to be back with the guy on the phone within a few minutes.

JANUARY 15,1993

I FELT I HAD grown ten years older in that one night. My marshmallow world had melted. I couldn't write about the robbery for a while. Likewise, with my RP, I wasn't able to write about my eyes when my therapist wanted me to.

I'm too traumatized by the bad news from my annual eye exam, and the changing amounts from Social Security contribute more to the trauma and feelings of helplessness that I've been living since my diagnosis day. No wonder my mind dredges up another drama.

Chapter Eighteen

CONTINUING ON

JANUARY 14, 1993

SARAH WENT SKIING WITH the band class from school at Afton Alps. She said she had such a good time.

She plays the trumpet that I built in Red Wing and also a French horn in a symphony band. I love to see her happy.

JANUARY 26, 1993

I rearranged the living room again.

"Bored again, Mom?" Sarah asked when she came home from school.

* * *

I WAS DEPRESSED EARLIER this month and wrote about all the disasters that had happened to me. I guess that helped me get over that for a while and allowed happier memories to become more prevalent, like in 1990, when we went kite flying at the Longville airport.

"Keep running, Alice," I encouraged. "You've almost got it up."

A gust of wind too strong for her tiny fist took her kite away. We watched as Donny ran after it like a gazelle and was able to retrieve it.

✳ ✳ ✳

ANOTHER FOND MEMORY FROM 1987 that occurred to me was cutting Christmas trees in two feet of freshly fallen snow. While living on Lake Wabedo, I walked with Sarah, seven years old, and Timmy, four, while pulling Alice, who was almost two, on the sled. As we walked down the driveway, all the pines stood tall like soldiers with their new white coats of snow. We journeyed the quarter mile to the end of our driveway for the best selection. The children stayed by the side of the road, while I trudged in waist deep snow to the bottom of the long ditch. Sarah directed me toward her first choice.

I grabbed hold of the soldier's trunk, ducked my head, and shook. *Flump!* The snow fell dumping me in a pile of cold winter white. All three of them giggled like little chipmunks at my display.

"How's this one?" I asked their waiting faces.

"No, try another one." Timmy suggested.

I trudged on a few feet, grabbed hold, ducked my head, and shook. *Flump!* This went on for about ten trees until I figured out they just liked the snow falling on me, so I threw a snowball in their direction, receiving more squeals and giggles. We ended up choosing the first one. I cut it down, pulled it up the steep bank, and gleefully, we sang Christmas carols on our adventure back with our reward.

* * *

YET ANOTHER FOND MEMORY was in 1990 on the 4th of July. While waiting for the fireworks to explode in Longville, Timmy was bored, so he showed us how fast he could run around the basketball court. Alice counted each lap. Faster and faster he ran with such joy on his face. Thirty laps! I grew exhausted just watching him.

JANUARY 27, 1993

TIMMY HAS BEEN BUSY with a science project for school. He had to choose a science question and show the class his observations. He looked through our science encyclopedia and decided to find out how a lemon can light a light bulb. He had Uncle Mark and Grandpa Lee help with this project.

Alice played *The Snake Dance* on the piano last night. I'm thrilled that she wants to learn. I showed her the D minor hand position and she played it with both hands on the first try.

I desire to always remember that each of my children will have their own passion. This is good to remember when Alice says she wants to be in Pom-Poms, gymnastics, and cheerleading.

My sister, Rita, started her new school aide job yesterday. She is at the school Sarah attends.

Now what am I going to do all day? I hope something productive happens.

REFLECTION, PRESENT DAY

THE SEED RECEIVED ANOTHER drop of water, encouraging it

to prepare for the shoot to start taking form.

FEBRUARY 3, 1993

THE KIDS ARE AT school. I've done my morning exercise and taken a shower. I was going to bake a cake, but I only have one egg and need two. Boy, I wish I could drive. The neighbors are gone, or I would borrow one from them. This is such a huge town, and has everything, but the closest store is ten blocks away. The bus takes too long to loop through town: I'll have to find something else to occupy my time.

Dad was admitted to the critical care unit yesterday with very high blood pressure. He's had problems for years. Last night, Mom was upset when I talked to her. Besides Dad not being well, her dad isn't doing well and keeps waiting to die to be with Grandma Allram.

We went to a Super Bowl party at my cousin, Julie's. Sue, her sister, rode with us. During our return trip on the freeway, the car quit. We were hoping someone would stop and help, but it didn't happen so Sue and Sarah walked in the snow and cold a mile to the previous exit to call for help.

We were towed to a service station where they discovered a coil wire had come unplugged. God was watching over us though, because a few other things needed repair. I had them take care of those too. Even though I could no longer drive, I couldn't give up the sense of independence totally; I still wanted to own a car and did.

Besides, it won't be too long before Sarah is driving.

FEBRUARY 5, 1993

I SPENT MOST OF yesterday at the hospital with Dad. Joan and

John came and took me there. I stayed until Mom came later in the afternoon. She also took me to get groceries.

Dad had a test to check his remaining kidney. He had one of them removed several years before because of cancer. The test showed blockage in an artery that comes from the heart. They wanted him to have surgery to remove the blockage at the Mayo Clinic in Rochester, Minnesota early the following week. He cried when they told him, happy that they finally found the reason for his high blood pressure after so many years.

FEBRUARY 9, 1993

ALICE AND TIMMY ARE doing so well with the piano lessons I teach them. Some of their lessons include me playing my own part along with them. They really love that, as do I.

Sarah likes to practice her trumpet in front of the window in her bedroom, and I've noticed a great improvement. Rita laughed when she saw Sarah practicing there during her visit yesterday.

I worked on my Braille yesterday, too, and finally finished another lesson to submit.

I noticed an ad in the newspaper for a sales trainee for Schmitt Music. It was for entry level sales on keyboard. I stopped in for an application and let them know about my disability. They said they could probably work around it.

Dear Lord, is this where I should go?

Dad went home from the hospital. His pressure had been stable for a few days. They went to Rochester to find out about the surgery and have to go back tomorrow.

I don't know if it's for the surgery or not.

FEBRUARY 18, 1993

IT'S BEEN A VERY emotional week for me. Dad had surgery in Rochester. Timmy and Alice stayed with the neighbors and Sarah stayed with a friend.

Mom, Rita, and I saw Dad go into surgery Monday morning, but Joan, my brother, Steve, and his wife, Julie, just missed him. The six of us patiently waited for reports all day. By 1:30 P.M., we were informed that the graft taken from Dad's leg to the one remaining kidney had complications. They had to reopen and discover why.

Dad had a couple rough days.

MARCH 17, 1993

SO MUCH HAS HAPPENED since my last entry that I hope I can remember everything.

Alice had a wonderful seventh birthday party with eight other girls. She said it was the best party she ever had.

Sarah went to the University of Minnesota for a NASA program. She really enjoyed it and was filled with conversation when she returned.

Dad took a turn for the worse, so Rita and I went to Rochester while the kids were with their father. Dad was finally able to come home on Friday, although he developed a hernia and will have to go back when he's stronger.

I completed three more Braille lessons.

I'm hoping to finish one lesson a month—I hate them. With each one, I feel the pull of darkness. I don't want to sink into this pit, but the lessons say to me that I don't have a voice in what is happening to me. Too many areas of my life are so out of my control, but Braille has a power of, well, making me spiral in outer space, into the darkness with no control over which direction I go or how . . . or even why. I'm spinning not knowing which way is up or down.

Where am I going? Will it be this dark forever?

In the distance though, there is a small spark, a glow that the tiniest distant part of me knows already. I will be taken care of. This journey will not overtake me. It can't because there is a reason for everything that happens. I don't need to know why now or maybe ever.

This is faith?

Listen . . . listen to that inner small voice that comes from that spark. It's whispering to me of a story that is mine. Listen, during those moments of complete loss.

I will listen.

It is telling of its love for me and the strength I have found but am not yet aware of.

Listen, listen, listen . . . hold on.

Chapter Nineteen

She Shall Not Be Discouraged

*And though you started with little, you will
end with much.*

—Job 8:7[15]

April 2, 1993

Yesterday was April Fool's Day and once again, Sarah
really got Timmy. When he awoke, she told him that all the
snow had melted, and the downstairs was flooded. He really
fell for it. I was trying not to laugh as she went into detail
on how the furniture was floating. He wasn't happy when he
realized he had been fooled.

Alice wore Timmy's arm brace to school and fooled
people by saying she had a broken arm.

---

15 Nelson, *The Holy Bible*

*A*PRIL 16, 1993

TIMMY HAD BEEN COUNTING down to his tenth birthday on April 18th. Tonight, he made an announcement at the supper table: "I'm going to be ten years old and I want everyone to now call me Tim!"

Oh my, my little boy, Timmy, is growing up. This will be an adjustment, but I will honor his request.

Goodbye, Timmy.

Hello, my young man, Tim.

*A*PRIL 19, 1993

TIM HAD A GREAT party yesterday as I gathered twenty-four of our family members to celebrate. Yes, he made his name change declaration to everyone.

"You will always be Timmy to me," some expressed.

He asked for a zip cord glider for his birthday, so I bought him one. He thoroughly enjoyed seeing how high the glider went each time he launched it.

A house full of people was a visual struggle for me, but I tried not to show it. I just slowed and took caution before I moved anywhere. I was so afraid I was going to trip over someone or something. Nobody knew how I felt, and I preferred it that way. *Just continue and act as if all is good*, I told myself. Besides, we had a great birthday party.

I've been so depressed again. I need to find mutual support—somebody who is experiencing the same challenges and learning how to handle them. I'm not sure I want counseling again. I'm just so tired of handling all of this alone.

*A*PRIL 20, 1993

WE BURIED GRANDMA ALLRAM on Tuesday, her spring
internment. Afterward, we went to Glenhaven, in Glenwood
City, to visit Grandpa Allram. He kept asking Mom and Joan
if they were coming to take him back home. At 93 years old,
the past few years were the first he's ever lived away from the
Allram farm where he was born and raised.

And now he is alone . . . without Grandma.

*A*PRIL 22, 1993

SARAH PLAYED A BEAUTIFUL solo with her jazz band during
the Renaissance Festival at her school. I love watching her
play. Her sense of rhythm is intoxicating, and I find myself
tapping my foot to her smooth version.

Other songs were well harmonized with the group.

*A*PRIL 28, 1993

GRANDPA EDWIN VALENTINE ALLRAM died this morning,
four months to the day after Grandma Ida Allram passed
away. It also is the birthdate of Grandpa Simen Lee, my dad's
father.

*M*AY 18, 1993

I MADE AN APPOINTMENT for counseling and will have
weekly sessions for a while. I've been so depressed and feeling
overwhelmed.

I've been working on crocheting an afghan to keep busy

and my Braille lessons.

JUNE 4, 1993

MY NEIGHBOR TOOK ME for another counseling session. I was hesitant about this one. The counselor had asked me to do only two things during the week and I hadn't done either. One was to contact a totally blind lady she knew in town. Second, to call the Chippewa Valley Technical College about women's career counseling.

Why did I make excuses not to do either?

I started crying during the session, because I hurt deeply about doing anything to affirm my blindness. Even writing this brought a lump to my throat and tears to my eyes.

If I acknowledge RP, more will be taken away. I don't even want to write out the whole name. Instead, I abbreviate it. It seems like there's an allotment of pain thrown at me. I can only endure one pain at a time so that is what is flung my way, only one at a time, no more, until I get a grip on it . . . then more . . . then more . . . then more . . .

Help me!

I remember last year when I attended counseling in Red Wing and discovered I hadn't written anything in my journals about my eyes. I tried to share this information with my new counselor, and I was shocked when she preferred talking to me about her cancer. Normally, I would try to reach out to comfort another, but this time I didn't. I didn't mean to be heartless, but I just needed the session to be about me.

JUNE 25, 1993

I HAD MY FIRST massage ever yesterday. I was nervous and not sure what to expect during the session, but it was a relaxing studio. Dim lighting set the mood, which at first stimulated my panic mode, but I adjusted.

Kay, the massage therapist, had a gentle style about her. The power of her touch was amazing. I had never had my hands massaged and that simple act reached throughout my entire body. Each stroke helped me to fall deeper into a zone that gave me such peace. I felt refreshed and calm like I never had before. I wanted more of this and to know how to help others feel this empowering self-love.

I'm thinking of going to school to be a massage therapist like Vicki suggested a couple years ago. The closest school is in Minneapolis. I'll have to get more information.

REFLECTION, PRESENT DAY

THE SEED THAT HAD lain dormant was watered, and its roots could grow. These roots would find their own way, each spreading a different direction, each at their own time, each at their own tempo. They would find their way through the darkness of the soil, pausing for strength and sustenance and then reaching out toward a destination yet unknown. All the roots knew was that they were strengthened and nourished and could not contain themselves by staying idle.

The journey had to continue.

An adventure could not be found by sitting dormant. These roots were the foundation to stabilize what would grow above the soil.

But wait, that time has not yet completely come.

July 20, 1993

A MAJOR REPORT CAME out last week on the benefits of Vitamin A slowing down the progress of retinitis pigmentosa. I requested more literature on it from my eye doctor.

I'm also working with the DVR, Department of Vocational Rehabilitation, to go to massage school. I hope to start fall classes in September. I have a lot to do before then like getting a physical, references, and finding and obtaining transportation. Next week, I meet with Social Services for the Blind to see if they will help with funding through their P.A.S.S. program, Program for Attaining Self-Sufficiency. I feel strongly that this is what I want to do.

Originally, when I was diagnosed with RP, I was adamant about staying within a musical field. My calculations seemed so simple. Blindness + music = piano tuning, 2 + 2 = 4, but instead it turned out to be 2 + 2 = 5. After the three-week piano tuning class, I came to another conclusion. I gained enough knowledge in piano tuning and repair to cause major damage to any piano!

Deep breath in, let it out. Yes, I think that is comical now. It's a journey in progress. I have so much to learn through every speed bump.

July 22, 1993

I TRADED MY CAR for another one, and I have deep emotions about it. I still feel the need to have a vehicle even though I can't drive. Someday, Sarah will be able to, but today, I can't give up that part of my independence. I feel the waterfall starting to flow over the dam again.

I can't drive and I hate my disease!

July 29, 1993

I HAVE A BAD cold, causing a concern about my central vision. I hope it's the medication.

Every moment of every day, I am waiting, aware I will be totally blind in five to ten years, or even next week. When? Will I know the signs and so what if I do? There's nothing to stop it. When I wake in the morning and open my eyes, will there be light? Will I ever see the faces of my children as they grow into adulthood?

I hate turning off light switches because I want to see all I can. I leave them on all the time. My fear is overwhelming, waiting for the black to take what I have left. He's smiling and creeping in the darkness, waiting for the moment when I will least expect it. That's when he will pounce.

"Why didn't you prepare?" Fear will condemn. "Why are you so surprised? You know you aren't good enough for anything but the darkness. You haven't earned the joyful life."

I want to run as far and as fast as I can away from this dark hole. I don't want to turn around when I feel its breath on my neck, but that feeling is always there. I try to focus on what is in front of me: I see a small glimmer of light when I think of this massage school. I don't know how it is going to work.

Red Wing didn't work even though I have a degree as a Band Instrument Repair Technician. Piano Tuning for three weeks didn't help, but I did learn one thing—

I *can* learn. That is a pride that glows within me, shining on my future path. It pulls me to reach out to see what else I can do.

Stay away, darkness. Stay away, Fear. I'm not ready for you. I never will be. I am going to win. In a very, very small voice, a whisper, I tell myself that if there is total blindness, I will be okay and find my joy somehow in that too.

But I don't want to.

So there!

August 5, 1993

I FINISHED A QUILT for my parents. I had asked Mom if I could use her parents' clothes to make it. I was able to add Grandpa Allram's shirts to the combination of Grandma Allram's dresses. Cutting them into squares created a loving pattern. A neighbor showed me how to use a flat sheet for the backing. I used the sewing machine my parents bought me. Threading the needle was the hardest part. While I sewed, I inspected where the material was and went slow so I didn't run over my finger. I was immensely proud of myself for accomplishing this task.

Each square spoke to me of the farm life they had lived. Grandpa loved the land and produced what he could, while Grandma occupied herself with what she could accomplish in her kitchen from her wheelchair. Her Multiple Sclerosis confined her to staying inside many years before. I'm sure she had many frustrations with her disability, but to me she didn't seem discouraged and kept moving forward with what she could do. She made the best chocolate chip cookies and chocolate cake. I have tried to make them but can't match the way she did. Maybe it was being at the farm that made them taste so good.

I'm inspired to continue with my RP journey, encouraged by her struggle and setbacks.

*A*UGUST 30, 1993

I HAD A PHYSICAL today for going to school. I'll start in January at Northern Lights School of Massage Therapy in Minneapolis, Minnesota, which is about 90 miles west from Eau Claire, Wisconsin.

The counselor I have from DVR is more interested in her soon-to-be retirement than helping me. When I finally talked about my future, she almost laughed about my thoughts.

Massage therapy remains the center of my focus, though I'm not sure how this is going to work out. The P.A.S.S. program has agreed to pay for my transportation after detailing a specific plan.

*S*EPTEMBER 14, 1993

SARAH HAS MADE MANY accomplishments in such a short time at school.

She's first chair trumpet and taking private lessons at Schmitt Music, the local music store. She is editor for the yearbook and made student council. I'm so proud of her. She can do anything with her drive and desire. That inspires me to continue on.

*S*EPTEMBER 20, 1993

I HAD AN IMPACTED wisdom tooth that really hurt. I also had an abnormal pap smear and had to have a colonoscopy.

I don't need any more health problems, thank you very much!

October 18, 1993

I've been very depressed for a few days. My colonoscopy came back bad, so I had to have cryosurgery. That was very emotional for me.

My eye doctor and I sent out letters to reach other RP patients. Three have responded so far. Last week, I called the local newspaper to advertise a support group. They expressed interest in doing a feature article on me. They said they'd be here next week for an interview and to take pictures.

I hope I won't be so depressed then.

I've been composing more songs and enjoying how relaxed that makes me feel. Words seem to be a problem—I had a dream that helped one song. I was searching through a huge house. It was very dark. I didn't know what I was looking for. I came to a room full of books. In a corner was a man sitting in a comfortable chair. He was Jesus, illuminated and glowing.

"You looked for me," he said as he turned toward me. "That's what I wanted you to do."

Within an hour, I had the lyrics to the song, "Jesus Said." The last verse impacted me the most . . .

*"Your troubles will not overwhelm you.
The trials that come will not hurt you. I'll be
there by your side."*

October 19, 1993

Alice had a Girl Scout orientation meeting tonight. Rita gave us a ride there and was going to pick us up later. The meeting was for signing up and we finished early. Several people offered to give us a ride home, but I didn't want to miss Rita. There wasn't a way to get in touch with her. We waited forty-five minutes, but luckily, the weather was nice. Alice was tired and hungry, so after waiting a while, we started walking. We were almost home by the time Rita pulled up. She felt so bad, and I felt even worse. But I wasn't mad at her at all.

I hate being dependent.

Yesterday, I had to wait forty-five minutes for a ride from a friend after an appointment downtown. Alice said she wished I wasn't going blind.

I'll never get used to this.

October 20, 1993

Sarah left a wonderful card for me.

"It's impossible to thank you for everything you've done," it said, "but I'll give it a try . . . THANKS! . . . hey, that wasn't so hard after all!"

Then she wrote, "I'm sorry that I get mad at you sometimes, but you're always the one who's there to help me get through everything. I love you! Sarah." What a very special way to start my day!

October 26, 1993

I taught a class of seven friends from church how to make lefse. I grew up having lefse as a special Christmas treat made by my Grandma Lee. It's Norwegian potato flat bread. The potatoes are boiled, peeled, put through a ricer, and mixed with flour. A small amount, about the size of a golf ball, is rolled out flat and grilled a few minutes on one side then flipped to brown the other side. Each sheet is buttered and sugared, rolled and enjoyed.

We had a lot of fun. Uffda!

October 30, 1993

It was a special day for Sarah as we gathered twenty family members together to celebrate her upcoming fourteenth birthday. I bought her a Black Hills gold and silver ring.

November 2, 1993

Sarah is fourteen and growing into a young beautiful lady.

She said she had a good day at school. For supper, we went to Chi-Chi's. The waiter embarrassed her by getting everyone's attention and singing to her. She did enjoy the free fried ice cream.

* * *

I had an interview with the *Leader-Telegram*, Eau Claire's newspaper, about starting a support group for retinitis pigmentosa. They said they'll be taking a picture next week and the article should be printed before the end of the month.

I've been in another terrible depression since the interview. Whenever I face the acknowledgment that I'm going blind, this happens. I'm not sure if PMS is a factor. I cry myself to sleep and cry sporadically during the day. I just have to keep busy and focus on other things.

* * *

I wrote another song. I heard it in my mind during last Sunday's sermon. I wrote the melody then started finding the right words.

I had an energy assistance appointment. Then at noon, I went to lunch with my cousin, Julie. That was interesting. She took me to a bar that serves food. It was very dimly lit and hard for me to negotiate the chairs as I tried to follow her to a table.

"So, Pam," she asked after we were seated, "how much can you see?"

"Well," I started, "when I look across the table at your face, I can't see your shoulders."

"Well, can you see this?" she asked.

Suddenly, I recognized that she was holding up her hand in front of her face and giving me the finger. We laughed, as I crawled into a corner on the inside. Once again, I felt the self-imposed shame of not being a normal human. I thought I was doing better than that. Hopefully, she didn't notice as I readjusted the happy face mask back into position.

*N*OVEMBER 5, 1993

I JUST FINISHED A game of *Pick-up-sticks* with Alice. I'm tired from the day, so I said, "Goodnight."

Alice and Tim are trying again to see how late they can stay up on a Friday night. The night is mysterious still to them. They're not sure exactly what to do, but watching TV is exciting. I'm sure they will both fall asleep with the TV on. Sarah is spending the weekend with her dad who is now living in Minneapolis.

ℓ𝒩OVEMBER 6, 1993

OUR FIRST SNOW OF the season came during the night before I had to be in Minneapolis for an interview at Northern Lights School of Massage Therapy. My support group was my dad and sisters, Rita and Joan.

I was nervous, but it went very well. I didn't feel any discomfort at all about my disability. I was only concerned about being accepted into the program as they only take sixteen students per semester. They did let me know of other possible contacts in Eau Claire for transportation.

I'll leave it in God's hands. He's done pretty well so far.

We stopped for pie on the way home then at Target. I was feeling constipated and needed a laxative. I giggled when I discovered the only two items I was buying were a snow shovel and a laxative!

I laughed so hard tears ran down my cheeks. Rita caught on to what was going on and acted out the part by walking behind me on the way out with the shovel. Dad just rolled his eyes and chuckled. I guess you had to be there.

ℓ𝒩OVEMBER 9, 1993

I WROTE THE VERSE and chorus words to my new song, "God Shines." Part of the chorus is, "*As He shines in what we do, let Him shine through me to you.*"

Teacher's conferences were this afternoon for Sarah. She made the A honor roll for the first time ever, making me very proud. Her teachers feel she contributes a lot to each class.

I played with Alice and the doll house today. We bought a small Christmas tree for it and made paper Thanksgiving turkeys. She liked mine better than hers and asked if she could take coloring classes.

*N*OVEMBER 13, 1993

I HEAR LOTS OF giggles downstairs. Sarah's friend, Amy, planned a surprise birthday party for her. There are eight girls here and I don't even know all their names. I hope she's having fun.

*W*EDNESDAY, NOVEMBER 24, 1993

THE ARTICLE ABOUT ME appeared in the *Leader-Telegram* today.

SLIPPING AWAY

DISEASE SLOWLY TAKES A WOMAN'S SIGHT

By Traci Klein

Leader-Telegram staff

Pamela Lee prepares for the day she will be blind.

"I get up in the middle of the night and stare at them sleeping," Lee says of her children, Sarah, 14, Tim, 10 and Alice, 7. "I put them in my visual memory."

Lee, 36, of Eau Claire has retinitis pigmentosa, a group of inherited diseases that causes the rod and cone cells to degenerate over time.

There is an increasing loss of peripheral, or side, vision, which creates tunnel vision.

In the United States 100,000 people have RP, but not everyone with RP goes completely blind.

"RP doesn't affect the vision that I have; it just blocks out vision," Lee says.

Lee's vision loss has progressed to the point that she has no peripheral vision, and when she looks at a person straight on, she doesn't see much above or below the person's face.

RP usually can be diagnosed in the teens, Lee says.

When Lee looks back to her teen years, she can remember being prone to tripping and bumping into things, having trouble parallel parking and backing up, and with night blindness.

Night blindness is the first symptom of RP, according to the National Retinitis Pigmentosa Foundation.

At a regular eye exam in February 1991, when Lee was living in northern Minnesota, she was diagnosed with RP.

At the time, she was a secretary for an insurance company but decided she needed to plan for an eventual sightless future.

She plays the piano, mandolin, and flute, so she decided to apply to a piano tuning program in Red Wing, Minn., and she and her children moved there in fall 1991.

That program hadn't started yet, so she went through a band instrument repair program first, but when it came time to start the piano course, she was told it wouldn't be offered because there wasn't enough money.

Within the same week, she saw a doctor at

the University of Minnesota in Minneapolis. He told her she would be blind in five to 10 years and took her driver's license away. "That was just another blow," she says.

She then took a piano tuning course in Shell Lake [Wisconsin]. And in fall 1992, Lee, a native of Glenwood City with relatives in Eau Claire, moved to Eau Claire to be closer to family. She recently applied to a yearlong program in Minneapolis to become certified as a massage therapist.

The piano tuning course, massage program, and Braille correspondence course are all efforts to make sure she is employable as she loses more of her sight.

"I need to do something where I can stay in town," she says, adding that she has contacted local massage businesses to express her interest in a job after the course. "My kids have been in four different schools in four years, and that's enough."

Learning Braille and how to use a cane for the blind forced her to acknowledge her disease.

"It took a long time for me to force myself to do it, and it still does," she says of Braille.

Depending on family and friends to drive her places is also difficult. "I hate to be needy," she says.

Once a year she has a visual field exam to monitor the progression of the disease. "That's about all I can do," she says. "It's just so I know what's going on."

She has looked into the palmitate form of vitamin A, which may delay the progress of the disease, says Dr. Lee Hofer, an Eau Claire ophthalmologist who treats Lee.

But the doses are fairly large, he says, and there are side effects, such as headaches, nausea, liver damage, and hair and weight loss.

Researchers continue to look for solutions for people with RP, Hofer said.

In a recent study, retinas were electrically stimulated with a light sensitive chip, which would allow people with RP to see flashes of light where they couldn't before, Hofer says.

In addition. Retinal cell transplantation, an intricate process, is being studied on animals now, a spokeswoman at the National RP Foundation says.

Hofer is impressed with Lee's attitude.

"She is a role model for people with RP or anyone with a serious affliction that will change the course of life," says Hofer, adding that he's found there are less than 20 people in the Chippewa Valley with RP. "She is taking control of her life despite her serious visual limitation."

Lee is looking into some natural products, such as carrot juice and bee pollen.

"They might slow down the disease but won't have the side effects (of vitamin A)," she says.

While she is not able to work now, she keeps busy with her church and Junior League.

Lee's disease is an open topic with her children, and she's even talked to their classes when RP has fit into the lessons.

They've adjusted well. For example, Sarah knows that when she wants to go somewhere, she needs to find a ride, and all three children know the importance of picking up after themselves so their mother doesn't trip over things.

But that doesn't mean it's not difficult for them, Lee says.

"Like the other night at supper—I went to pass something, and *I* was the one who spilled a glass of milk, not one of the kids," she says with a little laugh. "They feel so bad inside, but I can joke about it. I try not to show the depressing side to my children."[16]

ℛeflection, Present day

As I read these entries from my journal, my mind swirled with new kaleidoscopic facets revealed with each day, each event. Strengths and weaknesses whirled past, showing my course. I had forgotten most of the depressing events, living through moment-by-moment, following a path that would turn out fine. I wasn't discouraged and kept on moving. I remembered not really having a choice, that I was guided by something inside of me stronger than my weakness. I felt I could rest comfortably with a bowl of popcorn to enjoy the show.

The ending is always perfect, right?

---

16   Traci Klein, "Slipping away, Disease slowly takes woman's sight," *Leader-Telegram*, November 24, 1993.

Chapter Twenty

PREPARATIONS; ALL IN GOOD TIME

THANKSGIVING, 1993

DONNY CAME TO TAKE us all to Longville. The kids hadn't been here since the move over two years ago. They were so excited to see all their old friends. Tim thought he would see everyone, and I think he was disappointed that he only saw two of them.

We visited Darlene and her family. The kids so enjoyed going there for daycare when they were younger. Alice and Kylee chatted a lot, and Sarah liked visiting with Wade. It was wonderful to catch up on news about the area.

At the Edwards farm, Alice spent most of her time pestering David to help do chores. She *helped* by entertaining the kitties that stay in the barn to keep warm. Afterward, we went sliding on the hill toward the lake where an eagle fed in the middle of the frozen water. The ice was thick enough, but still slushy around the edges. When we returned to the house, Donny and I baked 14 loaves of bread from scratch like his mom used to do. It was necessary back then to feed the large family. Alice helped form the little loaves and called them baby loaves.

The smell of fresh baked bread wafted through the old two-story farmhouse. Our mouths watered in anticipation until . . . out of the oven, the first loaves came. We layered melted butter onto the first slices as we each devoured the freshness.

Later, I reunited with Alicia and Cheryl for a music jam session. We practiced the song I wrote a few weeks ago, "God Shines," and sang it Sunday at church. We received so many compliments I was pleased and humbled. I love composing and seeing people enjoy my work; it motivates me to do more.

I really miss playing with our trio. The service was recorded, so I hope to get a copy of it.

Donny had to travel thirty miles to Pine River to get a part for the faucet at the farm. Quite a difference from living in Eau Claire, where it only takes five minutes to drive most anywhere on an errand.

I still prefer the north though and hope to return someday to live.

It was sad to say goodbye for everyone, but we had a great time. Alice didn't want to leave. She wanted to stay at the farm forever and pester David, or it could have been the kitties she wanted to play with.

When we returned to Eau Claire, Rita brought me the paper with the article about me. That threw me into another dimension. Who was this person? It couldn't be about me, I didn't have that much non-normal happening, did I?

I don't like this. Why do I have to struggle through this? I'm so glad Rita was there to uplift me and point out how positive it was to have the support group where my questions would be answered.

Later, Rita and I went to sixth grade orientation at the middle school for Tim. I couldn't believe how fast he's grown. Next year, Alice would be in elementary school, Tim in middle school, and Sarah in high school.

Heaven help me!

December 4, 1993

I DON'T THINK I can cry anymore.

I cried all morning yesterday being so nervous about finally meeting other people with RP. Today, I attended my first RP support group session, and it felt as if I was riding an emotional roller coaster.

Rita was a wonderful support for me while we set the room up and waited, and waited, and waited. I had called the several that were interested in attending to remind them about the time and location. Two said they couldn't make it, two said they could.

Nobody came.

I wonder if they have the same roller coaster feelings as me? If I think about it that way, I'm able to better understand But oh, how I want to come face to face with another peer.

December 4. 1993

I'M AMAZED BY THE outpouring of support after the article about me was published. So many people commented how they now understand what I can't see. One friend said what a witness of strength I was to others. I'm so glad I seem so strong when inside, I feel like Jello. I cried because I would rather not have this happen. The article about me and my RP is just another acknowledgment of going blind.

I received a letter from a man who was concerned about my soul. The letter was written on the backs of three restaurant placemats. He had seen the article in the paper and wanted to save me. I was a sinner, according to him, and I didn't love Jesus enough. Through my sins I was being punished and could only be saved by repenting.

I should have saved that letter but was so furious when I read it that I immediately tore it up and threw it in the trash. I was too mad to cry at first but drenched my pillow during the night. How could anybody think like that?

My God loves me unconditionally, and him too.

DECEMBER 7, 1993

I JUST RETURNED FROM Sarah's eighth grade jazz band concert. She played a solo she had to write herself in eight measures. Wow, she did awesome! I couldn't be prouder as I let the notes flow throughout my weariness, uplifting me and helping me to focus on another positive in my life. My daughter, my first reason to be a mom.

Thank you for revealing our joy.

Mom and Dad came today to help me run errands. I had a chiropractor appointment with Dr. Best. He has been talking to me about magnetic field treatments and acupuncture treatments ever since he saw my article in the paper.

"They are all possibilities of slowing progress," he said, "but no guarantee for a cure."

I baked a double batch of peanut blossom cookies this morning. I just can't keep up on the Christmas cookies this year . . . Timothy? He's the reason why, and I smile at the thought of him savoring them saving the delicious chocolate kiss for last.

I sent in another Braille lesson. This one introduced the period and capital signs. I have found I'm more interested if I complete the lesson as soon as the kids leave for school.

Last night after supper, I played Christmas carols on the piano, Sarah played her trumpet, and Alice sang along. Tim was busy wrapping a special present for Sarah. What a wonderful memory.

DECEMBER 9, 1993

I JUST RETURNED FROM an amazing lunch with the Craft Club. The ladies took me out to thank me for forming this group. They paid for my lunch and bought me a glass statue, a dark green angel playing a mandolin I had commented on several weeks ago. These friends have really made me feel welcome in town and glad that I had decided to move to Eau Claire.

Yesterday, Tim's class had their Winter Warm Up program. He did a wonderful job doing his part. This morning I listened to Alice's class read again.

DECEMBER 13, 1993

I RECEIVED AN ACCEPTANCE letter from Northern Lights School of Massage Therapy in Minneapolis, Minnesota today!

I also worked on another Braille lesson.

It's really going to happen. I am going to become a massage therapist. The class is 600 hours. I will go Tuesdays and Thursdays and some Saturdays for almost a year. I'm so excited and have so many details to figure out.

Listen, listen, listen . . . hold on.

Reflection, Present day

The nurtured seed stretched as it prepared for the first breath of an awakening soul. The sprout filled with inspiration and desire.

All in good time.

December 16, 1993

Yesterday was truly a blessing. I received a gift certificate from an anonymous person through Pastor Kurt. I also got a Christmas card from my godmother, Aunt Barbara, which had a check. I called her to thank her, and she told me she's putting me in her prayer circle for transportation to massage school.

December 23, 1993

I'm at the farm in Longville while the kids are spending Christmas with their dad. This is another adjustment in my life that is hard to reconcile.

December 31, 1993

Mom told me of a time when Grandpa Simen Lee found a penny in the road in Ridgeland, Wisconsin. He picked it up and took it home. Later, he felt so terrible he went back to town and put it back right where he found it because it wasn't his. That story gave me a wonderful reminder what a caring man he was.

Rounding up the year on my wish list, I trudged on with my Braille lessons, not daily, but more often. I started a support group in Eau Claire for RP. Now, if I could only get those interested to come. It wasn't really a group with only me attending.

I've practiced more on the mandolin by playing with the church group, and I started to feel more confident. I also learned more about God's timing again this year. He has given me the patience to compose some beautiful songs.

I'll be starting massage therapy school in January for one year. After that, I will be able to get a job and hopefully feel better about myself. I hope to continue to be inspired.

It's been a wonderful year, indeed. My children have grown so beautifully, and I'm so very proud.

Each one of them always tries their best.

Reflection, Present day

AMAZING HOW I HAD such low self-confidence but endured. I accomplished a great deal in a little time: attending school for band instrument repair, mobility cane training, piano tuning, learning basic Braille, moving my family twice, and writing songs. If I could do these, why did I doubt my abilities to learn new things?

I felt the strong support of my family and friends lifting me as I soared on eagle's wings each day, and I smiled at that heartwarming thought.

Chapter Twenty-One

PATIENCE IS THE KEY

By night we have no light; no colour can we see.
Thus, light we learn by darkness, its converse. Agree!
A seeing of the light, perception is of tints;
And these distinguished are through darkness' gloomy
hints.
Our griefs and sorrows were by God first introduced,
That joy to sense apparent thence should be reduced.[17]

—*Rumi*

JANUARY 3, 1994

I WAS REFERRED BY my chiropractor to contact Dr. John Sunderledge in Baraboo, Wisconsin for acupuncture treatments. I called him and was stunned when he told me he could stop the progress of my RP and also regain the vision that I have lost.

Is this a dream? Do I dare even hope?

The doctors so far have told me I would be totally blind

---

17 Rumi, *Mesnevi*, 244–49

within ten years. That was three years ago, so in reality, I should have only expected seven years of vision according to their calculations.

He also read the article on me from the newspaper and wanted to treat me at no charge. He said, "It's to show the medical profession that it can be done."

Am I crazy to try or crazier not to?

JANUARY 4, 1994

Last night, I had a dream that two-year-old Connor, our neighbor's son next door, was sick. His mother, Julie, wanted me to wrap him in a blanket and hold him while she drove to the emergency room. He threw up into the blanket on the way and that was all I remembered.

I shared this dream with Adam, Connor's older brother, when he came to walk with Tim to school. I didn't think anything else about it the rest of the day.

While eating supper, the phone rang. It was Julie calling, frantic: "I need you to hold Connor while I drive to the emergency room at the hospital!"

"I'm on my way," I said and hung up the phone.

As I walked into the apartment, Julie yelled from upstairs, "Wrap him in his blanket. I'll be right down."

Connor was lying, lethargic but awake, on his colorful blanket. I wrapped him snugly as he melted into my embrace.

"You're going to be okay," I said trying to be confident as he spit up some more.

Julie ran down the stairs thanking me and explaining that her husband, Steve, and Adam were gone for the evening. We scurried out to her van.

I held Connor all the way while she tried not to speed.

It happened exactly in detail as it did in my dream: same blanket, same actions, same everything. In the ER, they discovered Connor had inhaled propane fumes at the daycare from an outside vent. He was okay but threw up on the way back home too.

I had never experienced a dream coming true before. It made me think about how something like that would occur.

Reflection, Present day

Precognitive dreaming is the internet description of this phenomenon.

January 11, 1994

Yesterday, I had my first acupuncture treatments. I worried all day about leaving the kids, but many neighbors called and helped.

One appointment was in the morning and another later in the afternoon. The first one didn't include my face. I didn't like needles. In fact, I was, and still am, a fainter. I couldn't believe I even tried it, but I didn't disbelieve what he told me, yet. He told me that my RP wasn't hereditary. He believed it happened from another source of deterioration. He mentioned my kidneys, pancreas, and liver were weak and could tell that only by feeling the pulse in my left forearm.

I asked him about the beams of light I see when there is a change in lighting. He said it was my retina fighting to function. To assist in the acupuncture healing, he instructed me to avoid coffee, chocolate, alcohol, and soda. They contained carbonic acid which would irritate the lining of the intestines and ileocecal valve. I had to eat two eggs daily, lots of fruits and vegetables, and drink eight to ten glasses of water a day. He also taped my insteps to help the digestive process. I wasn't supposed to sleep under an electric blanket that was plugged in. I could warm up the bed before I crawled in, and then I needed to unplug it.

He asked to see me every Monday for a few months to start a baseline. He looked into my eyes and saw the bone spicules from RP.

What am I doing having these treatments now?

I'm ready to try anything that will end this nightmare.

I took a bus with many others taking treatments. It was a long 138-mile ride east from Eau Claire to Baraboo. During each session, I lay on a table while he inserted these long needles all over on meridians or something like that. Somehow, I endured it without fainting.

I don't understand it, but I'm desperate. I hate needles!

I'm glad I have family and support to stay with the kids and get them to where they need to be. I don't think I thank them enough.

Chapter Twenty-Two

Quiet Angels

YOU'RE IT

by Hafiz

God
Disguised
As a myriad things and
Playing a game
Of tag
Has kissed you and said,
"You're it—
I mean, you're really IT!
Now
It does not matter
What you believe or feel
For something wonderful,
Major-league Wonderful
Is someday going
To
Happen."[18]

---

18 Ladinsky, *The Gift*, 30

Reflection, Present day

This next event is one of my most cherished memories. It shows me just how important God is in my life. God doesn't give us what we can handle. God helps us handle what we have been given by being there with us holding us as we walk through our tunnels toward the light. This story, this adventurous passage, proves it to me. My father, my angel, had such faith that he was glowing this whole day. May you be as blessed as I am as you travel with me through this next journey.

January 12, 1994

Yesterday, my dad, Selvin Lee, came with me on a trial transportation run to the University of Minnesota where my massage school would be within their science building. Without being able to drive, I had to make many choices regarding how to get myself there and back home and how the children would get to where they needed to be while I was gone. I'm so glad I decided to try this plan before my first day, because it didn't turn out at all like I had thought it would—it turned out better.

I have so many people praying for me. I know God was with us all day.

First, I sent the kids to school before Dad arrived. We were going to take the Eau Claire passenger service van ninety-one miles west to the Minneapolis airport. From there we would take the airport express shuttle to the university. I called before we left to see if they would take a check. No, they needed cash. My bank didn't open until 10:00 A.M. and I had thoughts of canceling, but Dad said we could go to the Royal Credit Union branch by Shopko South. They were open, so we left at 9:30 A.M.

I got the cash and went to Days Inn to meet the Eau Claire Passenger Service van. We boarded and left town at 10:15 A.M. The driver was nice and assured us of where to meet the shuttle at the airport and where to be picked up for the return trip.

We arrived at the Minneapolis airport at 11:50 A.M. and went to the Airport Express area. They told me they would not drop us off at the University. They only have specific drop-off and pick-up points. I felt as though I had to give up. I was tired of struggling so hard and things not working out.

My dad never wavered in his knowledge this would all work out and suggested we try a taxi. I couldn't afford a taxi. My P.A.S.S. program only allowed so much for transportation. I was in utter despair. Now what was I to do? My guardian angel stepped in and led us to the taxi line. We were directed to one that would take us exactly where we wanted to go.

A.Y.S., At Your Service, taxi was the next in line. The driver, Gary, owned his own company with four taxis.

We got in and Dad said, "I need someone to watch over my little girl. She's going blind and is starting a year of schooling to become a massage therapist."

Gary, without hesitation, looked Dad in the eyes and said, "Sir, it will be an honor to take care of your daughter. You can count on me."

Since Social Security paid for transportation, we decided this would be best. Gary would meet me every Tuesday and Thursday at noon at the airport and take me to class. He'd also pick me up at 9:00 P.M. when I was done with classes and drive me back to the airport to meet the return van to Eau Claire. I would also take a taxi from my home to and from Days Inn in Eau Claire.

Thank you, Dad, for your faith in God, for your constant loving care.

We drove to the university and returned to the airport. Gary got us back to the airport at 12:55 P.M., assuring us he would be here ready and waiting for my first day of school.

We weren't scheduled to return on the van until almost 3:00 P.M., but when we checked in at the desk, our same driver had waited for two other people who were late. We were able to take the earlier van trip home and arrived in time to pick up Tim and Alice as they were walking home from school.

God is good!

REFLECTION, PRESENT DAY

WASN'T THAT A WONDERFUL journey? My father's faith had been steadfast throughout my life, even when I didn't appreciate it. Dad never went to high school because he was needed on the farm after the 8th grade. Still, he went on to become an entrepreneur, owning his own electrician business, Lee's Electric.

How was Gary chosen to be at the right place at the right time?

I believe he was another angel sent to assist me.

JANUARY 20, 1994

I AM SO NERVOUS about starting school next week. I'm so lonely, I mean, I feel so alone on this new adventure. Donny said he would visit next Friday. The kids have been so helpful and wonderful around the house, most of the time. Without them, I wouldn't be able to pursue going back to school so far away. They give me the confidence and support I need. I hope I do the same for them and that they can feel it. We're a family and supporting each other is vital.

I had another massage this morning. It was relaxing. That and my prayers for peace, strength, and courage have helped my emotional self.

I feel more prepared for the coming week.

January 28, 1994

It's Friday, and what a week I've had! I'm pooped! I guess I'll get used to it.

Monday, I went to Baraboo. Tuesday and Thursday, I went to massage school.

My acupuncture treatment was frustrating. He placed needles around my eyes and about fifty on my back. They really hurt this time.

I'm getting more skeptical about the whole thing. And now, with going to school, I might be stretching myself too far. I've also noticed that I'm really getting tired of sharing my RP story with so many people—I hate the reactions that I get.

"Oh, how horrible!" I heard one say, and, "That poor lady, I'm so glad it's not me."

I sink with each person I tell. As if I'm standing in a deep dark pit and each time I recount my story, the listener lowers me further down into the darkness while they rise above me into the light, the light that I can't have.

For the most part, I don't mind kind people who gently ask about my vision. I usually give a brief reply: "No, I don't mind you asking." I smile to hide the hurt. "I have a tunnel vision called retinitis pigmentosa which means I don't have peripheral vision."

I'm shocked though at how frequently, mostly men, will

respond, "Don't hit me with your cane."

Or another reaction that's just as bad: "Hit Donny with it to keep him in line."

I hate those comments. They are rude and hurtful. Why would anyone think they are being funny? Would they mock someone in a wheelchair by saying, "Oh, please, don't run over my toes?"

Most people mean well, and it's a learning chance for them. Here's a great example:

Donny and I went out to eat, and in the next booth, a little girl watched me walk in. My hand rested on Donny's shoulder and my cane tap, tap, tapped until I found my seat and sat down. Her eyes really sparked with questions when she saw me fold up the cane and set it next to me.

"Why do you have that?" she boldly asked, pointing at my folded cane.

"My eyes don't work right. I use the cane, so I don't run into things," I replied.

Instantly, she blinked her eyes as fast as she could and said, "My eyes work. See!"

I loved that innocent honesty. Her parents tried to admonish her, but I insisted that she was fine and only being curious. I felt joy inside.

Tuesday was my first day of school. I got the kids off to their schools and called for a taxi to take me to the hotel to meet the shuttle. I was filled with nervous excitement as I traveled to the airport. A very pleasant delight waited for me as I approached the taxi line—Gary stood next to his A.Y.S. Taxi with a cold bottle of water for me.

"At your service," he said before he bowed, tipped his hat, and opened my door. I was a little awed at how tall he really was. I had only seen him sitting in his cab before.

It took twenty minutes for us to arrive at my school destination. He reassured me that he would be promptly waiting at 9:00 P.M. to hear all about my first day.

Classes started at 1:00 P.M. with an orientation all afternoon about school policies and getting our books. The Anatomy and Physiology books weighed a ton! How shocked I was that I would have to learn so much for just giving a simple relaxing massage. My assumptions had been so wrong.

I met my other classmates, a total of twenty, nineteen ladies and one man. The instructor then gave us each our own pair of nail clippers, instructing, "Clip 'em short."

One lady couldn't handle that and walked out.

After our supper break, class had information about massage tables, their different manufacturers, styles, and prices. The instructor told us to purchase one for at home use. The classroom had tables provided.

Class finished at 9:00 P.M. and Gary was waiting for me.

"So, Miss Pamela, how was your first day?" he asked as he opened my door.

I babbled on and on about details, the books, the classmates, the instructors . . . It was as if a floodgate opened for me to share my new world. I thought how much Gary would help make this journey easier.

I'm so glad Dad helped me find him.

He took me back to the airport, reassuring me he would be there Thursday. I waited an hour for the next shuttle to take me back to Eau Claire. When I arrived at the hotel and walked into the lobby, I asked the attendant, "Please call me a cab."

"Okay, you're a cab," he said.

I laughed from tired exhaustion and knew this was going to be fine. Alice really laughed when I told her the next day. I didn't get home until 1:00 A.M.

Thursday, I repeated the school routine. The schedule is going to be rough, but if I can do this, I can get through anything.

ℱEBRUARY 1, 1994

I HAD MY FIRST Anatomy class in the evening. Whew, one day at a time. I know I can do this. Listen, listen, listen . . . hold on.

Donny came to visit for the weekend. I hadn't seen him since December. On Saturday we went skiing. It was Alice's first time to try and Donny was so good at showing her how. She wanted to give up when the tow rope flipped her over the first two times, but he stood her between his legs, and they went up together. They also came down together for the first three times, and then she tried it on her own. She didn't use poles, but later insisted on getting a pair like everyone else had. Once she had them, she fell and hurt her thumb. The ski patrol looked at it and said to keep an eye on it. She put Tim's wrist brace on when she got home.

My Mom and Dad came to watch us and were thrilled at all of our fun. Tim and Sarah went nonstop on their runs. Donny skied down all the slopes but avoided the moguls. I enjoyed slowly meandering down three slopes, being cautious not to run into someone or something.

Sunday was Youth Sunday at church. Sarah played her trumpet in a quartet and then did a very nice liturgical dance: Well done, my dear, darling daughter. She seems so grown up at times like this.

FEBRUARY 6, 1994

I HAD A DREAM I was in a church so full of people that there wasn't anywhere to stand. A woman sitting next to me praised my courage for facing my RP and never being sad.

"You are totally accepting what God has willed for a purpose only He knows," she said

During the service, I was lifted up and could look down at the congregation. Nobody noticed as I drifted toward the front and into a small room to the left. As I sat there, one-by-one, people came in the room looking for something, not noticing that I was above them. They each talked about their loneliness or another need. I noted their concerns and told myself that I would be aware of these concerns when I met them next.

After waking this morning and remembering this dream, I feel guilt for having acupuncture. Maybe it wasn't guilt but an uneasiness from within. I felt a forced need to try anything to heal myself.

FEBRUARY 12, 1994

TODAY IS A BAD day because it's so cloudy. It's harder to see details.

I had acupuncture last Monday again. It didn't hurt as bad, but I'm not sure of any progress. He said I would be cured in 1 ½ years.

School has been going great. I truly love all the learning, and I need more study time. The kids have been wonderful; they help out with laundry, dishes, and any other way they can. I couldn't go if they weren't so good.

Rita has been such a great help to me also. I don't have to

worry at all.

I better get some studying done before I go to bed.

*F*EBRUARY 17, 1994

I'M AT THE MINNEAPOLIS airport waiting for the shuttle van to go back home. If the weather is good, I will arrive in Eau Claire at midnight. Tonight is a beautiful warm thirty-two degrees.

I've found that studying while waiting helps a lot, but there are so many distractions. I'm amazed at all the different languages I hear. People are interesting to watch. Some are in such a rush; others are enjoying their journeys, taking in all the new sights and sounds. A variety of shapes, colors, and moods occur every night.

This is a beautiful world, a kaleidoscope of facets, each one tempts me to peek into their world, where they are going, who they are seeing, how long will they be gone. I can tell the romances that are reunited; the families that are being temporarily separated. Love energy is everywhere and I'm embracing its warmth.

Class was good today. We worked on the legs.

Now I need to do six one-hour, full body massages by March 15. I'm sure I will have many volunteers as I'm unable to charge until I have my license.

There is a small quiz next week on legs and a major exam in Anatomy class. I feel pretty confident about my knowledge. I've created flash cards of all the terminology, constantly going through them while I'm waiting for my next mode of transportation.

I've been very emotional this week. I called my sister, Joan, in tears. I'm feeling too stretched out. In Communication class, I broke down and cried uncontrollably. Fortunately, I was able to leave the room. My instructor noticed and followed me; she listened as I blurted out my pain.

I went through this type of depression a month after I was at school in Red Wing. School is another acknowledgment of my blindness. Why do I look at it that way? This is such a wonderful adventure. I truly love every day of school. I have so many close classmates already who are so caring and concerned for me.

FEBRUARY 20, 1994

ALICE IS EIGHT TODAY!

It was her day for deciding what she wanted to do and where she wanted to eat. We ate breakfast at Country Kitchen. Afterward, she wanted to look at the Pencils and Play store at the mall and then go bowling. Her choice for supper was McDonalds.

We had a lot of fun. At one time, Alice had problems shutting her van door. She thought she could get it better if she got out and shut the door. She stopped, thought about it, and decided that wasn't such a good idea. Donny got out and shut her door for her. Donny and I really got a laugh out of that, and later, so did she.

FEBRUARY 22, 1994

IT'S 9:15 P.M. AND I'm writing again from the airport.

Today, there was a quiz in massage techniques. We also had to demonstrate on the instructor, who provided some helpful feedback.

The evening class was a review for Thursday's anatomy

exam. I did poorly on the pop quiz. I passed, barely, but that made me more nervous about taking the exam. I would really need to study.

Yesterday, I had an acupuncture treatment. Dr. John said my emotional roller coaster was because of the treatments. "It's releasing so much that the emotions are unstable," he explained. "It is common and will make a new you."

The afternoon acupuncture session showed so much progress from the morning that he didn't do the full treatment. "Too much energy is already there," he said. "Don't be afraid of the flashes of vision."

When I asked about that, he said I may see a flash of how I'm supposed to see, and then it will fade.

Is this just a power of suggestion or is he really helping?

March 1, 1994

I passed my first Anatomy exam.

I also had my yearly eye exam. Dr. Hofer says my vision has decreased to eight degrees, down from ten last year. That hurt deep inside. I couldn't describe it. Fear? Or just a deep pain of uncontrollableness?

Yup, that's a new word.

I talked with Dr. Hofer about acupuncture.

"Medically," he said, "it can't be done. Those cells are gone. They can't come back, but I really don't know enough about acupuncture."

He took pictures of my eyes with bright lights that burned. It felt as if the laser was boring a hole through my eye and out the back of my head. He wanted me to come back in four months to compare. Maybe there was a possibility that the acupuncture can help.

I'm totally depressed about it now, but I'll continue. At least it's no charge, just a lot of running back and forth.

ℭMARCH 8, 1994

ANOTHER ACUPUNCTURE TREATMENT IS done. I've grown to hate going. I feel drained, stretched, and emotional. The kids are being so wonderful, but I know it's a strain on them too. I'm gone so much—too much.

This time, while he put the needle in the back of my right knee, I felt an electric zap, a current running to my little toe. It tingled and went numb. This continued throughout the treatment and I could still feel it afterward. Dr. John said that was good and it meant it was clearing out my bladder. He talked about how healthy I am.

I'm also aware of a red dot between my eyes from another session. It doesn't hurt, but it is there, almost like a mosquito bite at the bridge of my nose.

Dr. John told me how, as he put it, clear and good my eyes are getting, while Dr. Hofer, my eye doctor said they were worse.

I don't know who or what to believe so I'm listening to my feelings, specifically, the one that isn't comfortable with the treatments.

The dream of me being in a room, elevated while listening to people drew me toward massage and away from acupuncture. It almost felt like I was accepting my vision journey. Would I learn to listen to my clients' bodies wanting to feel healthy? Could I feel that comfort toward acupuncture?

Listen, listen, listen . . . hold on.

I just called and canceled my treatments, and I feel better already. He was very kind and told me that maybe after schooling I would have more time.

We'll see.

I have another 25 terms to memorize by Thursday. These are the muscles of the skull. I didn't even know there were any there!

Chapter Twenty-Three

A NEW FOUNDATION

APRIL 28, 1994

MOM AND I WENT shopping at the mall. We watched as a mother walked by with a special needs child.

"I'm so thankful," Mom said, "that my children don't have those kinds of problems."

There I was, walking around with my white cane, feeling abnormal, ill at ease with all the stares, and she made a comment that there was no problem with me. I could very much appreciate where my mother was coming from, but I felt strongly that I could not ever feel better about my situation because of what someone else was going through.

We are all equals going through different chapters in our own journeys. I'm not better than anyone because I can do something they can't.

Mom was talking about the struggles that family had to go through and the pain. Through all my struggles, I grew and became better because of them.

*J*UNE 1, 1994

OH, MY GOODNESS, I didn't write anything in May or even about my 37th birthday on April 30th. It was a very busy month. Our apartment had been wonderful, but I found a duplex that would better serve our needs.

I've already started moving boxes.

My first term of school finished. I had an Anatomy exam that I passed with flying colors! During the practical exam, I had to give my instructor a massage and got 100% on that.

I really love this.

*A*UGUST 17, 1994

ANOTHER LONG BREAK FROM writing. There went the summer.

Every time I wanted to write, I found myself doing something else, mostly studying. I'd done well in school so far. How did I manage? Second term was tougher than the first, and the third term would be tough, too.

I'm so glad to have such a good support group.

The friends I found through church gathered and made a sign-up sheet for delivering meals to my house on Tuesdays for the kids while I attended school. I was overwhelmed by this generosity. They delivered on Monday nights so that on Tuesday, the kids had an after-school snack, an easy dinner to heat up, a dessert, and a bedtime snack. This helped the most, so I didn't have to worry about meals.

I'm so excited to become a massage therapist. Hearing

how good people feel after they receive an hour-long full body massage brings me joy. Just like in my dream, I feel so energized afterward. In September, I'm taking a weekend seminar on On-Site Chair Massage. I hope to make that a part of my future business. Second term will be done September 1.

In one week, school starts for the kids. Sarah will be a freshman in high school. Tim will be in 6th grade at the middle school, and Alice will be in 3rd grade at the elementary school.

I decided to stop the taxi transportation to school in Minneapolis with Gary and A.Y.S. I met a student in another class who lives in Hudson, Wisconsin, and I started riding with her for the last part of my trip. The Eau Claire shuttle could drop me off and pick me up in Hudson where she lives.

I missed Gary. We became good friends. He would often quiz me before school when he knew I had an exam. In the evening on the ride to the airport, he would take a special route down the river road for a change of scenery and buy me a candy bar and root beer. On my last night riding with him, he took this route, and when I handed him his check, he tore it up and said the ride was free. What a blessing he was.

I'll never forget him.

My eyesight has gotten worse over the summer. It feels like I've taken a big step backwards in my tunnel, and my field of vision has narrowed. I find it harder to focus on so many objects. My depth perception is harder to control. I still have moments when I wish my sight would be gone completely. This waiting and slowly going blind is torture at times. I'm thankful that it isn't painful, except when I run into things. I'm doing that more often and knocking things over.

Argh! Could I please have at least one week where I don't drench one of the kids during our meals?

FEBRUARY 28, 1995

FINALLY, I'M WRITING TO you again. More than seven months of exciting events have happened, and I didn't find time to write them down.

"Why bother?" my mind says frequently. "You won't be able to read it later anyway."

Some of the events I never wrote about were major. In December, after completing 500 hours of the 600-hour massage school, I passed my exam and became nationally certified in Therapeutic Massage and Bodywork.

I didn't sleep much the night before the exam. I had too many facts swirling in my head. I was fearful that if I didn't keep repeating them, they would all fall out and be lost forever.

Most of my classmates chose to take the exam before graduation as I did. We gathered outside the college lecture room, gave each other hugs with boosts of confidence, then proceeded to enter. We formed a line to register, collected our test material, and found seats. The steep stairs in the amphitheater style room were a challenge as I tapped, stepped, tapped, stepped, up the ladder type stairs until I was able to find a seat.

"Begin," a voice commanded.

A flutter of pages sounded as students opened their exams. A booklet contained numbered questions and the corresponding sheet had numbers followed by five circles, labeled A, B, C, D and E. My mind started to panic at the size of the font used. Could I use that as an excuse to not take the test that day? But I need to take it then or I would lose all my information.

Listen, listen, listen . . . hold on.

On February 12, 1995, I graduated from Northern Lights School of Massage Therapy. I did it! I had become a massage therapist and could develop it into a career. I proved years before that I was able to learn when I had attended school for band instrument repair and piano tuning. Those both proved to not fit what I needed, but oh, massage therapy felt so right.

I am proud of myself.

Family and friends came to the graduation, supporting me. Even the taxi driver, Gary, attended. Dad gave him a hug and thanked him for taking care of his little daughter.

"She did fine on her own, and she's going to go far," Gary said.

I gave a speech to my massage class during graduation. I told a story of an acorn wanting to become something more. But the acorn also knew it would take time, time to be nourished, time to take root, time to send out sprouts, time to reach for the sun, and time become a strong oak tree. I then handed each of them a carved acorn to remind them of what they had accomplished throughout the year.

Those were two of the biggest accomplishments of my life, and I didn't even acknowledge them. I wrote about so many other trivial things. Did I really feel that I still wasn't good enough? Or was I just doing what I need to do without the fanfare because I needed to do something?

Regardless, I did.

Reflection, Present day

THE NOURISHED, SPROUTING SEED had begun its journey, a journey of new thrills, joys, and experiences. That triumph strengthened my soul, my heart, and my mind. Those accomplishments reassured me I could soar on my new wings. I felt serene momentum, satisfied with what was and eager for more as I enjoyed my eagle's ride.

I grew each new day, learning how to take this path and stretch toward another. I felt freedom and yearned for even more. I had a free spirit, able to uncover the me that I had buried, the me who never took the chance. I took it then. I was on track. My words weren't completely written in my journal, but the feelings that'd grown could never be stopped.

My journey had taken me from order to disorder to reorder. I built a foundation for which I would continue to rebuild my life. How had I done it? I trusted my source, my inner-being, my God. I allowed Him to be in charge when I had to let go. I leaned into my family and graciously accepted their support. I took action by going to school, moving my family twice, learning to use the white cane, and learning Braille even though I sometimes hated it.

I soared on my eagle like in my dream from four years before. I remained silent in my support, knowing that I had no need to fear. A calm clarity enfolded me as the wings glided with ease. I allowed and received so much when my focus was directed inward. Light joy of love's energy was always there. Everything would be fine. I felt secure when I rode, being guided toward a voyage free from my self-imposed limitations.

All was well.

Chapter Twenty-Four

FINDING A NEW DREAM

*M*ARCH 21, 1995

ON FEBRUARY 23, I opened Horizon Therapeutic Massage on Brackett Avenue in Eau Claire. I never thought I would be self-employed, an entrepreneur like Dad.

Today is the first day of spring and I'm writing from my new office. It's like a dream come true.

There are four rooms in the office: a waiting room, an office, and two therapy rooms. I also have a private restroom and closet space.

I hope for another therapist to join me soon. There are four students from Eau Claire going to school now. Hopefully, one of them will join me.

I had an open house/graduation party at my office on March 5. It snowed that morning, but about fifty people came after seeing my announcement in the paper.

The first day I was open, Mom and Dad came to help. I

was so nervous I forgot something back home. Dad drove me back and while I was gone, Mom took an appointment for my first client. He was coming in the afternoon—I was so scared.

Listen, listen, listen . . . hold on.

The session went very well as I relieved some pain in his neck area from a tractor injury. He made an appointment for another session.

REFLECTION, PRESENT DAY

THE ROOTED SEED SENT out a shoot, feeling sunshine's first warmth. "Come out," it called. "I'll embrace you, strengthen you, and nourish your way."

MARCH 8, 1995

I HAD MY ANNUAL eye exam. This time I went to the University of Minnesota to see Dr. Knoblach. I hadn't been there in three years. He didn't do as extensive testing as he had the time before. He just had his assistant look in my eyes with bright lights and write down the results.

"You don't need to know the number of degrees remaining," he said. "That's too depressing."

He then told me he could tell there has been a decrease and checked for glaucoma, cataracts, and other infections that are common with RP.

I told him I was learning Braille.

"Good for you," he said. "But you're cheating, aren't you?"

"Yep." I replied. "Well, I'm not really cheating, but I find it difficult to tell how many bumps are in each cell. It's hard to tell where one letter ends and another begins."

March 11, 1995

Mom, Dad, and I went to Milwaukee. I had a meeting with the Wisconsin Council for the Blind for a small business loan. I was so nervous, but they were so kind. They had approved my loan before they even met me because of the business plan I had sent to them. Clearly, they'd been impressed. The plan had been a requirement for massage school.

Very worthwhile.

March 28, 1995

It's a slow day at the office but it gives me a chance to catch up on other things. I'll do my Braille lesson today. I'm on lesson twenty-three in book one, and I am learning dollar signs and fraction lines. Lesson twenty-four is the last one in the book. Then I move on to book two.

Later today, I'm having cryosurgery for the second time. They will freeze my inside female parts because of pre-cancerous cells found during my yearly exam. I hope this is the last time. It's painful and uncomfortable for several weeks afterward.

April 25, 1995

Tonight, there was a program at Alice's school: Star Search 95, 5th Annual Manz School Talent Show. Alice gave her first piano performance, playing, "Reindeer Rock." She had been so nervous while practicing that I stood behind her and massaged her shoulders. I told her to imagine me doing that during the show. She played wonderfully, and I was so proud of her.

April 26, 1995

Two gals came into the office selling roses today. I decided to buy a dozen for $12.99. I'd never had a dozen roses before—besides, my 38th birthday is on Sunday.

Business is going so well. I'm so pleased with the progress. I just counted and tomorrow, I will accept my fiftieth client already. My average is between eight and eleven clients a week.

I advertised a $5 off coupon in the Leader Telegram. That brought in eight clients. I had been hoping for many more, but at least it put my name out there.

My business loan came last week. I had my sign put up, got my business cards, and ordered a water cooler. I placed advertising in the yellow pages and started with a laundry service so I wouldn't have to bother everyone to help me transport laundry to and from work.

I still hate not being able to drive.

In Sunday's paper, I was featured in the Small Business Spotlight. What a thrill it was to see a picture of me sitting in my massage studio. I'm becoming the taxpayer that Ralston told me to be.

I'm getting a computer from DVR (a government assistance program called Development for Vocational Rehabilitation that supports persons with disabilities). They are sending me to Wausau, WI to meet with someone who can set me up with the right equipment for my needs. This should take a couple months.

* * *

MY BUSINESS WAS VICTIM to a burglary that happened Saturday evening. Luckily, all they did was go through my desk looking for money, which I didn't keep at the office. I'm so thankful they didn't take or destroy anything.

I feel violated though. Someone going through everything is such an eerie feeling, like they are still watching me and could enter anytime I'm at work—I hope I get over this feeling.

MAY 26, 1995

LAST TUESDAY EVENING, I was a guest speaker at the Evening Eau Claire Lions Club meeting. They asked me to speak about retinitis pigmentosa. I'd talked at the Red Wing Lions Club before and decided to share similar information.

Speaking to these groups feels normal, as if talking about my vision impairment is as common as making an apple pie: slice the apples, toss in flour, add to the crust, and bake. Anyone can do it with the right knowledge.

I began my discussion describing my vision entering a room. "I need to pause to let my eyes adjust to the new level of darkness or brightness," I calmly said. "My cane is a part of me, giving me confidence to continue when I feel I am ready."

I shared then with the group a few specifics about retinitis pigmentosa. "There is no cure, no prevention, and no surgery."

Next I explained what I accomplished in schooling, strategies I employed to assist me like Braille, how I learned white cane travel, and finally finding an occupation I loved and would be able to continue.

They said I was informative and easy to listen to. I'm humbled that each club offered to pay for a Seeing Eye dog if and when that time arrived.

Later that night, as I lay in bed, I felt proud of how the evening went. I relished the praise and acceptance, but still, a slow chill surrounded me and I felt my common dreadful doubt calling me back to my corner of darkness. When would I ever be completely free of this anguish? Hopefully the episode would be brief.

May 28, 1995

My neighbor, Liz, drove me to Wausau. Two men, Al and Greg, showed us a room containing about ten computers. Each had a different configuration. Three were hooked up to a device that output speech. DECtalk, a "voice synthesizer unit that can 'read' aloud ASCII text messages,"[19] was the best and easiest to understand. The others sounded like they had a very bad Norwegian accent.

Each configuration read exactly what was on the screen of the computer. An Oscar scanner was attached to one of the computers. It could take any printed material, scan it onto the screen, and then it could be read by DECtalk. Wow, it felt like such a burden had been lifted; I was no longer so afraid to go blind.

Al was totally blind, and Greg had RP with ten degrees of his vision field remaining. I was at eight but had better quality

---

19   Peggy Zientara, "DECtalk lets micros read messages over phones," InfoWorld 6, nos. 2-3 (Jan 9-16, 1984): 21–23.

to the remaining sight. Greg had his nose to the screen unless he enlarged the text. I felt comfortable with them, I think, because they were so happy in their jobs. They didn't seem to have any problems managing the computers.

They also showed me a CCTV (closed circuit television). This enlarged any printed material to the size the viewer needed. Greg said he uses it a lot to fill in forms. They also showed me a Zoom Text program[20] that, when added to the computer screen, enlarged the text to one quarter of the page.

I went into DVR a computer illiterate, but I learned so much. Heck, if I could learn human anatomy, this would be a cinch!

Lord, thank you for all this knowledge and help. It has set me free from my worries and anxieties about going blind. Setting me free . . . how unusual that I might think that my fears are all gone. They aren't. They're always there, but I am trying to portray the essence of being strong, that I can handle this, that there isn't a problem here as long as I don't focus on it. Focus on a solution instead.

I can feel the dreaded gloom of the black cloud off in the corner. It peers at me, waiting for its chance to creep in and make itself comfortable. It has a purpose as it forces me apart from the rest of the world. I don't belong there anymore. Never again will I be there—part of the "rest of the world."

My retinas dying eats into my future, but I am going to fight, to adjust, to adapt, and show myself that I will shine on.

---

20   "Company History," AiSquared company website, WayBack Machine, last modified April 7, 2010, https://web.archive.org/web/20100407090547/http://www. aisquared.com/about_us/categories/category/company_history.

*J*ULY 21, 1995

ONCE AGAIN, TIME HAS slipped by. I'm teaching myself to slow down and enjoy every moment of every day that God has given me.

Taking it one day at a time and asking myself, "What can I do today?" Instead of looking at what I can't do. "Who can I help?" Instead of, "Who can help me?"

Lord, which path do you want me to take?

* * *

I HAVE SOME EXPLOSIVE ideas for expanding my business. I want to create more awareness for the healing benefits of massage.

This week I participated in the International Massage week by putting myself out in the community. Tuesday, I talked to the headache support group at Luther Hospital. Wednesday, I gave twenty free on-site chair massages at the local TV station. Thursday, I gave eighteen free on-site chair massages at a car dealer.

In October, I will do an expo at Oakwood Mall in Eau Claire.

* * *

SARAH GOT HER DRIVER'S permit. I think I put too much pressure on how important this would be for me, but I was sad too. It wouldn't be the independence I had hoped because she would get a job and work every weekend. We wouldn't be able to just go when I wanted to. I would have to learn to adjust, again.

* * *

I'M STILL WORKING ON my office computer. I'm seasick from

the movement of the CCTV and have decided to get a talking computer. Hopefully, things will be figured out soon.

* * *

I'VE DEVELOPED A DESPERATE urge to have my own home. After three short years, Sarah will be off to college. I'm thirty-eight and have only rented. That hurts so much. There must be a way. It looks so easy when I see so many houses. There are so many homeowners. How can I do it?

I've applied to Habitat for Humanity. I don't want to worry about finding housing. I want to feel more stable in my own home while I'm losing my sight.

JULY 26, 1995

SARAH DROVE YESTERDAY FOR the first time. She was so scared and upset because nobody was able to take her driving before. I wished I could have. I would have let her go anywhere.

Have I said enough times how much I hate not being able to drive?

Well, I do, I hate, hate, hate it!

AUGUST 5, 1995

I'M THE ONLY ONE awake so far. We'll be leaving in a few hours for our first vacation ever. The kids, Rita, and I are going to South Dakota for a week with the church group. We will spend a week on a ranch.

"It's almost like we're a normal family!" Tim said.

All his other friends went on vacations. But this would

be the first time for Tim and Alice to see a state other than Minnesota and Wisconsin. Sarah had vacationed before with her friend Georgia.

Tonight will also be their first night in a hotel. They are so excited. I'm so grateful I'm able to do this, but I'm a little frightened. I don't travel often, and I'm self-conscious. I try to avoid running into the unknown, so I'll be happy when we get back home.

"Vroom, vroom, vroom."

A line of 15 motorcycles passed us as we ventured west toward our South Dakota destination. We had seen fifty of them so far. Carefree passengers held onto riders, hair wiping in the wind for those who chose not to wear a helmet. It was Sturgis motorcycle rally time, and with each stop— Wall Drug, the Corn Maze, Mount Rushmore, and Crazy Horse—parking was limited. It was ninety degrees, and the earth radiated heat.

With each tourist attraction, we saw more and more delights. Tim wondered how they could wear the leather chaps in the heat. His thirteen-year-old eyes couldn't decide which sight held more interest, the rock formations or the biker chicks.

Chapter Twenty-Five

WALKING A THIN LINE

REFLECTION, PRESENT DAY

(AUGUST 1995 – DECEMBER 1997)

I found it very odd, that as I started with another round of journals, I stopped in August 1995 and did not write again until December 1997. And then, I only wrote in brief format. Why did I not write in 1996?

From reading the last entries in 1995, I know I was sinking deeper and deeper, trying to hang on. I swirled downward in the rushing vortex of a cyclone. I had no way of knowing what would come next, and I couldn't grasp anything solid to give me strength. Blindness was the main topic of every day—it forced me from the rest of the world.

My massage business became my source of power as the one thing that I could do and do very well. I was making a difference in people's lives, even when I couldn't do anything for myself.

Using my cane was stressful for me, and I couldn't be sure if those were the years when I chose not to do that anymore. The looks from people hurt me to my core. I kept telling myself that without my cane, all I had to do was try harder and I wouldn't run into anything.

Once, when Donny and I decided to go see a movie, the lady selling tickets seemed baffled by my wanting to see a movie.

"How many tickets?" the lady behind the counter asked.

"One and a half," Donny said.

She looked at him, then at me, then my cane, then back at him.

"She's only here to listen to the movie," he said with a smirk.

She wasn't sure what to think, but I thought it was funny. Donny had a way of making my pain fly away, lifting me out of my darkness.

I assisted myself into the dark theater by holding his elbow and tapping up the stairs to find a balcony seat. The further back I sat, the more of the screen I could see at a time. Donny developed a routine of quietly guiding me to look toward any action that I might otherwise miss during the movie. Gently, he helped me to remain normal, in control.

I appreciate that part of him.

✳ ✳ ✳

ANOTHER TIME, TIM MET me at work after he finished school for the day. We walked the seven blocks back home, enjoying how each of our days had been. I was using my cane while he strode next to me on my left, curbside. Suddenly, a tree branch struck me in the head. It startled me, but I felt even worse after Tim's reaction. He blamed himself for not seeing it for me. He was protective that way.

The next week, he worked on a project with Donny's help. They placed a rolling ball on the end of an extra cane that I had. This was to assist the glide of the cane so as not to jolt into a crack and cause me to trip. He didn't know how to handle the tree branch situation, but I was so proud of him for wanting to help me in any way he could. Secretly, I held my head out of the darkness pulling me down. I so wanted to be strong.

DURING 1995, I GATHERED information for people with Fibromyalgia, a painful muscle disorder that has no known cure. Massage helps clients by assisting their muscles to feel calmer. I created a day-long seminar with information from about ten different vendors, who each had their own ways of relieving the pain. It was a great success.

I MOVED MY BUSINESS closer to my home to a salon/spa, Mane Attractions and More. There, I had the use of the receptionist to make appointments and other spa features that assisted my clients. The new location increased my clientele and made my business an instant success.

BEING PULLED IN SO many directions, I felt as though I was no longer in control of my life. I went through the motions of pretending to be happy. My children were busy in their worlds. I could hear them and sense them, but I was not the full mother I should have been.

I was an empty shell.

Nothing mattered; nothing had meaning to me. I waited for the morning when my eyes would open, but there would only be dark.

I didn't want to bother anymore.

This was when Donny and I clashed. My heart stopped beating when I chose for him to go his own way and let me be. Part of me didn't want him to see me crashing as I watched the world spiral into another galaxy, a galaxy that didn't include me.

"Leave me alone," I told him.

I would care for my children the best I could, right or wrong, I would make decisions with their input. And hopefully, I'd find a way.

Listen, listen, listen . . . hold on.

I couldn't hear it. The Veery Thrush remained silent, but her vibration still flowed into my heart, my hurting, beating heart. This pain deepened, an open and raw wound worse than my divorce. Then, I didn't have any more love; I couldn't allow myself that luxury. As a non-human, I would separate myself from the loving part of me and continue into my blindness.

✶ ✶ ✶

I HAD PLANNED A surprise birthday party for Donny in July of 1996 for his 50th birthday at a resort in the Longville area. I was going to cancel it, but my dear friends, Cheryl and Alicia, convinced me that I had other friends to see. So we went. Sarah drove us to Kee-Nee-Moo-Sha Resort on Woman Lake four miles from town for our seven-day vacation over the Fourth of July. I knew Donny would probably be home during this time and I didn't want to accidentally run into him. So, I wrote him a note letting him know my plans.

Tim, Alice, and Sarah enjoyed the resort's amenities, the swimming, sand, other kids, games, and weather. I wanted to just sit and relax. I wanted to feel refreshed and hopefully be able to find my way back to myself.

"Vroom, vroom."

I heard and knew the familiar sound of Donny's motorcycle, and my heart leapt into my throat. Could it really be? It's been six months without a word.

"Donny!" Tim and Alice squealed.

As I walked out of the cabin to the front porch, the breeze gently blew through the wind chime hanging from the branch of the sugar maple. The warm fragrance of a nearby pine wafted past. The world sang to me again as the chickadees chirped their merry twitter.

And there he was.

It was the scene from *Sleeping Beauty* where all the animals of the forest came out to see the prince. Time stopped long enough for our eyes to meet. There . . . that spark from before. It hadn't gone, but what was I to do?

He parked his bike and listened to the chatter from the kids telling of all their excitement at the resort.

Although my heart sang, I felt a brick wall quickly being built inside me. I didn't want this, even though I did. The wall would protect me from being hurt again, from hurting him, and from hurting my children. We said our hellos from a distance as each brick found its place. He wanted to spend the Fourth with us and I thought that would be okay. I could enjoy my other friends, too.

The Fourth celebration in Longville has always been exciting. The small town with a population less than 200 swelled to thousands as tourists and cabin owners traveled to town by car or boat for the parade and other activities. The kids and I were reunited with many friends, picking up where we had left off. Joy filled our hearts throughout the day and into the evening as we watched the fireworks. Parades and fireworks were always my favorite delights. With the loss of vision, I found that I enjoyed them even more because I only had to focus in one area for the enchantment. I didn't have to look for it, and that gave me a small sense of being worthy.

Another day of rest and then the week was over. Our journey back to reality would begin in the morning. I wasn't ready, but thankful for the time we had and the memories made.

Donny asked to take me on a motorcycle ride before I left. I went, letting my heart soar and sing silently inward with joy. The brick wall around my heart was finished, but I had left a window open. The window allowed for a passionate kiss before he left, unlike any other we'd ever shared.

"You know I always loved you," he whispered to me. "I always will."

"It's too late." I heard someone else say. Was that really me?

"It was never about your eyes," he said, his voice trembling.

He roared off as I slumped to the ground, lost once again, alone and broken. *Goodbye, my love.*

Two weeks went by and I received two dozen multicolored roses at work.

I hope you enjoyed your vacation, Don, the note said.

That was it! I knew in that moment. I couldn't live without him, vision or not. I wasn't sure how, but I knew I had to call and thank him for the beautiful flowers. As a friend of mine once said, "Stop and smell the roses."

When I called, my brick wall crumbled, and he said he had something to ask me. I told him to go ahead.

"Not on the phone," he said "I need to ask you in person.

Can I come and see you Friday night?"

I said yes. And when he arrived, we embraced again with passion.

"If I asked you to marry me," he asked, "would you say yes?"

"I don't know," I smugly replied. "You haven't asked me yet."

"Will you marry me?

"Yes, yes, yes!"

Thirteen weeks later, on October 26, 1996, after dating for eight years, we were married. I prepared my small version of the church wedding that I never had.

Donny was now working for Veit out of Rogers, MN, doing heavy equipment operation. We never knew where he would be working next or for how long. Weather permitting, he had work, but if it rained, he would be home.

Another shoot joins the already established sprout. While taking a deep breath and feeling the warmth of the sun, joy ignites nurturing the small, persevering plant that was once only a seed.

Chapter Twenty-Six

IN THE DEEP

DECEMBER 23, 1997

I HAD A FULL schedule of seven clients today. I started at nine in the morning and went until 8:00 P.M. I was invigorated from giving but felt mostly fatigued when I finished. I loved the sense of accomplishment when I received compliments from my clients. I made a difference. I did something useful, but still, I couldn't shake the feeling of pain deep inside.

JANUARY 27, 1998

MY SISTER, JOAN, WHO is two and a half years older than me, visited an eye doctor. The doctor diagnosed her with the start of retinitis pigmentosa. She was such a support for me when I received my diagnosis that I want to be there for her while she adapted.

My heart sank with the news.

Not someone else! Now the whole family is getting exams to see if anyone else has it. It's very scary. Mom and Dad are heart broken and blame themselves. How can I help them when I'm weak? I'll have to put my big girl pants on and do whatever I can.

FEBRUARY 5, 1998

I CAN'T STOP THINKING about Joan having RP. I want to talk to her about it, but she isn't ready yet. I told her I would always be here for her, like she was for me. Somehow, we'll get through this with each other's support.

＊ ＊ ＊

TIM'S PAPER ROUTE USUALLY started by two-thirty in the afternoon, but they didn't arrive until half past seven that evening. He had to miss confirmation class. He loved delivering the papers with the new fat tire wagon I got him. I went with him one day, and his work ethic impressed me.

"A precise placement is required at each delivery to keep the clients happy," he told me.

＊ ＊ ＊

I HAD A FULL day at work and extended my hours to make room for another client. A man stopped by, wanting his wife to receive a massage that night and paid for the session. She didn't show. When I called her, she seemed upset about the whole thing. I was too but did not let her know that. I let her know that she could reschedule.

I don't think she will.

*C*March 2, 1998

I took long breaks between clients today. Yesterday was the biggest day I had so far—nine clients without any breaks. I needed to take care of me, or I wouldn't be able to take care of others. My clientele numbers rocketed after doing the chair massages at businesses. Last month, I made more than I did the entire year of 1996. What a great feeling that was, but I needed to know my limits. I was already booked out 2 weeks with a growing waiting list.

Donny surprised me after work with a pint of raspberries, my favorite.

I love surprises like that.

Alice had her first babysitting job yesterday. I couldn't believe my baby was old enough to babysit. She took classes through school and even got a certificate. She looked so professional with her small backpack filled with creative fun for the children. She carried a form for the parents to fill out before they left, informing her of their contact phone numbers and emergency care. She already had many plans for the money she would make, but also wanted to save part of it in her pink elephant bank.

Sarah's band had a wonderful concert. The concert hall was filled with hundreds of others, but I only saw her. I focused as they played the Irish hymn, "Be Thou My Vision." Chills lifted me as I heard the familiar tune, filling me with the hope that I had lost.

March 11, 1998

I got a massage from Kelly, another therapist in town. We do exchanges which are so important for self-care.

March 16, 1998

For my CEU's (continuing education units, which are necessary for maintining my massage license), I gave a class for *Loving Pregnancy with Partner Massage*. Only one couple attended, which worked out very well.

March 20, 1998

We went to Longville yesterday for a vacation. I wanted to see Brainerd, so we drove south 60 miles to look at the changes since our last visit. On the return trip, I had a sudden urge to drive. It had been six years since I had been behind the wheel. I knew I shouldn't, not with the kids in the car, but Donny obliged and found a back road that was straight. He said I should be fine.

It wasn't like riding a bike, I soon discovered. I was so nervous.

"Gee, I don't remember all these gadgets!" I teased as I tried to find my right adjustments.

"NO!" came a trio of screams as the children ducked in the back seat.

Check the mirrors, foot on the brake, put the car in gear, gently apply pressure to the gas . . . and we were off. White knuckled, I decided 20 MPH was fast enough and a quarter mile was far enough. That satisfied me.

Later that day, Alice had her friend, Kylee, over to the farm. Tim spent most of the day hitting golf balls in the yard with Donny's brother, David. Donny went for coffee in town to talk with guys he grew up with. Sarah and I just relaxed.

Donny was so happy at the farm. I wished we could stay. My mind wondered how it would be to have my massage business in Longville.

I saw my first robin, which, according to Dad, means there are only 3 more snows till spring. It's a yearly tradition to keep track of, and he was usually right.

REFLECTION, PRESENT DAY

AS I READ THE end of March 1998 and into April, I remembered the trying times of those days. I wished I would have been a stronger mother then. My written words showed how hopeless I was and how I wanted to know the right thing to do. I was torn in different directions as a mother and wife among other obligations. I was afraid to make my own choices because I would have upset someone with each contrasting feeling that arose.

"God never gives us more than we can handle," a friend told me.

I don't agree. I believe that we can only handle the tough stuff knowing He is there to go through it with us, no matter what the outcome is. It's not easy and it doesn't get lighter when we think we're at the bottom and we've had too much.

I wrote in April that I wanted to have a nervous breakdown, but I didn't know how. And besides, I still had to work from 9:00 A.M. to 7:00 P.M. that day.

APRIL 8, 1998

MY YEARLY EYE VISUAL field exam was today with a new machine. My right eye lost some, but the left seemed unchanged. Dr. Hofer was good at boosting my spirits with compliments. He said he was impressed with how well I've done with my business.

I get so nervous about my eye exams. I think I will finally get the news that today is my last day to see and tomorrow will be dark. Or I hope for the news they can't find anything wrong, that the RP is completely gone.

* * *

THE REPORT CARDS CAME back today with all three children doing great in school. We celebrated by going out for pizza.

APRIL 16, 1998

MOM AND DAD WERE in town for Dad's stress test. He was having pain last week and they wanted him to come in. I'm so glad it turned out to be okay.

I worked another long day from 9:00 A.M. to 7:00 P.M.

APRIL 18, 1998

TIM TURNED FIFTEEN TODAY. He spent the day with his friend, Ben, four wheeling and had a great time.

APRIL 23, 1998

I WENT HOME FROM work today with flu symptoms. I felt bad

about missing the money from cancelled sessions and having to fit them into my already busy schedule.

Stress is my main problem.

April 30, 1998

It's my forty-first birthday.

The kids got me a beautiful bouquet of purple irises, my favorite, along with purple orchids. I had a beautiful day, even though I was busy at home: I washed and hung out four loads of laundry, scrubbed floors, and cleaned the bathroom before walking two miles for my massage from Kelly.

I stopped at the office afterward and found that Donny had delivered a dozen roses for me— Oh, how beautiful.

I went to lunch with Mike, a quadriplegic client of mine. I visited his house two times a week to work on his neck. His place was on my walk home. I'm sure we caused quite a scene as we made our way the few blocks to the restaurant. He was in his wheelchair, going down the road because the sidewalks were bad, and I walked next to him, tapping my white cane.

Tap, step, roll, roll, tap, step, roll, roll.

We joked about it as we went. Sometimes, you just have to make an impression and laugh about it.

In the afternoon, Mom and Dad came to help in my celebration. We played croquet in the backyard.

What a wonderful day. I will always cherish making joyful memories, which blow the dark clouds away.

May 5, 1998

I HAD ANOTHER FULL schedule today.

Alice had a softball game and lost for the first time. Mom and Dad came to watch. Afterward, we all went to listen to Sarah play in the pop concert. I was sad to realize this would be her last band concert as she would be graduating soon. She played the trumpet I built while in Red Wing in band and would play the French horn in the symphony concert next week.

I love listening to her play.

May 11, 1998

I GAVE CHAIR MASSAGES at Meadowview Elementary to the staff. A client of mine paid for all the sessions as an appreciation of what the teachers do. Hopefully, I recruited some of them as clients.

Sarah had her final symphony concert tonight. I had tears throughout the evening, as I focused, trying to memorize her face and the lulling sounds.

May 17, 1998

WHAT A SPECIAL DAY, as we celebrated Sarah's graduation and Tim's confirmation. The house was full of family, joy, and laughter. It was a beautiful day so that we could be outside as well as in the house. Sarah and Tim each invited their friends to join us.

Two big events, stepping stones in life came and went, making me wish time would stop for a moment. I still hadn't had enough time to memorize each facet of their lives. If

I could only stop waiting for the darkness, maybe then, I could relish in the joy of their special day. There was so much activity and I tried to navigate the busy house without my cane.

Slow down, you've got this, I told myself.

And there's Joan, my sister, who still wasn't ready to talk yet. I tried not to take notice of her navigational skills. Was she having problems? I really couldn't tell.

May 19, 1998

DAD CALLED AND ASKED if Tim would want to go to Canada fishing with him in June. He will be so excited. My brother, Steve, is also going with his two sons. I can't wait to tell him.

I've always wanted to go with Dad, but it's a guy thing. This is a big annual event, Dad has traveled with the same men for years. As time goes by, sons are included and now grandsons are going.

The Foundation Fighting Blindness, RP convention is in Chicago in August. I'm hoping to go, but my sisters have informed me they have decided not to go.

May 26, 1998

TODAY IS THE SECOND time I seriously thought of ending my life. How can I go on?

Typical teenage behavior entered our lives, and my husband, parents, and siblings have reprimanded me for not controlling it their way. The kids were doing so well in school, I tried to focus on the positives. Everyone had an opinion and they hurled them at me. Expectations that I follow their edicts burned my soul. Each comment about how to treat my children, how to run my business, how to be a mother and wife tormented me. As I tried to please one family member another chastised me.

I have nothing left. My losses are too overwhelming. Hateful words come from every angle, as if I'm being stoned. The words, the looks, the actions . . . I'm told that I'm a horrible mother by my kids, husband, parents, and siblings.

"You don't let me do anything!"

"You're letting them get by with too much."

"Why aren't you listening to me?"

"I can't believe you let him do that?"

"Mom and Dad are always doing things for you."

"Where did that money go?"

"I'm going anyway, and you can't stop me."

I love each one of them. Can't they see I am trying to please everyone? I'm going blind, trying to run a business, trying to raise my children, trying to be a wife . . .

In the middle of it all, I've lost me. And I don't . . . even . . . care.

There's nothing left.

The non-person wins, and I succumb to the darkness. Within its depths, there is a chilling comfort as I realize I no longer need to try. I give up. It doesn't matter. Nothing matters. I will stop trying and, maybe in that, I can find me. Maybe, the hard shell will crack, and I can become who I was really meant to be, a happy person. Perhaps I can find my inner-being and listen, listen, listen . . . hold on!

*R*EFLECTION, PRESENT DAY

HOW DID I CARRY on? Where was my help? Who pulled me through all this pain? I didn't feel it. My vision tormented me throughout these days. I wish I would have written about those thoughts, but how could I when I had so much else to handle?

I kept reading and glimpsed where my path was going. Oh, this was so hard for me to read. With each entry, I saw my past self as a frightened little girl, trying to be a mother, a wife, or just a person, but feeling she failed miserably.

Growing, stretching, feeling, the plant knows its direction. It is upward, sending out a branch, an idea of what she is to be.

Chapter Twenty-Seven

A RAY OF LIGHT SHINES THROUGH THE CLOUDS

*Deep in your wounds are seeds, waiting to
grow beautiful flowers.*[21]

—*Niti Majethia*

MAY 27, 1998

I RECEIVED A NOTE from a lady in Longville, reminding me
how much I dislike living in Eau Claire. I would love to move
back to Minnesota and only work part-time. I rarely have any
openings or breaks during the day. I feel burned out from
lifting up everyone else, when my whole life has crashed.
Who is helping me?

REFLECTION, PRESENT DAY

DONNY AND I WERE married in 1998 and living together

---

21   Niti Majethia, *The Battle Cry: A Little Book of Comfort and Strength* (United
States: Partridge Publishing India, 2020).

in Eau Claire, but he traveled for work. Combined with his work schedule, I felt a strong sense of responsibility for my own career and raising my three children. Independence was something I had always valued. However, when I wrote the entry above, I must have realized somewhere deep inside that I needed help, but I had no clue who or where to seek assistance.

*M*AY 29, 1998

I GAVE DAD HIS first ever massage. He loved it!

"Now I know why this is the perfect occupation for you," he complimented. "You have such a relaxing touch. I feel so good. Thank you."

Mom has never had a massage and probably won't.

"You know what that is?" she said when I first told her I wanted to learn massage. "That's just a cover for sex." Yup, she even said the word.

Sure thing Mom, that's why I'm doing it!

Many shared that thinking years ago, and some still do. But people have come to acknowledge the health benefits from relaxing their bodies: letting natural energy flow, releasing toxins built up in stressed areas, and bringing relief.

Tim went with Mom and Dad to stay until their fishing trip.

He's going to have such a great time. I want to go too someday. I hope I can.

*R*EFLECTION, PRESENT DAY

THE NEXT ENTRY IN my journals took me to a really dark

place. Many of the specific events that led to this entry were not pertinent to my journey with retinitis pigmentosa, but I've given a glimpse below into my personal state of mind.

Teenage years for children and their parents can be full of conflict. My family in this regard was no different than thousands of other families. Raising children with a man other than their father compounded the problem. Donny was raised on a farm where the children were expected to be up at the crack of dawn, helping in the fields or with the livestock. He was also expected to help after school. Furthermore, Donny was a Marine through-and-through. He took a black-and-white, non-democratic approach to raising children, whereas I wanted to nurture their desires. Our differences made cohabitating difficult at times. The bottom line was . . . I felt stuck between those I loved in my life. I wanted to run, but there was nowhere to go. I wanted to fly, but I couldn't find my eagle. I wanted to hear the music, but my Veery Thrush was quiet.

There were so many things to endure at the time, but my children, Donny, and I came through them all. Stronger.

*J*une 6, 1998

Donny got rained out at work yesterday and today. He was home, but the kids were all away. Alice went to Six Flags Great America near Chicago with the church youth group for four days, Timmy was fishing, and Sarah moved to the Cities to live with her dad.

Life will be so different without her here. I hope she finds happiness. I know she has her own journey that is calling her, and I wish her well.

Mom called to tell me about the fishermen having a great time and catching lots of fish. They'll be home on Monday—I

237

cried afterward.

I miss my children when they're gone, even though there is such chaos here.

Life isn't peaceful anymore. Donny and I are at odds again, and it seems like he doesn't want to talk to me. I can't stop my thoughts or planning suicide. I wish there was someone to talk to, but I have to take another step forward, into this dark cloud, surrounding myself with its numbing effects.

It doesn't matter what I do or say anymore.

JUNE 10, 1998

ALICE CAME HOME THIS afternoon and talked non-stop for an hour about how wonderful it was to be at Six Flags. She fell asleep in the chair at seven, so I put her to bed at eight.

JUNE 26, 1998

DAD WAS TAKEN BY ambulance to Luther Hospital. He had a severe headache, had been throwing up for two days, and couldn't stand. They thought he had a possible inner ear virus or a slight stroke. After a CAT scan, they discovered a slight stroke in the cerebellum and admitted him to the ICU.

* * *

AN ARTICLE IN THE Eau Claire, *Leader Telegram*, paper caught my eye today.

There is a competition for people with disabilities in the surrounding five states. I guess I qualify. I'm going to apply and see what happens. I'm to write, in 250 words, or less, why I think I should win an award and what I would do with it.

*J*une 28, 1998

THIS WAS A DAY of many emotions. Dad was still in the hospital. Donny, Alice, and I left for the Minneapolis/St. Paul airport early in the morning to connect with Donny's daughter, Ann, and two-year-old granddaughter, Rebekah. They were arriving for a three-hour layover between Kansas City and Hibbing, MN.

We had a great time letting Bekah entertain us.

"The plane got really, really loud!" Bekah said. "Then, it went really, really fast! Then I got gum!"

She sat on Papa's lap for a little while before they boarded another plane. We didn't see them often, so it was fun.

We visited in an area where the intercoms couldn't be heard, but we were being paged. Joan had been trying to let us know that Dad was in emergency brain surgery to relieve fluid. We arrived home to messages on the answering machine telling of the surgery and outcome.

At 2:00 P.M., Alice had her championship softball tournament. They were playing the undefeated team, the Eagles, for the title and won! It was an exciting game. Alice got a trophy and took it everywhere for the next couple days.

After the game, we went to the Midway Hotel for a wedding reception for Rita's daughter, Tammy, and her husband, Garry. This was their first visit from Alaska since their wedding last September. Tammy was five months pregnant.

Next, we went to the hospital to check on Dad. I felt uncomfortable seeing him with so many attachments from the surgery. I could only stay in the room a few minutes before feeling woozy.

$\mathcal{R}$EFLECTION, Present day

READING THIS ENTRY, I felt like I was watching a tennis game. My emotions bounced back and forth from high joys to low despair. I continually felt the pull of the darkness tugging from below and refusing to let my bobbing head above water. *Act as if everything is normal in my fading world,* I told myself. That was my mantra.

I crumbled when I saw my dad hooked to tubes and heard the swooshing sounds of the machine assistance he was receiving.

Then, I was elated to see the joy in my husband's eyes. Donny delighted in his daughter and granddaughter in our brief moments together.

Alice's championship game caused thrills of accomplishment with her team's victory. All those practices really paid off in the skills they honed.

My niece's wedding reception continued, a celebration regardless of Dad's surgery. It felt okay, because they had traveled so far and planned so long. All gathered shared in this joyful event while sending prayers of healing for Dad.

$\mathcal{J}$UNE 29, 1998

THEY TOOK ANOTHER CAT scan on Dad and found the fluid was gone, so they let him wake up. His headache was gone.

$\mathcal{J}$UNE 30, 1998

I TOOK THE DAY off to relax, but God had other needs for me. I helped Mom move Dad from Luther Hospital to Sacred Heart Hospital on the other side of Eau Claire for a few days of physical therapy. Maybe he would be able to come home by the weekend. Dad thought it was interesting that his therapist was totally blind. I had considered that occupation at one point, but I discovered a four-year waiting list to attend the school in Duluth.

I received a letter from the disabilities competition. I'm one of the top four finalists for the Judd Jacobson Entrepreneurial Award! I have an interview on August 11.

Sarah called from her dad's in the Cities. I miss her so much. I was thrilled to hear that she found a data entry job at Fairview Hospital.

While I was still working, Donny called me to say he had just gotten home from working in Mankato, Minnesota, and didn't work this Saturday. I'm having deeper desires to move back to Longville. The drama with the hairstylists at Mane Attractions Salon is frustrating, but I love my clients.

𝒥ULY 1, 1998

WE WENT TO THE Lee Family Reunion on Lake Holcombe, an hour northeast of Eau Claire, at Uncle Don Lee's cabin. I was thrilled to see Mom brought Dad, but I felt even more surprised when I saw Sarah. She had arranged to ride with my parents and spend several days helping me redo my old business plan so I could have a fresh one for the award. I was pleasantly surprised to realize that I had already accomplished several of the goals I set three years ago.

𝒜UGUST 11, 1998

MY FRIEND, MINA, WHO is also a massage therapist, drove me to the Cities for my Judd Jacobson Entrepreneurial Award interview at the Courage Center in Golden Valley,

Minnesota.

Deep breaths in, feel the calm, slowly let it out: listen, listen listen . . . hold on.

"Pamela," a voice called from the opening door. "They're ready to see you."

My heart jumped into my throat as I stood, extended my cane, and strode confidently toward my awaiting purpose.

I can do this.

One wall of the room was a window from floor to ceiling, giving the much needed light that I hoped for. That gave me a tiny boost of confidence. An attendant guided me to a podium in front of the window, which faced the middle of the room. A large oblong table with five smiling faces greeted me. Each one wore a comforting look as if I was a normal human being. There wasn't an ounce of sympathy.

"Good afternoon, Pamela. We're so glad to meet you," a lady announced, wearing a brilliant blue scarf, leisurely adorned on her shoulders, emphasizing the curve of her neck.

Barbara Jacobson introduced herself and the other four board members surrounding her. She explained how the Judd Jacobson Entrepreneurial Award came to be. Her husband, who passed away several years ago, had become a quadriplegic as the result of a diving accident when he was young. The award was started in his honor.

"We are very impressed," she continued, "by what you have outlined in your business plan and we would like to hear more."

They allowed me 20 minutes to share more about my plan, tell what I had accomplished so far, and outline what I would use the award money for. I didn't think I had ever been so nervous, but I also couldn't believe how calm I was on the outside. If I didn't think I was good enough, how would I convince them I was?

"I'm very interested in the health benefits through massage," I said. "In order to deepen my interest, I was directed toward providing an effective environment for my clients."

I described my mission statement: To promote an alternative form of healthcare that provides a natural treatment to both mind and body through therapeutic massage.

I shared then my philosophy of massage, followed by my needs.

"I may be selfish in my venture as a massage therapist," I said. "When I was diagnosed with retinitis pigmentosa, I was told to find a job where I didn't need my eyes. I was told that by helping others, I could forget my disability. I truly believe this has been the right choice for me. I enjoy helping other people feel better, especially seeing the difference between the way the client feels when they start a treatment and when they leave."

The time was up, and I felt I had covered everything that I had intended to share.

When I arrived home, there was a message on my answering machine.

"Congratulations," The voice said. "You have been selected as the recipient of this year's Judd Jacobson Award."

I would receive $1,200 at a ceremony next month. I was in shock. I really did it!

REFLECTION, PRESENT DAY

WARMTH FLOWED THROUGH ME, lifting a dark cloud from around my heart. As it rose, I felt rays of hope, giving joy to my seeded plant. Courage, hope, and empowering love swooned into me. Finally, a ray of light shone brilliantly on the, once upon a time, seed. A plant took shape as the first few leaves began to form hesitantly, but it knew everything would be okay.

Grow my beautiful plant. Breathe the breath that fills your joys.

Chapter Twenty-Eight

STUCK IN THE MIDDLE

AUGUST 13, 1998

THE GALS AT WORK got me flowers for winning. A stunning bouquet of vibrant, bright colors, including a few purple irises.

I worked until noon. Tim went to stay with Ben at their cabin for the weekend. Alice and I had a great afternoon making a three-layer white cake with a lemon filling and fluffy white frosting. Later, we did facials and played scrabble.

AUGUST 18, 1998

I FOUND OUT TODAY that my award is for $2,500. Wow! The Celebration for Courage Banquet is planned for September 13 and Smokey Robinson will be the entertainment! There will be 800-900 people in attendance and several other awards are to be presented. Barbara Jacobson is sending more details.

My mind is racing with all the possibilities for how I can use this money. I've always wanted a table that adjusts electronically toward the desired height. That would ease the strain on my body and be easier for my clients. But for now, I need to pack for the RP convention in Chicago. I decided to go even though my sisters changed their minds.

AUGUST 20, 1998; MORNING

MY EYE DOCTOR WAS able to connect me with Patty, who also has RP, and her husband, Joe. They live in the Minneapolis area and were able to pick me up on their way to Chicago for the convention. They were friendly, making it a nice trip. We played the car alphabet game, finding words starting with A and working our way to Z. Each word had to start with the letter and we each had to find our own. It was fun, but it really strained my eyes. After we arrived, they went their separate way with friends, and I went to my room.

I am trying to relax in my room at the Palmer House Hilton on the 15th floor before the retinitis pigmentosa convention. I wish my sisters would have joined me. The view out my window looks at the next skyscraper. It's comfortable with all the amenities: two queen beds, a beautiful whirlpool tub, and even a refrigerator bar. I see that I will be charged for each item, so I'll have to do without. I'm not going to pay $4.50 for a bottle of water.

The opening session is starting soon, so I need to find my way to the elevator.

AUGUST 20, 1998; EVENING

I WENT DOWN THE 15 floors and watched the doors to the auditorium open. The scene made the inner me drop to my knees. There I was, lost in a different world where disabilities surrounded me, from the totally blind to people with Usher Syndrome who have their hands cupped around their assistant's hands reading the sign language by feel. Guide dogs, guide people, wheelchairs, canes tapping, it was all there. How could they all look happy and satisfied with their circumstances? Weren't they devastated like me?

I gasped and realized I had to step into this world.

It's my world now, one I have become a part of.

"Dear God," I prayed, "carry me through this. I can't do it alone."

I walked to the reception, talked to a few people, but I felt a strong desire to be alone. I wanted to run back to my room and isolate myself from the rest of the world. The dark cloud approached from behind, placing its cold hand on my shoulder. I let it win again and returned to my room.

I think I'll order room service and watch TV. The news comes on the screen, the U.S. bombing terrorists. Click! That's not relaxing, and I have a toothache.

AUGUST 21, 1998

THIS MORNING WAS A struggle as my depression set in hard. It took me a long time to stop crying and go to the opening session with scientists, followed by a luncheon.

There were several sessions during the afternoon. One was just for RP. Another talked about the current technology. I was disappointed when a speaker forgot his handouts at his office. This was the one session I really came for and they didn't have any information except to get it on the web. Many people walked out.

In the center of the huge hall, there were exhibit booths.

247

I became frustrated, because my expectations were to find useful assistant information. My toothache was getting worse and I had a headache. I found Tylenol in the bar in my room that slightly helped. It cost $4.23 for two capsules.

AUGUST 22, 1998

I ATE IN MY room last night. I went to the gift shop to buy a small bottle of Tylenol for $6.50. I couldn't locate the exact tooth, but my whole right jaw was throbbing. My ear even hurt. I called Patty's room. She said it sounds like when she needed a root canal.

Yuck! I hope the pain goes away, it's terrible!

AUGUST 23, 1998

I FELT A LITTLE better and went to the morning session, Therapeutic Approaches to Retinal Degenerative Diseases. It was a good presentation.

I had a nice conversation with a man from Washington who told me about the Microsoft assistive technology session. It sounded like it would be what I needed, but it was only for a large print, no voice, like I was hoping to find.

My tooth was so painful by the afternoon and I had taken too much extra strength Tylenol, so I spent the afternoon taking a hot bath and a short nap. Jets zooming past the building woke me. The Blue Angels were having their air show, which I could see from my window. That was a delight.

After falling back to sleep, I heard a loud crack. I thought they were still performing but discovered there was a thunderstorm. I felt like I was in the middle of the sharp booms because of being up so high.

I called Donny and shared how my day had been going. It was good to talk to him, and it made my toothache feel a little better.

I went to the final reception in a room filled with over 100 elegant tables. There must have been at least 1,000 people. A string quartet serenaded the crowd from one of the corners. Conversations almost overpowered the sound, but I chose a table near them so I could enjoy their music.

A fancy dinner was served starting with a fruit plate and salad.

I think it's a salad, I thought. So, many different colors and vegetables had been added. *Oh, and which fork do I use?*

The main course was a delicious small slice of roast beef, three asparagus spears, two carrots, and two small potatoes. Dessert was an exquisite Chicago-style cheesecake with raspberries in whipped cream and a mint leaf on top. There were swirls of raspberry puree decorating the edges of the plate, pretty fancy for me.

Wine was served during the main course, and twice someone bussing dishes cleared my glass before I even had a taste of it. I was embarrassed when the lady next to me told our waiter and he insisted on doing something for me. He brought me some Bailey's Irish Cream to go with my coffee during dessert—that worked.

Awards were handed out, although it was hard to hear and see what they were doing. Entertainment started with musical impressions of Cab Calloway, The Blues Brothers, and Aretha Franklin. When they were finished, it was 10:00 P.M. My tooth hurt so badly. I really wanted to stay, because everyone was having such a great time, but I went to bed.

August 24, 1998

I was amazed that I could do a "zip-check-out" on the TV in my room. Why did they have that technology, but I had nothing to tell me what's on my computer screen that I could understand? I went downstairs to have them put my luggage in storage while I went to the last meeting, Future Directions: From the Lab to the Clinic.

All in all, it had been a wonderful weekend. I met many people with RP, many with most of their sight remaining, and many my age with seeing eye dogs already. Numerous conference attendees still used canes, but I could tell they had less sight than me. Others didn't use a cane at all. I used mine during the weekend even though I hadn't used it much in over a year. I couldn't stand the looks from people. I should have just looked elsewhere and refused to care what they thought, but it had been easier for me to just give it up.

In the final session, I learned that Axokine, a medication that works on the brain and nerves behind the eye, is currently being studied with hopes of finding a cure for RP. Scientists felt they were around the corner from a discovery.

I hope and pray it happens before I go blind. I would like to attend many more conferences if I'm able.

Many emotions went through me during this weekend. Mostly, I realized just how much Donny would have to help me. I hoped he would be able. There were so many people with RP that had family support in attendance. I didn't think that would bother me, but it did. I felt lonely.

Reflection, Present day

I felt sucker punched once again. The details of my 1998 journal ripped my breath out of me. I relived that spiral down into the depths of the darkness where my RP kept me captive, but I never hit the bottom. Painful, self-defeating, and negative hate surrounded me as I read and fought desperately to tweeze out the fragments of positivity or a ray of hope that kept me going. It was there.

It is here. Keep looking, Pamela. Keep going. Don't give up!

God, help me to forgive the girl I was . . .

Listen, listen, listen . . . hold on.

Chapter Twenty-Nine

AN EVENING AT THE BALL

Be still, sad heart, and cease repining;
Behind the clouds is the sun still shining;
Thy fate is the common fate of all,
Into each life some rain must fall,
Some days must be dark and dreary.[22]
—Henry Wadsworth Longfellow

SEPTEMBER 13, 1998

TODAY WAS MY SPECIAL day to receive the Judd Jacobson Entrepreneurial Award. Being a Sunday evening, Donny wasn't able to get away from work, so I asked my friend, Mina, to drive and attend the occasion. On our way, we stopped to pick up Mom. Dad wasn't feeling good enough to attend but gave me a wonderful hug of congratulations.

"I'm so proud of you," he said. "You continually amaze

---

22 Henry Wadsworth Longfellow, "The Rainy Day," Henry Wadsworth Longfellow, A Main Historical Society Website, https://www.hwlongfellow.org/poems_poem. php?pid=39.

me as you take on challenges and win awards."

My heart felt sad that he wouldn't be there to share in this victory. Along with Mom he has been heavily involved in supporting me in my schooling and career in the earlier years. Now it had become my children who increasingly showed support in their own ways.

We arrived at the Marriott City Center Hotel in downtown Minneapolis in plenty of time before the start of the awards reception. Sarah, living in town, arrived before we went in. I was so glad she was there.

This first reception was a warm and intimate gathering of about thirty people. A very fancy table of chilled vegetables along with a delicious cranberry beverage was set up. The five Phillips Award recipients and a representative from Northwest Airlines for their Partners Award were also there.

Soon, one of the workers escorted me, along with the other award winners, to a separate table in front. I was nervous because I had to give a brief talk about myself after I received my lovely plaque.

The plaque was silver framed, a block art design in one corner, and had an inscription from my eye doctor that read: *Pamela has not allowed her physical status to change her drive and motivation at any point in time.*

Photo sessions with presidents from sponsoring organizations followed. Escorts showed us the way toward the next reception. A silent auction filled the hallways with exquisite art, baskets of fine wine, vacations, and more—at least seventy-five items to be bid on. As we passed, I glimpsed the asking prices and the current bids and decided this party was way out of my league.

The grandest gala room I had ever seen brought a small *wow* to my inner being. Scanning around the room at the outer walls reminded me of trying to see distant shores of a lake in northern Minnesota. People at tables resembled distant pine trees. The escort guided us to our tables located in a dark area, far on the other side. There must have been over 1,000 people there.

Barbara Jacobson, Judd's widow, told me that the richest of Minneapolis were there, but she seemed unimpressed with that. Barbara wanted to make sure that the evening focused on the award recipients. She sat at my table along with her niece, Maureen.

Barbara told of how Judd broke his neck in a diving accident off a gravel pit into a shallow pond when he was sixteen; two other friends were with him. Daniel Gainey was one of them and remained his lifelong friend—he set up this award through the Courage Center after Judd died in 1991.

I learned I was the first female to receive the award and the first one with a sensory impairment instead of a physical disability. This lifted me more than anything that evening, making me feel almost normal. Maureen told me that it was a tough competition between sixteen applicants, but she knew I had won as soon as she read my application.

Dinner was an elegant display of many courses. Sarah looked at me when they asked her if she wanted wine.

"Of course, she does," I told the waiter.

It meant so much to have my daughter with me along with Mom and Mina. I was really hoping that Donny would want to participate in this wonderful event—something that I accomplished through all the hardships. It would have been so much easier for me with the transportation, but he wouldn't take any time off work. Not even for this once in a lifetime event. I was crushed and I really missed not having him by my side.

After dinner, the award recipients went backstage. I was nervous when I met Don Shelby from WCCO TV. He was the emcee of the ceremony and a very friendly man. I told him how honored I was to meet him.

"I'm more honored to meet you," he said, shaking my hand. "I'm proud of your accomplishment, congratulations."

"My mother would love to meet you too," I said.

"I will make sure to stop at your table later in the evening."

One by one, Don talked about each of us on stage before presenting our award. During this time, there were several big screens showing pictures that had been taken of us in our work setting. I wish I could have seen them. Sarah said they were beautiful and impressive.

I received a second award, a lovely hard wood plaque that read: *Judd Jacobson Memorial Award presented to Pamela Edwards in recognition of achievement in an entrepreneurial business endeavor. Celebration of Courage, Courage Center, September 13, 1998.* A check for $2,500 was attached to the back.

I was Cinderella at the ball. Chandeliers hung from the ceiling and a spotlight shone on me. My beautiful apricot dress flowed perfectly around my knees—I felt special; proud. I held my cane with confidence and without embarrassment. Applause just for me was thunderous.

I looked out into the crowd, beaming, unconcerned that I had a disability as I caught the eyes of Sarah, Mom, and Mina.

Back at my round table of eight, I received more congratulations.

Don Shelby made his way toward us, stopping then at my side. "Okay,"—he grinned—"where's your mother?"

I'd never seen Mom blush before; it was wonderful to see her glowing.

"I loved the smell of his expensive suit!" she said after he left.

A live auction followed raising a lot of money. Music by Gwen Matthews came next, and then . . .

"Ladies and gentlemen, Smokey Robinson!"

What a thrill I had to see and hear one of my favorite entertainers. He performed a medley of all his hits, while the room exploded in applause. Smiles, foot tapping, clapping and singing along, filled the room. I didn't want my Cinderella evening to end.

When he finished the set, we were able to meet Smokey Robinson in a private room and have our picture taken with him. Embarrassed, I couldn't find words when my turn arrived: *Flash!* the camera snapped. Then it was over, but I could still feel the glow of that moment, a cherished lifelong treasure.

* * *

AFTER THAT NIGHT, I had two plaques and $2,500 to show for my accomplishments, but it all felt hollow. An empty pit opened in my heart, proving once again that it didn't matter how hard I tried or what I did—I wasn't worthy. I wasn't a whole, normal person. I was nothing.

My sensory impairment is because of my own unworthiness to be anything else. A plaque and money will never bring back my sight.

So, I retreat, and once again silence my Veery Thrush.

REFLECTION, PRESENT DAY

WAS IT ALL A dream? I remember feeling so important, encouraged and empowered, but I also remember not allowing myself to continue feeling that Cinderella moment.

I returned home and went back into my unworthiness mode, packed away my joy, and settled back into who I thought I was. It was a brief moment of light, it seemed surreal, and I extinguished it with my reality. Each attack at my decisions felt as though another nail was being pounded into my coffin.

Chapter Thirty

VICTORY WITH A TRAP DOOR

SEPTEMBER 21, 1998

ALICE HAD HER FIRST diving meet today. She let me know how scared she was, but she was going to try to be brave.

* * *

MY AWARD ARTICLE WAS in the *Minneapolis Star and Tribune* paper. They also published it on the internet through the Associated Press. Wow, what a surreal feeling to see my name on the internet with a story about my accomplishments. It almost made me feel proud, but I still felt numb.

* * *

I went to an organizational meeting for Wisconsin Women Entrepreneurs.

If I act as if I'm important and worth something, maybe I'll feel it?

SEPTEMBER 23, 1998

I RECEIVED A LETTER from a man in Madison. He read about me and my award in his paper and sent me $100.

Oh my goodness! I'm not sure what to think of this. I must send him a thank you for his kindness. Or is it pity? Either way, I accept.

* * *

BARBARA JACOBSON ASKED ME to be a travel agent for her. Judd Jacobson, being in a wheelchair, started a business that made travel easier for people with disabilities. Barbara thinks I could open an office here in Eau Claire.

I'm very curious., but I have too many other issues to consider that addition to my hectic world.

SEPTEMBER 27, 1998

SARAH IS LOVING HER college experience. I miss her so very much, but it pleases me to hear that she is finding her journey and is happy.

* * *

PATTY, MY FRIEND, WHO drove me to the conference in Chicago, was right when she thought I'd need a root canal to cure my toothache. The dentist gave me penicillin afterward, and I broke out in a rash that looks like little mosquito bites. A penicillin allergy, what next?

* * *

ALICE HAD A DIVING meet again today and they won. Yesterday at practice, she did a perfect back dive and was able to replicate it. She has been getting good grades, too.

* * *

I'M FEELING DEPRESSED. I have to keep thinking about all the positives instead of the negatives. Change the negatives. Can I do that? The negatives are so burdensome and all-encompassing. I'll focus on my children. They are always my source of joy.

October 1, 1998

DAD WENT TO THE hospital with an irregular heartbeat. He stayed overnight because his blood was too thick. I went to visit him with Mom. They said he might come home tomorrow.

October 3, 1998

MY EYES ARE BAD today. The central vision is usually clear, but today it's blurry. It scares me and reminds me I don't know when I'll be totally blind. The anticipation is so dreadful. Sometimes, I want my vision to just go and stop teasing me. But, NO! I can't let that happen.

I focus on my children, memorizing each smile, each skinned knee, their faces when they try something new and succeed, like Alice with diving. They are my treasures and when I can't see them anymore, I'll at least have the memories.

Reflection, Present day

I HAD TO FIND courage as I stepped back in time in my journal. How frightened I was, a mother facing so many challenges and insecurities with the fading light.

What choice did she have? She did the best she could for all of those around her. She tried to support them while she felt tempted to surrender to the inevitable—going blind.

When would the last beam of light disappear? In 1991, they said five to ten years, uncaringly it seemed. In 1998, they couldn't tell me because they didn't know, but time was expiring. I was approaching the ten-year mark. No wonder I had lost hope. The blurred vision was more evidence of my demise.

October 7, 1998

I HAVE BEEN GETTING very annoyed with situations at Mane Attractions. The atmosphere is not what I want for me or my clients, so I'm thinking of joining Designer Edition Salon. I'm impressed with the professionalism there.

Lord, guide me to where you need me.

October 13, 1998

I'VE MET WITH DeAnn at Designer Edition. I don't have a lease where I am, so I can give notice anytime. I need to think more about this.

I talked to Donny and he was supportive.

My clients complain so much about the clamor of hair dryers, the smell of cigarettes, difficulty parking, the busy location, and street traffic noise. I know there will be problems anywhere, but I feel that it's time to leave.

October 27, 1998

ALICE HAD HER FINAL diving meet, and wow! Mom and Dad came to watch with Tim and me. She showed a lot of focus when she performed her dives.

* * *

AT 4:00 A.M., WHILE making Donny's lunch, I accidently forgot to take off the paper from the sliced cheese. Oops! I guess I wasn't too awake at that time. He said he had a good laugh about it though.

"Damn, blind wife!" he teased, shocking his co-workers.

He then told them of another time when I didn't see that the bread twist tie was included in the sandwich. Luckily, he didn't swallow it.

* * *

I HAD A FRIEND doing a business mailing list for me. She said she would be done last week, no problem. I got them back, and she had only done A through C. I have to hurry to get them done now to notify my clients of my move.

October 30, 1998

TIM IS PROUD OF a kitchen design he has been working on at school.

He has asked me what my perfect kitchen would look like and suggested the perfect layout would be to have the sink, refrigerator, and stove in a triangular configuration for ease of use.

I love to see him so happy. Maybe this will be something he'll pursue when he's older.

*O*CTOBER 31, 1998

HALLOWEEN.

I worked in the morning and discovered that Donny had a dozen red roses delivered there in honor of our wedding anniversary. They were gorgeous! He stayed at his brother's house in the Cities while he worked all week.

Tim went to a party at his friend's house. He said he had a great time.

Alice couldn't find anyone to go trick-or-treating with her, so I went. It was perfect weather. We were only gone for an hour while Donny stayed home and handed out treats.

*N*OVEMBER 2, 1998

SARAH TURNED 19 TODAY. Tim, Alice, and I called and sang "Happy Birthday" to her.

I went to the doctor for a physical. The doctor said my thyroid felt too big, so she ordered blood tests.

I pray it's nothing. How am I to survive if anything else happens to me?

*N*OVEMBER 3, 1998

I HAD A FULL day at work, but it was hard. I felt tense, knowing that I'm moving my business soon. I prayed for a smooth transition.

I received the results from the blood test. They were normal, but the doctor ordered an ultrasound because of the increased size.

*N*OVEMBER 14, 1998

I STARTED AT DESIGNER Edition Salon today. What a wonderful new atmosphere, so professional. I'm going to like it there.

Tim started working at Randall's grocery store a few blocks away. He loves it and has shifts every day this week.

I received a letter from Social Security, notifying me that they paid too much according to my earnings. The letter stated the matter was under investigation and instructed me not to cash any checks starting in July 1998. I haven't cashed them but can't get through on the phone to find out why.

SOCIAL SECURITY IS GONE. I owe money on my business phone. My computer and the move to Designer Edition took most of my award money, and I don't make as much money at the new location. Child support stopped in October. Donny is laid off for the season.

What else do I have to endure?

I thought I had already hit bottom, but I didn't see the trap door.

There is no bottom.

*R*EFLECTION, PRESENT DAY

THERE WAS MORE TO this entry that I couldn't write in the same words I used then. I felt like there would always be more pain, and it weighed on me. Some conversations I had at the time made me feel like I was too stupid to be able to figure out what happened with Social Security. Illogical though it may have been, it felt like going blind was my punishment for struggling financially.

I prayed, but there seemed to be no help. I felt empty, like I was useless.

I contemplated suicide again. The doctor prescribed Zoloft, but I hated taking pills. They didn't take away the pain, and it entered my mind that it was a way for someone else, the doctor, to control me like a puppet.

December 8, 1998

THE TV STATION CONTACTED me to help with an article about how massage could relieve headaches. They came and did an interview. Instead of pity for my blindness, they asked about my profession and knowledge.

If I pretended everything was wonderful, maybe it would be.

December 30, 1998

I DIDN'T WANT TO leave my last entry of the year on such a depressing note. Nineteen ninety-eight was a very emotional year for me with many unhappy, disturbing memories.

There was one happy event that overshadowed the rest: winning the 1998 Judd Jacobson Entrepreneurial Award out of a four-state competition. That gave me the confidence, strength, and courage I needed to go on.

Now I need the wisdom.

Chapter Thirty-One

WALKING THROUGH THE VALLEY OF DEATH

JANUARY 1, 1999

LIFE CHANGED DRAMATICALLY WHEN we purchased a computer for the home. I have the internet on my office computer, but now the kids would be able to work on homework. And we set up an email account.

I'm not sure what online is all about, and it's probably just an expensive fad.

Time will tell.

JANUARY 3, 1999

I CRIED MOST OF the night about finances, and to top it off, the toilet broke, flooding the bathroom at midnight.

I'm stuck in the middle again between Donny and the kids. Tim has been sneaking out of the house at night, causing issues. There seems to always be something that someone isn't happy about, and I feel stuck in the middle.

My vision seems so much worse. I don't know how to give up or I would. How do you even have a nervous breakdown?

It is five below zero and there is too much snow to go to church. I made a turkey breast to help warm the house. I feel a little more strength, I think, than I did last year. I want to hold on to that feeling.

Because of the love I have for my husband and children, I'll take another step, a baby step.

January 11, 1999

WE WENT TO WATCH Alice do her Pom Pom routine at halftime of the school basketball game. I loved watching the synchronized movements and the girls' enthusiasm. Alice did a great job and had a lot of fun.

Afterward, while walking through the dark parking lot toward our car, I hit my head hard on a truck's side-view mirror—just another thing I didn't see. I had a bad headache and needed ice. It startled me, because I was getting too comfortable with what I could see and forgot the dangers of what I couldn't.

January 12, 1999

DONNY AND I WENT to see the movie *At First Sight*. It was a true story of a blind massage therapist with RP and hit too close to home for me. I cried through most of it.

The story told of a man who, at age three, lost all his sight from cataracts. He had surgery and adjusted to having sight only to lose it later from the progression of RP. The man in the movie seemed happier when he returned to blindness. It seemed to remove his wondering about when it would come, but at the same time it's so painful to know that's in my future.

FEBRUARY 1, 1999

I HAD TO TAKE the taxi to my dentist appointment because Donny was gone for an OSHA class that was required before the season starts.

I'm ignoring my inner voice that's pissed because I can't drive. That recording is getting old—deal with it!

I'm getting used to getting and sending emails. I love hearing from Longville friends.

FEBRUARY 13, 1999

THERE WAS A BENEFIT concert at church tonight. Tim helped and made sure I was where I needed to be. I really appreciated that. It must have been a horrible feeling to watch out for your mother. Tim has become my guardian son.

I rarely ask for assistance, but I'm getting more comfortable at doing so. I would rather ask than hurt myself or someone else.

FEBRUARY 17, 1999

DONNY'S EX-WIFE LYNN'S FATHER died this morning. After they took the hospital bed out of his room, they let in three-year-old Bekah, Donny's granddaughter.

"Great Grandpa has gone to heaven," they told her as she went to find him.

"But he forgot his slippers!" she said, bringing them out

to show.

That was a rainbow moment during their storm.

*F*EBRUARY 20, 1999

ALICE TURNED THIRTEEN TODAY. It was fun to have her decide what kind of a birthday cake we should make. After looking at different selections, she chose a baseball mitt and ball. She had friends overnight to celebrate. They had pizza, did facials, watched movies and giggled a lot.

*M*ARCH 1, 1999

I DON'T WANT TO live in Eau Claire anymore and want to move to Longville. My vision is getting so bad. I want to be settled before it's too far gone, before the ten years are up from when I was diagnosed.

Is God watching over me, guiding me, uplifting me?

He must be.

*R*EFLECTION, PRESENT DAY

As I READ BACK over the words I wrote and never revisited, I became so much more aware of His presence now. I have had to pause often and realize my blessings, but not only that, I paused to love the me who was.

I cheered her on with each day I read.

*A*PRIL 3, 1999

IT'S EASTER VACATION AND the kids are spending it with their dad in the Cities.

After much discussion, weighing the pros and cons, Donny and I decided we could start the paperwork and the process for a move to Longville. We visited over Easter and met my friend, Alicia, at the bank where she works. We talked to her about completing loan papers before we leave.

As a Vietnam Veteran, Donny qualifies for a VA loan. I almost hate to hope. Donny seems so happy about the possibility of moving back home, and I pray things go smoothly and swiftly.

*A*PRIL 30, 1999

I TURNED FORTY-TWO TODAY. That sounded old and I really felt it at times. My high school friends, Kathy and LuAnn, took me to supper to celebrate. We laughed for over three hours. I sure needed that.

*M*AY 2, 1999

I STARTED TAKING VITAMIN A Palmitate several years ago, but I haven't taken it for three months. It's supposed to slow or stop the progression of RP but could also cause liver damage. I'd rather go blind.

*R*EFLECTION, PRESENT DAY

LIFE IS SLAMMING ME very hard as I read entries in May 1999. I feel like I've lost control of everything. The pain is too deep even now. I'll continue reading with a very heavy heart.

May 28, 1999

I TOOK TODAY OFF for some much-needed organization, physically and emotionally. Papers arrived from the Social Security Administration Office that were required for the home loan.

I'm excited for the possibility.

* * *

DONNY AND I WENT to Longville to stay with David at the family farm for the weekend while Tim and Alice were with their dad.

Sunday, I played my mandolin at church. It felt so wonderful to be with the group again. After the service, I talked to Pastor Monson about the parsonage next door. I'd noticed it was listed for sale and thought it would be a perfect in-town, location for us. I could run my massage business out of the house, and while Donny would be out of town working, I could walk the half block for groceries.

I feel at home here and pray we can move back soon.

Reflection, Present day

THE FIRST PART OF June 1999, Tim decided to move to the Cities to live with his dad and sister, Sarah. I couldn't write about that pain then. Life moved on but felt empty, so my journals focused on the move to Longville.

In the middle of June, I felt my world crashing and crushing me from every angle. There were too many personal issues weighing on me. It's amazing that I never once wrote about my RP or used it as a *poor me* crutch during that time. It was the first time I'd not done that. I had choices and directions with the other issues, but not my vision. RP was and is something that I can't change and need to adjust each day, each moment.

Given that none of my journals focused on my condition, I will skip through the trials of those summer months and only share this one joyous entry.

AUGUST 25, 1999

I RECEIVED A CURIOUS email from Ann, Donny's daughter. She and Bekah were living in International Falls, MN with her mom and stepdad.

"Hi Dad and Pam, I wanted to let you know that I had a baby girl three days ago."

Lexi Miranda Edwards was born August 22, 1999, and she had been keeping the pregnancy private. With busy lives and such a distance, we didn't have a clue. We were invited to her baptism and fell in love with her adorable big eyes and smile.

Bekah adored her already.

NOVEMBER 15, 1999

THIS IS THE WORST day of my life, even worse than the day I was diagnosed.

The car has arrived and soon Alice will be gone too. My eyes are still red from crying so much, but I see such joy in her as she has prepared herself for this transition.

Gather up your courage, I prod myself, trying not to show

my gut punch feelings.

Tim and Sarah get out of the car and are here for a brief moment. I plaster on the make-believe-you're-happy face. They have come with their dad's girlfriend to take Alice away.

I venture outside to embrace my beautiful children. I hear them, their exuberance about the new road ahead.

Tim and Sarah chatter about their jobs, friends, school, and how happy they are. I'm so happy for who they are becoming in their new worlds. I pray for them daily and take comfort in knowing they are always protected.

One last long hug, then the traditional wave until I can't see them.

Alice is now reunited with her siblings and her dad.

I failed.

I tried yet failed.

My heart stops beating.

REFLECTION, PRESENT DAY

I HAD GREAT JOY when my dream of living in my first home ever came true, but it was tempered with such pain when Alice, too, decided to go to the Cities and live with her dad. My children were invaluable. At times, they were my only source of joy. My dream was to return to Longville, but it was not theirs. The thrill of the Cities called each of them one-by-one like birds leaving their nests. This was a hard and emotional event to allow even though I had no choice. I had truly given this up to God and where He needed her to be.

All three of my children—gone.

My only peace came with knowing they each had their own journey to travel. I was blessed to have had so many years with them. Now, their dad could share in that chance. I would still be a part of their lives, always.

Chapter Thirty-Two

NEW VISION

From all that was familiar,
I broke away.
Now I am lost, without a place,
wandering.
With no music like a fool
I dance and clap by hands.
How am I to live without You?
You are everywhere
but I can't find You.[23]

—*Rumi*

REFLECTION, PRESENT DAY

WORKING THROUGH MY JOURNALS, I recalled how lost I was in the time after my last entry in 1999. Five years had drifted by without my attention. I didn't feel worthy enough to write, but my seed formed into a bush, encouraged me, whispered to me, and guided my heart. It nurtured me without my

---

23   Maryam Mafi and Azima Melita Kolpin, *Rumi's Little Book of the Heart*, (United States: Hampton Roads, 2016), 87.

knowing.

My next journal started in 2004.

My reason for starting a journal many years before had been because I thought my kids would enjoy seeing what they did in the past. But in 1999, they were gone, so I figured why bother writing? And then I heard my Veery Thrush: *Continue for you, find who you are . . . listen, listen, listen . . . hold on.*

I wrote this section to summarize how we adapted to our new home in Longville and one life-changing event that happened between my journals.

✳ ✳ ✳

WE MOVED TO LONGVILLE on Thanksgiving Day, November 1999. I setup my massage business out of our home, which worked well for me. Although, I had to lower my session rates from what I was making in Eau Claire to account for the smaller town incomes.

From my home in town, I could walk to the bank, post office, grocery store, and the quaint tourist shops within two blocks.

Donny left early Monday morning and returned either late Friday night or sometimes on Saturday to work in other towns such as Duluth or Minneapolis. His return time often depended on the job and weather. He was usually assigned as the heavy equipment operator to finish the jobs, smoothing the end results to perfection.

So, I adjusted to being home alone all week. I didn't drive and became well adapted into having a list of household needs so that I was prepared when someone asked if I needed anything. The organizational tool I had learned years ago was still good.

I became very involved in the contemporary music group

at church which thrilled me so much. I even coordinated the performances at times. Composition highlighted my days, singing through me with such urgency I had to play and write the melodies during the night before I forgot them. I loved the inspiration, the joy that the opportunity brought to my heart and my soul, encouraging me, and making life worthwhile.

* * *

MY DAD DIED ON September 13, 2001. It was two days after the tragedy of 9/11.

Alan Jackson sang, "Where Were You When the World Stopped Turning?" Well, the world was in shock over the violence in the United States. Many families instantly felt a need to reach out and contact the ones they loved. Donny called me from where he was working that morning. Our hearts were raw with disbelief, unable to understand the cruelty to so many people.

* * *

MY PARENTS CALLED ON that fateful evening too. They talked about Dad's surgery in Rochester, MN scheduled on the 13th. They wanted to repair the aneurysm that had developed in his aorta. With Donny out of town, I wouldn't be able to be present for his surgery. I was heartbroken that I couldn't find another ride. These were the times when my vision disability made me feel like such a failure and added to the torment of how unworthy I felt.

"It's okay," Dad said before we ended the call. "I'm going home."

After talking to Mom and Dad, my pastor called, asking about some music for Sunday's service. He then asked how I was getting to Rochester for the surgery, which is 258 miles away. I told him that I couldn't go because I hadn't found a ride.

"What time do you want to leave?" he instantly asked. "I'll take you."

I was stunned and excited. What wonderful timing! I also shared that, if I could get a ride to Minneapolis, I could ride with my brother, Steven, who was going at noon after he was done teaching at Dunwoody.

My pastor drove me to Dunwoody. First, my brother and I had to go to Glenwood City, WI to pick up Joan. Rita was traveling with her husband from Eau Claire to Rochester.

While I was with Steven on our way from Dunwoody to Wisconsin, he got a phone call and pulled over. We received the horrible news from Joan on the side of the road.

"Dad died before the surgery," she cried.

Steve and I hugged and cried.

I'm not sure how we made it to Glenwood City. My heart was broken like everyone's in our family. Dad had just turned 74 on September 8.

When Steven, Joan, and I finally arrived at the hospital at the same time as Rita, Mom greeted us, sharing the details of the morning.

"Dad wanted me to get settled in the hotel room while the nurses checked him in," she struggled to say.

While she had been gone, and the nurse had been in the room, he had commented about a back pain . . . and died. The aneurysm had erupted. The nurses had met Mom at the elevator and had taken her to another room where they had explained with comforting words what had occurred.

My mom finished the story with: "'But I got him a candy bar, and I was going to let him have the bigger one.'"

We cried and hugged.

I felt relieved that Joan informed me before seeing him that Dad would be cold by the time we saw him. I never knew that and was thankful for the information when I kissed his cheek goodbye.

We gathered in a circle, holding hands, and said the Lord's Prayer before we left.

When we arrived back at Mom's home, she found a note on Dad's nightstand. He had left several scriptures for his funeral.

> Blessed is the man who walks not in the counsel of the wicked, nor stands in the way of sinners, nor sits in the seat of scoffers; but his delight is in the law of the Lord, and in his law he meditates day and night. He is like a tree planted by streams of water, that yields its fruit in its season, and its leaf does not wither. In all that he does, he prospers. (Psalm 1:1)

I now knew why his last words to me were, "It's okay. I'm going home."

The following week, Donny's brother, Bob, died of a heart attack. His daughter, Gina, tried to perform CPR on him without success, but it sent her into labor. That evening, she delivered a baby girl!

Many mixed emotions for both of our families.

January 7, 2004

I read the obituary of Hazel Bombeck in the Longville paper yesterday. I named my cuckoo clock bird after her. When Sarah was little, and before Tim was born, Joe and Hazel were our neighbors on Lake Wabedo. Sarah and I would walk a quarter mile to their house to visit. At 9:30 A.M., she would serve coffee and cookies and at 2:30 P.M., tea and cookies. Sarah always preferred to go in the morning, so that she could see their cuckoo clock chime ten times instead of three.

"Cuckoo, cuckoo . . ."

Sarah grinned and watched its peek-a-boo rhythms. She was excellent in keeping her enthusiasm under control though, knowing that Hazel could not take loud noises because she had had brain surgery years earlier. She had to learn how to walk, talk, write, and many other things all over again with the assistance of Joe. She also had to walk briskly two miles every day to keep the circulation going. She walked in every kind of weather.

They were great companions to me in those years, 1980-1983, when I was new to the Longville area and didn't know anybody.

ℛEFLECTION, PRESENT DAY

WHILE READING ENTRIES FROM February 2004, I sensed how strongly I had forced myself to be normal. It had been 13 years since I had been diagnosed with RP. Thirteen years of sight, when I had only been given 5-10.

I've written about my diagnosis day, but I wish I would have done more in depth writing that first evening. It was comforting to realize that the intense depression with this disease had eased by 2004 and I barely even thought of that aspect. I've found that if I could do more, it helped me to take the focus off of what I couldn't do.

I was tired of all the yearly eye exams, upset for weeks before each appointment. New glasses were required in 2004, not because of vision loss, but due to a change in prescription.

Anticipating a loss in vision each year had become a familiar, deeply darkening feeling yet one I was able to disregard. I felt hopeful that one day I wouldn't remember its sting, that I would know it had disappeared; that it would have been replaced with strength and comfort. I hoped I would have confidence that I was okay, that life was okay.

My journey has always been a path of facets, a kaleidoscope in which I had to constantly see things in different ways than I ever had before.

Other emotional trauma existed in my life at this time with my music position at the church. I was trying not to fail, but I wasn't succeeding.

Bruised and battered, bobbling forward, limping with the energy that somehow kept me going, I embraced strength and found joy in the journey that guided me through the paths that needed to be altered and recalculated.

And I found my peace.

JANUARY 23, 2004

As PART OF MY CEU classes, I registered for a yoga class in Minneapolis. I studied the material sent to me. A letter came with my acceptance that there would be an exam before the class started. I had to pass it before continuing. Yikes! These class credits would be part of my annual choice of credits for my massage license. I read the book twice and was familiar with most of the thirty poses. I was nervous but confident that I would be fine.

It was a three-hour drive to the class, so Donny and I left in plenty of time to He brought me to the registration area and said he'd return at 4:00 P.M., when the class was scheduled to be over.

"Deep breath in and slowly out," I said to myself while trying to compose the inner me that wanted to run after Donny.

Part of me hungered to whine about my eyesight, that I needed special help, but a bigger part of me knew that I'd be fine. And if I needed help, I could ask for it. I had my cane to rely on. I'd grown accustomed to my new glasses, and they made a big difference in clarity. They proved I wasn't experiencing further loss in my field of vision like I had believed was happening.

"When are we having the test?" I asked a classmate during our first break.

"Oh, that was just a ploy for us to read the material beforehand," she said.

What a wonderful way to have the class more in focus toward the results desired. Class flashed past as the instructor demonstrated poses and we repeated them.

Feeling stretched and refreshed, I slept most of the ride home.

FEBRUARY 27, 2004

BARB ANDERSON HAD BECOME a cherished friend since the day I met her in 2000. When I was introduced to her, she said in a spunky confident voice, "You can call me Barb, Mrs. A, or Barbara, but never call me Barbie!" She's fifteen years older than me with a very joyful spirit.

We soon became close friends and spent a day every month going to Brainerd, sixty miles south of Longville, for hair days. While there, we would shop, eat, laugh, and enjoy our friendship.

I rode to Ash Wednesday service with Barb and her

husband Craig. After the service, I was talking to a few people when I heard Craig say, "There she is!"

Evidently, they had gotten ready to go home and went to the car, when Craig asked where I was. They came back into the church, but didn't see me, so Barb called Donny and asked if I was there.

"No," he said. "You took her."

Barb knew I wouldn't have taken a ride with someone else, as that is a policy that I have adapted. I ride home with whomever I go with. There are some crazy drivers out there, I've learned. Not having control of the steering wheel, I take control of who I ride with.

When Craig found me, they were so embarrassed, but I just laughed.

The next day, while shopping with Donny, I noticed a big display of seed packets. I told Donny I needed to get a packet of Forget-Me-Nots for Barb.

I made a card to go with it.

On the front it said: *You're such a good friend, that if we were on a sinking ship . . . and there was only one life jacket . . .*

Inside, I wrote: *I would miss you VERY much!*

When Barb arrived that evening to pick me up for the Maundy Thursday service at church, Donny had me wave to her to come inside. He sat at the top of our split-level entry steps and tried to look stern.

"Hey!" he growled with a smirk. "The next time you take my wife somewhere and forget her . . . make it further out of town."

Then he handed her the card.

"Yes sir!" she said.

She opened the card and laughed hard as she held up the packet of Forget-Me-Nots. He told her to keep the seeds on the dash to remind herself.

What a joyful fun moment that was.

I love when I can enjoy life.

ℳARCH 25, 2004

DONNY LEFT FOR WORK at 2:30 A.M. and I couldn't sleep after he left, so I got up and accomplished a lot. I finally wrote the alto part to the song, "Do you see the shining star?"

I want to add a flute part. I think I'll record the song on the keyboard and then play along with the flute several times to see what I like best. I can tape record what I do and then play it back and write it on the music program I have on the computer.

Whew! Sounds complicated, but I find so much joy in doing all of it. I have written a few other songs many years ago, but none have touched me as much as this one has. I pray that God will inspire me to do more.

Throughout my early years with RP, I searched for answers, cures, hopes, dreams, anything to make it somehow make sense or go away.

A friend once asked me an interesting question: "Who don't you want to see?"

My first internal reaction was anger. It felt as if she was telling me that I brought this diagnosis on myself, so I didn't have to deal with someone. I couldn't think of anyone, not a soul who would cause that kind of reaction in me—the mind has its own ways of dealing with emotions.

For many years, that question sat back in my mind,

waiting for a moment of clarity.

As I progressed through my struggle to heal myself through massaging others, I felt the question piquing my interest again, and I wondered if there was someone. A possible answer came to me, but I wanted to rephrase the question. It wasn't *who* I didn't want to *see*, it was *what* didn't I want to *feel*. The answer was my divorce that happened two years before my diagnosis.

How interesting that insight was. My religious upbringing in the 1970's instructed me that divorce wasn't allowed. Women were meant to marry and obey their husbands forever, no matter what. Men were in charge of every situation, and my duty, as a woman, was to raise the children, take care of cleaning, and defer to my husband for decisions.

Times have changed and so have I by allowing myself through journaling to discover who I am. I am not a puppet bowing to the whim of a dictator. Divorce is not something to be ashamed of.

I found my path, followed my heart.

My intuition told me I deserved to be happy, and I was not happy in that marriage.

*A*PRIL 12, 2004

I'VE BEEN THINKING ABOUT my business and how I can make it more profitable. I accepted six to eight clients a day in Eau Claire, but I no longer want that many. Four to five a day would be effective. I have too many days, especially in the winter, that I don't have any clients. It's nice to have some time off, but I would rather be able to afford a vacation. In a few years, I will be fifty, and I have never traveled outside of the northwest or northcentral United States as an adult other than briefly into Canada.

There is great emotional pain when I dwell on the possibility of going totally blind tomorrow, next month, or next year. Now my work season is starting again, and I have to just wait and hope that next winter we might go somewhere. Ouch! I hurt thinking about it, and I try so hard not to get jealous when I hear of others going places.

Ouch, ouch, ouch!

I talked to my children's dad about his eyesight. He has glaucoma and told me that, this week, he was declared legally blind. His left eye is like looking through a steamy shower, and his right eye is also deteriorating. It looks like he is looking through a letterbox at a movie.

He said he quit driving two months ago. I know this is devastating to him and the kids. Sarah has mentioned it to me. She's traumatized that both her parents are legally blind, with hereditary diseases.

I spent all week washing the windows. My mother and her mother, Grandma Ida, loved to do their spring-cleaning during Lent to prepare for Easter. I've carried on that tradition. I love being outside with all the spring nature excitement as the birds sing their chorus.

There was a robin, once again, eating the fermented fruit of the crab apple tree in our front yard. It made him tipsy and he attacked the window, thinking that he saw an invading robin there to take over the territory.

Years ago, I considered adding a tablespoon of vegetable oil to my window washing water. It would add smears. Maybe Donny would declare that I shouldn't be doing them anymore because of my vision. The thought made me chuckle inside.

I'm easing my spirit, adjusting to tomorrow's unknown.

Vacuuming and dusting can be challenging too. I've injured myself several times when I don't pay attention to my surroundings.

BAM! Rude awakenings can spiral me into despair in the blink of an eye, literally!

April 20, 2004

ALICE HAD THE STAR role in her high school play, *Wait Until Dark*. She played a blind woman and had asked me for some suggestions. I don't have enough wonderful words to say about how brilliantly she portrayed the role. Awesome, outstanding, real to life are only a few.

I felt drawn into her acting. Her movements as a blind woman were so realistic. It didn't seem like she was acting at all but living the part. I'm so proud of her. It seemed like she grew into a woman in two hours.

This gives a whole new dimension to who Alice really is and can be. Did I say how proud I am of her? Not enough; I'm so proud of her. My heart is lighter knowing how happy she is in her life in the Cities.

May 12, 2004

A CLIENT TOLD ME that I truly had a gift from God. What a wonderful boost and exactly what I needed to hear.

I pray daily that God will guide clients to me that I am able to assist.

I'm a little depressed today because I really felt a vision loss while I walked to the post office. It could be the cloudy weather or the increase in traffic for the beginning of tourist season that made me aware of it. I just feel like darkness is closing in on me, little by little. I wish I could make it stop.

Comments like the one from my client help me to appreciate what I do have instead of what I don't.

June 22, 2004

A VERY SPECIAL CLIENT has helped me through many trials throughout the years. He is a retired pastor. Yesterday after his massage he talked about my vision and told me to claim the healing that Jesus has to offer me. I shared with him how much I want to be able to do that, but I've gotten so depressed when I do, and it hasn't happened.

The doctors told me I only had five to ten years vision left in 1991. I guess it is a miracle that it has been thirteen years and I still have about eight degrees remaining, down from the fifteen I had back then. Maybe I can claim not to lose anymore? How can I have the desire to heal others if I can't even heal myself?

My friend's daughter got married in Duluth on Friday, June 4. Erin's wedding was a beautiful celebration as the sunset on the shores of Lake Superior. I went Thursday with Alicia to help get things ready; Donny hadn't arrived from work yet. Thursday evening while everyone was at the groom's dinner, I went for a walk around Canal Park, alone. After watching the ships, I ate supper then walked back to my hotel room. On my way, I heard some guy yelling in my direction from a car in the parking lot.

"Hey lady, you blind?" He repeated several times, getting louder and louder.

I can't believe how rude some people can be. I tried to ignore him and kept walking with my cane. After his third yell, I turned, looked straight at him, and said, "No, I'm fuckin' deaf!"

I turned and continued walking.

The crowd walking the canal gasped and paused. *Tap, step, tap, step.* I couldn't retreat to my room fast enough.

He cut me deeply as he called out, very publicly and rudely, the very thing that makes me different and has been causing me so much heartache and suffering for thirteen years. He stole my joy in that moment of freedom.

*   *   *

I RECALL A GAME I would play as a child with friends in my small hometown, Glenwood City, Wisconsin. In the 60's, life was so different and safe. We would gather at a street corner and toss a penny to see which direction we would go next, left or right.

We enjoyed the freedom, the adventure of not caring where we were going, but we were also excited in the anticipation of the journey. I'm not sure why that story came to me, maybe to just embrace the feeling and allow it to surface again. Or as my friend, LuAnn, said, "There's no moral to that story. I just like it."

June 26, 2004

IT'S THE SECOND ANNUAL Turtle Town Art Fair in Longville. Kim, Alicia, and I developed this event named for the town being the turtle racing capital of the world. It brings area crafters and artists together to sell their products.

The elementary school across the street from my home has been a wonderful venue for us as we gather close to fifty vendors, each displaying their unique gifts. Jewelry, wood creations, rugs, quilts, clothing, and paintings are just a few of the items sold. We even have food vendors for the crowd. Our trio works hard year-round, making the details enticing for all who attend.

The school has a tennis court with a high fence surrounding it near the road. I use Styrofoam cups, tucked in the diamond shaped wire, to create a large, eye catching sign, reading, "ART FAIR," with an arrow pointing toward the location.

I was surprised this year to find that someone had moved the F and placed it in front of "Art." "FART AIR" was what it now said. That was funny, but I had to change it back.

September 12, 2004

Donny has been working in the Cities for the past couple weeks. We traded in our truck for a new one. I was very offended by our salesperson and finally called the owner of the business and let him know what had happened.

The salesman was fascinated with my folding white cane and when we were looking at our choices of toolboxes for our new truck, he grabbed it from me and wanted to use it himself.

Well, I took it back to show him because he was doing it wrong. I didn't mind that so much and could have tolerated it, but then he started saying, "Hit me with it! Go ahead, I don't mind, hit me!"

He wouldn't stop.

I looked at Donny who was upset but didn't say anything. I finally took my cane and put it to the other side of my body. "We're here to discuss trucks." I firmly stated.

I later realized that Donny had never encountered this and was too shocked to say or do anything.

"I thought you could handle it," he said, "because you did in Duluth last June."

"When it happens next time," I said, "I expect you to step in and say something."

I later called the business and told them that we were pleased with the company and wanted to do business with them again; however, I never wanted to have that salesman contact us. The manager apologized and was just as shocked. He said that the issue would indeed be taken care of.

"I don't want him to lose his job," I explained. "I just want some sensitivity awareness to this issue."

I felt so humiliated and degraded. It was another time I allowed the darkness to pull me deep. I tried to fight it by standing up for myself, but I wasn't used to that.

People have been shockingly rude over the years. More than one man has told me to hit Donny with my cane, and then they'd laughed. Maybe they had been trying to make light of a horrible situation in the only way they'd known how or because they were in a situation they had never encountered before.

September 18, 2004

I had an incident at the end of one of my massage sessions today. When I was with a client, I always locked the front door and posted a sign to tell when the session would be done. In the main area of the house, I also blocked the sliding glass door. I went to open the door to my studio, and it wouldn't budge. The doorknob had broken.

My client was very patient as I tried to take the bolts off the hinges. The top one came off, but the other ones needed a screwdriver or something. Throughout the ordeal, I really, really had to go to the bathroom. I eventually had to crawl out the window into the front yard. Good thing, I have a key to the front door hidden outside.

What a sight that must have been. My client and I laughed so hard afterward.

October 13, 2004

It's a beautiful fall in northern Minnesota. Most of the brilliant colors have gone, but the oak trees are a vibrant rust color surrounded by blazing yellow poplar trees. Donny and I love to travel the country roads through the wooded scenery.

He asked me if I wanted to drive and I did.

The new truck is a F250 turbo and boy does it have a lot of power. I didn't think I was nervous, but after about a quarter mile when I went back to passenger mode, or the negavator (as I mispronounce it), I was shaking.

November 14, 2004

I talked with Alice and she gave me the most wonderful compliment as I told her that I was planning my ten-year anniversary for my business.

"I'm so proud," she said. "You have accomplished so much throughout these years and even won an award. You amaze me as you overcome the obstacles with your vision."

I was overwhelmed by her comments. I never knew if the kids realized how much I had done.

* * *

The Uffda Ladies is a musical group of six. We dress in old lady style dresses wearing hats and playing kitchen type instruments, such as spoons or clanging pot lids together. Who knew that after our debut signature song, "Lime Jello, Marshmallow, Cottage Cheese Surprise," we would be requested to entertain again?

Yesterday, we amused a group at the Women's Expo in Remer, about twenty miles away. We sang two new songs, "Yust a Little Lefse" and "Dupsha Dove." We also did a skit called The Uffda Ladies Amalgamated Lefse Association, U-La-La for short. We made things out of lefse to show for each verse.

"Vy by new, Ven Lefse Vill Do!" we chanted.

That was great fun. Full of belly laughs.

Rehearsals are a real hoot, don't cha know!

I also gave a talk at the expo, that I titled, *Relax, Adjust, Endure, and Trust.* I enjoyed doing that and had a great response. I told about my RP journey and how I've gotten through to this point.

REFLECTION, PRESENT DAY

I LAUGHED ALOUD WHEN reading my journal entries about the Uffda Ladies. For those who are unfamiliar, the songs were a play on Norwegian traditions and dialects. "Uffda" is the equivalent to "Oh geez" or another show of slight shock or exasperation. We pronounce Ws as Vs, and the lime Jello . . . that's a real thing at family get-togethers. Yum! Lefse is a Norwegian flatbread made from potatoes, flour, butter, and either cream or milk.

As for my journey, the seed turned into a bush and grew vibrant and strong. It soared in the sunshine with clarity, joy, and laughter. All was well while I followed the path of least resistance, even throughout the upcoming speed bumps.

December 7, 2004

Donny was having chest pains. He said he had had them for the past month, but only let me know about it last night. The pain was enough that he needed to go to the emergency room in Crosby, an hour away. He drove instead of calling an ambulance.

I hate my RP for not letting me drive.

Donny's pains turned out to be what they were a couple years ago, his GERD and acid reflux. The doctor suggested he should take some Maalox liquid to see if it helps.

My world crumbled thinking of the what ifs. How would I go on without him?

I'm not strong enough to walk this crumbling path without him to lean on.

The following week, he had a stress test that went very well. They said he had a very healthy heart and although they couldn't guarantee that nothing would happen, from the test results, it would be unlikely.

Recap of the Year 2004

It's the last day of the year. Many channels on TV are going through the events of 2004. I thought I would like to mention a few but knew I would overlook some of them.

Alice's graduation and play last spring comes to mind first. My youngest is taking on challenges in her new world, adjusting and finding her own desires. I'm so pleased to see her so happy. Sarah and Tim have discovered challenges in their journeys too, but I'm so proud of each of them.

Erin's wedding in Duluth was wonderful. I was honored to help my dear friend, Alicia, as she made arrangements for the celebration to be as elegant as her daughter.

I'm grateful for the songs that I was inspired to write and perform at church. "Do You See the Shining Star?" and "Ring the Bells" were so transforming for me as I heard the melodies, the harmonies and the unity of the music pulsing through me. It's ease of flow gliding through me, releasing me from the pains of the past.

I celebrated my ten-year anniversary of Horizon Therapeutic Massage with an open house. I was surrounded by supporters and loving clients who attended the event in my home office.

I kept myself very busy with many activities. I feel content when I have things to keep my mind busy and stay on a routine. I find that I don't dwell on my RP when I look to contrast situations that keep me busy. Instead, I put the focus on other facets in my kaleidoscope life. Maybe doing that helps me adjust my thinking that it's not so bad and there are other events to be concerned about.

Most of all, I thank God for all that I have and where I am. I pray He will hold me through this next year along with my family. Also, I thank God for the vision I still have. I know it's decreasing, but slower than predicted. I try to use what I have left a lot more than I used to. I gave up for the first eight years after I was diagnosed, but now I feel like not acting blind—I'm acting sighted!

REFLECTION, PRESENT DAY

WOW, WHAT A YEAR of challenges, disappointments, giving up, getting back up, and finding a spark of inner strength to continue.

When I sat down to write this book, it was the first time I read my journals from 2004. I didn't share all of that journey here, but because I now see who I was and how far I have come, I am inspired to become stronger.

My kaleidoscope life is shining brighter than ever before.

Chapter Thirty-Three

BREAKING THROUGH

JANUARY 2005

ONCE AGAIN, I'M PLAYING the *poor me* game while I hear about several groups of people going on winter vacations in warmer climates. I dwell on the fact that I've never been on one. I keep having the horrible thought that I might as well go totally blind now because I won't be able to go anywhere for a visual vacation, ever! It hurts so badly to think about, but I can't stop. Is this why I have such a headache?

A client told me that she saves every $5 bill she gets and uses it toward her annual vacation. I hate to raise my hopes by trying that, but maybe, by doing that, I will pivot my thinking toward a more positive aspect.

I'm having an emotional time. That's normal—this morning is my annual eye exam. I'm trying to hold up. I think I've cried enough, but I'm a mess. My thoughts are, "Why me?"

The doctors told me I would be totally blind by 2001. Why can't I focus on how grateful I am for the vision I do have? Why do I find myself thinking about the independence that's been taken away?

Oh, how I wish I could just get in the car, drive away to where I want, and do what I want.

February 2005

My eye appointment went very well.

"You won't need to have the Visual Field exam every year," said my doctor. "Every three years should be fine, unless you notice a change."

I thought that was great. She did want to test the thickness of my cornea, so she numbed my eyes before probing them. I didn't feel a thing and was glad she didn't tell me what she was going to do . . . I would have fainted.

Of course, it was a sunny day, so with my eyes dilated, even wearing sunglasses hurt.

March 2005

I was asked to play keyboard for a friend during church when she sings special music. I had a new client who works at the Family Center in town. She asked me to teach a class on infant massage. The second-grade teacher at the elementary school across the street asked me if I would be interested in talking to her class about my vision. A client of mine asked if I would do yoga classes for the staff at Deep Portage Conservation Center, which is about 20 miles south. I got an email from a vendor of the Turtle Town Art Fair, asking me if I would be interested in talking with a friend of hers about my vision.

Interesting that all these requests came in the same week. Was it because I had such a pity party last week? God only knows, but I felt better about myself. Focusing on positive things has always helped.

That reminded me of my mom's advice: "Change the subject."

✳ ✳ ✳

I TALKED TO A client about my vision. I went on, I think, too much and then found out that she only had a little vision remaining in her right eye, which went out several times a day.

She is writing her 38th book and wants to include conversations from me and others.

I asked her if I could send what I had written so far of this book for review. She said she would need it sent on the computer, because she couldn't read anymore.

During our talk, I had some very insightful thoughts. One was that, when I was first diagnosed, I hated to go to sleep at night. My thinking was that I hated to waste my vision by having my eyes shut. There was too much that I wanted to see and too short of time.

"When did your transformation from depression to gratitude come?" she asked.

"I didn't have a certain, aha, moment," I shared. "It was very gradual as I tried to focus on better moments."

I continued by telling her the past five years had been the best for realizing what a gift God gave me through massage. I'd also, for once in my life, been happy for who and where I was. I talked to her about trying to write my book and getting stuck. She suggested I talk it into a tape recorder, instead of writing it. Then I told her about my journals.

"You have a book right there!" she said.

I didn't know if I really put my feelings into my journals. I usually just wrote what was current for the day. Maybe, I would be surprised if I went back, read them, and attempted to remember how I was feeling when I wrote them.

Hmm, I'd have to think about that.

Reflection, Present day

I AM MORE THAN surprised at what I am accomplishing as I write my story. I can see and feel that I have been two different people with two different lives filled with facets that sparkle as they come together creating one bright, shining person, one me.

April 2005

I TALKED TO THE second graders this morning about my vision at the Longville Elementary School across the street. It had been a couple years since I'd done that.

I had Braille bookmarks for them from the Foundation Fighting Blindness organization. Their teacher wrote their names on the back of them. I then used my Braille label gun and punched dot versions of their names to stick to the backs.

It was a good class, but I couldn't help thinking about Alice and all her classes that I talked to when we lived in Eau Claire. I also thought about Dad; he would always drive me to the classes and listen to my talks. He was such a support for me, and still is as I hold his strength dearly within my heart.

May 2005

I HELPED MY FRIEND Alicia with spring cleaning some cabins at Doc Holiday Resort on Woman Lake in Longville, Minnesota. Her brother owns the resort while her family manages it. We started in cabin six, in the bedroom. I dusted the walls and she vacuumed out the windowsill. I shut the door so I could dust the back then tried to open it—I couldn't get it to open, so Alicia tried. Same results.

Luckily, her husband, Doug, was in view from the window. Alicia called to him and told him that we were locked inside. He came over and tried from the other side, but he couldn't get it open either.

"Is it locked?" he asked.

I replied, "No, umm, well yes."

The doorknob was an old-style box with a lever on the side. While I had been dusting, I flicked it down.

I unlocked the door and opened it.

"Every time the two of you are together," he said, "something happens."

We all laughed. But did a part of me blame it on my vision?

June 2005

I HAVE STARTED WRITING in the journal Alicia gave me for my birthday. I wasn't sure I wanted to write by hand. The past few years it had been easier typing my entries on the computer, but I like having the journal with me anywhere I go instead of waiting until I had time to type.

I want to use it as much as I can and avoid acting like

I'm blind. This will help focus on the positive things in life, I think. We'll see how it goes (pun intended). I think there will be times when I will want to type it too.

September 2005

I LOVE MASSAGING AND helping others. It really helps me to stay in a positive place when I focus on what their body is whispering to me.

I had new clients this week who praised me. They said I was the best massage therapist they'd ever been to and they'd been to a lot around the world.

"Your hands are filled with chi energy," one of them said. "You probably hear that from many of your clients."

I do hear that and have throughout the years. I just find it hard, at times when I'm down, to believe it.

Shut your eyes, Pamela; it is true, speaks my inner being. *You know it when you feel the guiding of your client's body crying for assistance in the comfort that it seeks. It is true. Feel the ease that flows through you.*

Angels are lifting me higher into that positive place, surrounded in love, helping me to focus on my joy.

October 2005

THROUGHOUT THE PAST YEARS in my journals, I wrote about events that seemed insignificant to my RP journey.

Yet now, I think they were important. I'm reminded of an incident that occurred in 1990 before I was diagnosed.

Donny and I went to visit his daughter, Ann, when she was still in high school and living with her mother and stepfather in International Falls, Minnesota. We took Ann out to eat at a local restaurant. While we were leaving, I walked right into a wall! I was so embarrassed. That same week, when Donny and I were going to the farm where he lived, I grabbed the stair railing and proceeded to walk on the wrong side. I had no clue that anything was wrong with my vision. I just thought I wasn't paying attention.

Reflection, Present day

As I read further, in my 2005 journal, I told about a Via de Cristo music team that I served on. It reminded me of another incident that happened when I was on the team the year before I was diagnosed.

We were in Duluth, Minnesota at a beautiful large church overlooking Lake Superior. The team had a break in our day, and another member and I wanted to listen to the beautiful music of the organist practicing for the Sunday service.

From the kitchen, the two of us found a stairwell leading toward the balcony where the mesmerizing music serenaded. It was dark and narrow as we ascended toward the top, reaching an enclosed area. I stood still listening, feeling the hypnotic song embrace me. I thought my friend was doing the same and after several minutes, my eyes adjusted to the environment. I could see the image of her standing in front of me. Trying to be respectful of the masterpiece, I whispered to her, "Should we go further?"

No answer.

I repeated myself slightly louder, with the same results. I stretched out my hand to tap her shoulder and was shocked that the person that I thought was her, was actually a mirror. I whispered her name without any response. I was so startled and scared, that all I could think of doing was running back down the stairs.

I made my way to the kitchen, found her and asked where she went. I described what had happened, and she said I shouldn't share that story with anyone. We had a good laugh, but this occurrence and the one at the restaurant always haunted me. How was I to know that I was losing my night vision?

Later, after my diagnosis and during the summers, Ann asked me to babysit her girls. I enjoyed taking them across the street to the school playground. But I hesitated to interact with them, because I was afraid of hurting them or myself with my lack of peripheral vision.

I allowed the RP to be in control of me.

I acted like I was blind.

✳ ✳ ✳

REFLECTING ON THESE EXPERIENCES after so many years, I feel a comfort and have better understanding of my RP journey. I can move into a life of gratitude for what I do have.

I was mentally blind to my vision changes prior to diagnosis, denying they were there. And now as I read in 2005, I have become more accepting of my diagnosis and therefore more awake to what was happening back then. I was blind, but now I see things in a new light.

As a few leaves withered from my growing seed, new ones replaced the ones lost. Buds, future flowers surrounded the branches, offering hope and creating joy within.

I am listening. I am holding on, enjoying my expansion, enjoying who I have become. I am grateful for the journey I have traveled.

Chapter Thirty-Four

LET YOUR LIGHT SHINE

FEBRUARY 2006

LAST FALL, I WROTE the song, "He is Heaven Come to Earth."

I've been inspired again working on another one based on a poem my aunt, Connie Allram, wrote that moved me. I think I'll name the song, "The Waiting Shores of Home." I have the melody mostly written, but I'm not happy with it yet. It just needs a little more tweaking.

* * *

DONNY AND I BOTH had eye appointments. We both had our eyes dilated and of course, it was a bright, beautiful sunny day. Ouch! My good news: there wasn't any change and I wouldn't have to have a visual field test for a couple years.

I think this is the first time an eye appointment didn't upset me for weeks. Was I adjusting to it or just too busy with other life situations to care? Distraction took the focus from a negative toward a positive, just like Mom had said.

AUGUST 2006

I JUST FINISHED HOSTING the loon and wildlife calling contest at the centennial headquarters as part of the weekly activities celebrating Longville's Centennial. It went well, and the weather was perfect.

I had several categories for contestants to sign up for: adult wildlife calls, sixteen and under wildlife calls, and adult and youth loon calling. Before the contest, I explained the four calls of the loon and played a recording of each. I then shared about a friend of mine who made a loon call by putting her hands around her mouth and then very dramatically yelling, "Here Loon!"

Everyone laughed over that.

I demonstrated my hand loon call that I've done ever since I learned in grade school from the neighbor kids. I also taught my children how to do a loon call. When they were young, they each had their number of calls: Sarah was one, Timmy was two, and Alice was three calls. I would call when I needed them. I've done the call to find my children at games, graduations, or whatever activity they were involved in. It always let them know where I was and that I was proud of them.

The winners were chosen by applause. The adult wildlife winner sounded exactly like a barn owl.

He told us his secret: "Who-cooks-for-you, who-cooks-for-you-all is what it sounds like."

The youth winner of the wildlife call contest was three, performing an eagle screech. It was very good. After the contest, I handed out instructions on how to hold your hands in a clasped position and where to blow to do the loon call.

I received many compliments and enthusiasm from the crowd of about fifty. How exciting it was for me personally to have something positive to focus on instead of RP. This helped me to soar. I love doing loon calls.

I also can whistle with an acorn cap.

October 2006

Donny was asked to go to Georgia to do some slope work for a friend of Vaughn Veit, his boss. The request was for the best operator.

"That would be Donny," Vaughn said.

What an honor and great pat on the back for all his hard work. They decided that Donny needed to drive there and take his wife . . . me!

There were so many things to see on the trip, and we made so many memories. I enjoyed every moment and spent days walking the streets of beautiful Rome, Georgia while I stayed at the hotel in town. I felt so free and independent, even without driving.

Donny had a cell phone and was able to call me during his breaks. I had to sit in the hotel room at these designated times to hear from him, because I didn't have a cell phone. He worked long days at a horse farm outside of town, landscaping with a dozer in the red clay, preparing the land for a new horse barn. I took a taxi to watch him one day and was fascinated at his ease and joy while performing his skillful dance across the land. In all the years we'd been together, I'd never had an opportunity to watch him.

During our time in Rome, we were able to see a living history display and encampment from the 19th century. We saw many period-dressed people, even an actor dressed as Abe Lincoln. During one event, we were able to watch a war reenactment with both Union and Confederate sides along the river through town. We both learned a lot about the Civil War.

January 2007

Here comes another song.

Funny thing about this one is that the entire song, with words, came to me in the shower. I toweled off as quickly as I could to get to my piano, play it, and write it into a notebook. I named it, "Let Your Water Fall Over Me." I've had several people tell me that I should have my song, "Do You See the Shining Star," published.

I write songs for me, from my heart, to me. It's my gift to me only, because I'm not good enough to really have others care about them. I find words to convince myself of my worthiness, but actually don't believe that, do I?

* * *

I've wanted to add some color to the walls of our home. This is the first home I've ever owned, and when renting, I wasn't free to choose colors. We had a mirror in my craft room with a lake and forest scene painting on it. It was lavender, so I used those shades for picking out the color. I used a lighter shade on three walls and a deeper tone on the fourth.

I really like it.

With my RP, the cone cells of the retina responsible for color vision have changed. I can see color, but it's different. At times I feel embarrassed about asking the color of things. I see a blue sky and green grass, my brain knows that and registers it, but if I take those colors out of that context, like a blue car, I'm guessing. Pink/orange and purple/brown are also tough for me to tell. I've learned to write on the tags of my clothes the color to help coordinate.

I was once shocked and hurt to find out I was wearing a purple sweater. I thought it to be a beautiful deep shade of chocolate brown.

"Not many could pull off wearing that deep shade of purple," someone said.

Argh! Anyway, back to painting the wall story.

Alicia is fantastic with colors and had just painted her kitchen and dining area a deep red, so I wanted her opinion, but there was a miscommunication somewhere. I knew what I wanted, and she was kind enough to try to make it work. I thought I was choosing a soft sage for the downstairs wall, entryway, and stairwell.

"Maybe if you add another coat, you'll like it," she said.

So, Donny rigged up scaffolding for the stairwell and we applied another coat. It took three days for me to finally say I didn't like it.

"Good," Donny said, "because it's lime green!"

We repainted a soft shade of simple, boring beige. I still get teased about green at times, and that's okay.

Chapter Thirty-Five

LETTING GO OF THE FIGHT

The secret of change is to focus all of your energy, not on fighting the old, but on building the new.[24]

—Dan Millman

FEBRUARY 2007

I HAD MY ANNUAL eye exam and learned some delightful news. I have been stable for so long, I probably won't lose any more vision than what I already have! Wow, I can handle that. I feel that I function very well. Most people don't know or aren't aware of my vision situation until I use my cane. My friends have said that they even forget that I am legally blind—that's nice.

So my "act as if . . ." attitude works to the outside world even though my inside is still tortured daily. I must keep

---

24   Dan Millman, *The Way of the Peaceful Warrior: A Book That Changes Lives*, (Peaceful Warrior ePublishing, 2000), 130.

aware of my RP at all times or accidents happen and I get hurt or break something.

It's become common for me to knock over anything on the table when reaching for something else. Especially when dining out, I try to keep my hands in my lap. I've also noticed how messy I can be while eating without even knowing it until later. I don't see what is happening between the food on my plate and my mouth, so sometimes I become a target.

A little trick I have is to place my left arm in front of my plate while eating with my right. That way, I feel if anything drops and I don't have to be told about it.

April 2007

IT'S MY FIFTIETH BIRTHDAY.

I've decided I want a sewing machine, a Baby Lock Quilter's Choice, similar to what Barb and Alicia have. When Alicia got hers six years ago, I remember thinking, *I would love to have one like that, but I'm going to be blind soon, so don't even think about it.*

Well, I'm not going to go blind, according to my last eye exam, and I can sew. I do have a sewing machine my parents gave me, but it's difficult to thread. This new machine is self-threading, has three font alphabets, does buttons, and *sew* much more.

Last year, while reorganizing and painting my guest bedroom, I wanted to have a quilt made to enhance the rooms décor of houses and pine trees. I asked Alicia and Barb if they would show me how to create the perfect quilt. Searching through their stashes of quilting books, we decided on a design with rows of houses and pine trees. They each had scraps of fabric that worked perfectly in the creation.

"Press, do not iron," Barb reminded as she handed me each piece that Alicia had finished sewing.

I learned many techniques helpful in simplifying our task, such as nesting seams, setting the seam with the iron, and trimming. This quilt quickly became a cherished item in my home, a constant reminder of what I can do.

REFLECTION, PRESENT DAY

THAT WAS THE CATAPULTING seed planted in me, a desire to use my central vision and create fun items for myself and others. I could tell by reading my journals, that I progressed toward a new me. I felt my sewing machine became a major factor in this sensation.

A strength grew from a tiny spark, it occurred to me when I learned the vision I have would probably remain stable. Reading how the light started shining from deep within thrilled me, as if an extremely slow sunrise gleamed just for me. It encouraged me to take another look at who I really am.

I am a wonderful being, filled with joy, if I allow it. I am filled with creative talents that I can use my vision for. Whatever comes to mind, I am willing to try. What else can I do?

Since the purchase of my sewing machine, I created countless quilts, baby items, room darkening curtains, flannel pajama pants, and many other things. It's a very long list of enjoyment, which I have documented with pictures and details about who the item was for.

I always have at least one creation going.

Due to my limited color vision, I usually ask Donny when I have a question regarding color. He's also good at critiquing what I have finished, looking for stray threads or anything that I need to adjust. I also am pleased to be able to take my pattern and ideas of colors to my favorite fabric store where they are helpful in choosing the right fabrics.

I've only sewn over my finger once. Ouch! Now though, I use a tool made by a friend. It's a wooden kabob skewer with beads glued to the non-pointing end. The point assists the fabric through the sewing, instead of using my finger.

How crazy it is to take a perfectly good piece of material, cut it up, sew it together, cut it some more, throw a part away, then sew it all together?

"They call it quilting," Alicia said.

May 2007

I FINALLY HAVE MY very own raspberry patch. Donny and I planted shoots given to us by his sister, Sara. I can't wait to enjoy the first one. Raspberries have always been my very favorite food.

July 2007

I HAD A CLIENT who had a twelve-year-old a son with RP. He was diagnosed at four. His dad is on the Foundation Fighting Blindness board. He had so much hope and information for me. He told of genetic testing and the importance of finding out which type of RP I have. He also told me my children should be tested to ensure they aren't carriers.

I didn't know they could do that. I got their newsletters but had no idea of the progress in the past few years. He mentioned an implant, a tiny capsule that produces a sustained release of a potentially vision preserving protein, to strengthen the remaining sight. I have the last newsletter telling about this research and looking for participants.

Maybe hope was on the horizon. I've realized that I have stopped thinking and hoping for a cure. I never believed it would happen, so I settled for what I had remaining and used it to the best of my abilities.

July 21, 2007

I WENT TO A sewing class on my new machine. Wow, the things I can do! Now I can't wait to have time. I learned so much and don't want to forget. I've decided to make pajama pants for Christmas gifts, and knit matching slippers that I will felt by shrinking them in hot water.

* * *

WE GOT HIGH SPEED internet today, no more dial up, slow speeds, waiting for long periods of time to see anything. It sure makes a difference. I can check emails and go to any web page without disturbing the phone line.

August 2007

I TALKED TO MOM and she told me about her cousins. She just found out they also have retinitis pigmentosa. Avis, 66, and Mary, 65, are the daughters of Grandma Ida Allram's youngest brother, Ingvold.

Mom gave me Mary's phone number, so I called her. We had a wonderful conversation. Avis also has macular degeneration, which takes away the central vision, along with her RP. Mary said that her vision doesn't allow her to see colors very well. Only if she gets very close to the TV, can she detect variations.

Getting this information from Mom depressed me, because they seem further advanced in their decline of vision. I don't want to go there.

"I can see some today!" Avis joyfully said.

I'm going to try to focus on the positive with what I have left.

November 2007

Barb drove me to a massage class in Bemidji, MN today, about sixty-five miles northwest of Longville. I wasn't sure of Donny's work schedule for my transportation, so I had her take me. It was a good class, and I got to meet new therapists in the area.

Every four years, I need to turn in my Continuing Education Credits to keep my American Massage Therapy Association certificate and my national license. Currently, Minnesota is one of the few states that doesn't require any license, but many local, larger cities do. Longville, with only 191 populations, does not. However, I want to be prepared for if and when they pass a law requiring it. Plus, it's a great way to connect with other therapists and stay current on techniques.

I'm getting better at letting the transportation solution to get to my classes flow. There's always a way and I know it will work out. I don't get as depressed when I ask someone and they aren't able to help. I'm particular about who drives because I've found several people that aren't good drivers. It's probably my lack of depth perception, but it scares me when I feel we are constantly tailgating the vehicle in front of us.

December 2007

IT'S A SAD TIME for the Edwards family as Donny's sister, Mary, passed away. She had Alzheimer's for fourteen years and was only sixty-five. I was asked to sing at the funeral: "Somewhere," "The Lord's Prayer," and "On Eagle's Wings." I choked during "On Eagle's Wings," but then was fine for the rest. I also played a flute duet with Donny's niece, Nikki.

I love singing "The Lord's Prayer" the most.

I'm honored and feel blessed with the gift of music. I love the soaring, uplifting presence during my singing and hope I will be asked many more times, but not that I want anyone else to die, of course.

January 2008

STATE SERVICES FOR THE Blind has free books on tape service. I have a cassette player, so I signed up for books and receive a variety throughout the year. I'm currently listening to a new one by Louise L. Hay: *You Can Heal Your Life*. She talks about positive affirmations and loving yourself while releasing anger. She says people create every illness in their bodies and that every thought we think creates our future.[25]

How does that happen? It's so contrary to what I've been told all my life. There is something in her message that feels comforting.

February 2008

ANOTHER ANNUAL EYE EXAM has come and gone. This time I had a visual field test, which hasn't been done in four years.

---

25 Louise L. Hay, *You Can Heal Your Life*, (California: Hay House, 2006).

It showed improvement in my left eye and the right eye was stable.

"It might be the machine," the doctor said when she couldn't find any other explanation.

She suggested a multi-vitamin to help the macular vision, not that she found a problem, but so that one didn't evolve.

"These are going to strengthen the remaining cells," she said. "It's impossible to bring back the dead retina cells."

That sounded fine, even though I knew there wasn't a cure or prevention discovered. However, when I read the label, I found out they were not recommended for patients with retinitis pigmentosa because of the high vitamin E content which has been proven to increase the effects. I shared what I read with her.

I won't be taking them. I'll stay positive, mostly. I've seen other miracles happen and I'm expecting one here.

REFLECTION, PRESENT DAY

A NEW SEASON HAS arrived, and the bush took form. The warmth found in confidence enabled her to stretch her joy and present buds just under the surface, ready to swell. They would multiply into blossoms, listening to the inner peace that sang of ease: *Relax, dear one, you are loved. You don't always know what to do, but you always know how you want to feel. Listen to the song, the feeling from within as it nurtures and blesses you.*

Chapter Thirty-Six

UNBREAKABLE

*M*ARCH 2008

WE BOUGHT A FIFTH wheel RV. I can't believe it. It's beautiful. Donny will use it when he travels for work. It will save so much on hotel costs. I'm so excited and hopefully, I'll be able to take time off from my clients and stay with him at times.

*A*PRIL 2008

"YOU HAVE COMPANY AT the front door," Donny said.

I went to check who it was, but I couldn't see anyone. I heard a quack, looked down, and found my friends Huey, Luey, Dewey, Daisy, and Floyd, my five mallards, wanting corn.

I walked them around the house toward the back yard where the river is.

Yes, I named them. I had to after they've been here as my

outdoor pets for almost two years. Even in the winter as the river stays open with the flowing from the falls.

Daily, the group waddles to the back door, pecking at it until they have my attention. I scoop their daily supply of corn into a bucket and they follow me until I sit on the ground, place the bucket next to me, and let them feed. They've gotten so used to me, that I can sit next to them while they eat. Floyd is usually pushed away from the group and has been adopted by the one pair of geese that also stay.

Gary and Gladys are a pair of Canadian geese that frequent my dock. Gladys has a broken wing and stays here throughout the winter while Gary flies south with their summer's young. It's a sad occurrence when Gary teaches the goslings to fly weeks before the long journey and Gladys can't go. She comes to me at the dock, and I console her with corn.

The glorious spring reunion brightens my heart as I watch her the few days before his return. Loud honks, increasing in intensity, signal that Gladys knows the time has come—Gary flies in for a landing. Their new season of courtship begins as they show their appreciation and love for each other, a lifelong joining. Last year's youth have found their own journey.

I love life here on the river. It's always a wildlife adventure, but I still desire a quiet home on a lake. Someday . . . someday . . .

✶ ✶ ✶

I'm having a lot of fun sewing a quilt for Mom. It's a colorful *Dick and Jane* throw quilt. Mom taught in a one room schoolhouse and used these books for teaching. The fabric has pictures and words from those books. I'm *sew* excited for her to see it. I have to force myself to go to bed or take a break from working on it.

I remember, when we moved back here in 1999, how

concerned Mom and Dad were because of the stairs at the front entry. I was a little stunned by those words and almost took offense. However, they have been an issue several times. I've learned to be completely aware of them and count them as I go up or down. This way I'm focused on the task instead of everything else. That has worked.

Last year, I raced down the stairs, a vase filled with water in one hand and carrying scissors in the other to get fresh cuttings from my lilac bush. I slipped down the last three steps, sending the vase and scissors crashing to the floor. Shards of glass went everywhere, and I was barefoot.

Don't move!

Donny was gone for the week, but Barb was coming soon to have coffee. I stayed there until she arrived and then allowed her to help me in my predicament. Luckily, I didn't break anything but the vase and a little pride.

September 2008

We went to the ethnic fest in Walker, twenty miles away. I was stopped by a vendor and was gently asked about my mobility cane.

"Excuse me," he said, "may I ask why you use a white cane?"

"Yes," I replied. "I have retinitis pigmentosa."

"So do I!" he exclaimed.

His name was Paul, lives in Bemidji, and makes clocks from his spin art designs. He and I had many similarities. He was also diagnosed in 1991, has about the same degree of vision remaining, and also remarried in 1996. His wife is a contemporary musician at their church, and she has taught piano lessons for many years.

I bought one of his lavender colored clocks and have it in my craft room.

He wanted me to choose any of his cards with quotes on them. This one he thought was especially for me:

> *A thought for you today. God in His infinite wisdom decided that His creation would not be complete without YOU. Think about it...before all creation...God thought about YOU! Thank Him and have a Great Day!*

Paul is a very gentle and kind man. I found myself giving him a hug through tears while he whispered a prayer in my ear: "I pray that God continues to have us be friends and to be able to help each other through this journey."

✳ ✳ ✳

I HAVE CONTACTED A friend about my desire to write a book. Connie is an editor who was very supportive and thought I had a great story worth telling about my vision journey. She sent me handouts from her writing classes with four questions that she said I should answer and pray about.

"Give my questions to God," she said. "And if He still urges you to write, then go for it."

I plan to set aside some time most days to work toward this goal that I feel burning within me. I pray for guidance, assurance, peace, and time.

REFLECTION, PRESENT DAY

WAS IT REALLY OVER ten years ago that I made an attempt at writing a book? The desire has been there all along but lacked the sustenance to flourish. My journey, the facets on my kaleidoscope, needed courage. I felt that someday, I would be daring enough to soar on my eagle's wings and let the words flow. I've had to allow the journey of the book to come on its own timing. I'm so thrilled with its birthing process, as it whispers its desire and words to share and what not to share at this time.

*O*CTOBER 2008

DONNY WAS SENT TO Louisville, Kentucky to do dirt work on the new Cardinal stadium. It was so hard to see him go, but I've just been told that the company is going to fly me there for an extended weekend.

Today, I was able to look on my computer at a webcam positioned on the worksite. I saw him working. Well actually, I could see a figure and tell where he was when he was talking to me on his cell phone. I'm amazed at this technology and the blessing of being able to keep in touch this way with the vision I still have. It helps me to not feel so lonely.

My eyes are sore. I've noticed a slight change, but I'm not sure how to explain it. Something is different. It is probably from the stress of Donny being gone. I'm so glad my central vision is good enough to see him on the computer.

*O*CTOBER 9, 2008

DONNY'S BROTHER, JOEY, TOOK me to the Brainerd airport for my flight to the Cities, then on to Louisville, Kentucky. This is my first flight since 9/11, so I was nervous about all the security changes that had been established. Would I be able to see where I needed to go? I wasn't concerned about asking for assistance, but I didn't want to run into things.

I was pleasantly surprised to find a lady from my church, who was also taking the flight to Minneapolis. She was very helpful through security and when we got to Minneapolis, her next destination gate was only four gates from mine, so we chatted for ninety minutes before we departed. That was a great comfort.

* * *

It's later now, and I'm here at Donny's Extended Stay America hotel in Louisville, Kentucky. He's still at work. The flight went well, and I wasn't afraid to ask for help. I took a taxi through town to get here. My, this is a huge town.

There are 24 red roses in a water jug on the counter for me. How sweet! He called me after I arrived, and I thanked him for the beautiful roses.

"Look in the refrigerator," he said.

I found a bottle of raspberry wine to go with the roses. I smiled. His thoughtfulness warmed my heart. I couldn't wait for him to finish his day at work and return to the inn. He said when he bought the roses, the lady asked if they were for an anniversary.

"No," he told her. "My wife is coming to see me for the weekend."

How sweet is that?

The time flew by with so much to see and experience. During the days, while he was working, I explored the new surroundings, venturing on walks. Donny had suggestions and caution areas for me as guidelines.

I'm so glad that I have learned to love my cane. It's a dear friend, when I allow it to be. There are times when I don't pay attention to its bumps and run into things, miss a curb, trip in a hole, but they are few.

I took a taxi one day to see where Donny and his crew were working. A fence enclosing the work area surrounded a huge hole. It was so deep and wide, it looked like a smaller version of the Grand Canyon. Equipment of every kind hauled or dug piles of dirt, excavating them to their new locations. Workers far away looked like ants.

Donny found me and took great pleasure in pointing out the different areas and giving me a detailed description of each worker's part. I listened without comprehending but still found it fascinating.

It was hard to say goodbye at the airport. Hopefully, he wouldn't be gone for much longer. Someday, we'd return and see the finished results of the stadium.

✳ ✳ ✳

THE FLIGHT HOME WENT well. Barb met me at the Brainerd airport to bring me home. I was pleasantly surprised that Alicia was also with her. I chatted the whole way back about my adventures.

Donny's stay has been extended. He asked me to send him warmer clothes and a few other items. I included an anniversary card for him and wrote him a love letter.

"I am proud of the work that you do," I wrote. "For all these years, my favorite sound is the beating of your heart as I lay my head on your chest at night."

I told him how hard this is for me, not knowing when he'll be home. I'm doing my best to be strong, to not feel pity for myself and all the challenges my limited vision brings. I can do so much when I take the focus off my woes and see my many blessings.

I took the box to the hardware store in town so they could ship it to him. I didn't realize how emotional that was going to make me. I even cried last night before bed.

ℓNovember 2008

Donny made it back earlier in the month. So good to have him home.

My writing seems to have issues, so I asked Connie for more information. She replied to my email within the hour. After reading her suggestions, I walked a few blocks to the library for books on the writer's market. Those would give me information on guidelines for articles and books. It's overwhelming, but, just like my massage classes, I'll focus on one day of learning at a time.

"1, 2, 3, 4, 5, 6, SCREAM!" I yell.

I just went down the first flight of stairs to the front door, focusing on each step, slowly, but concentrating on making it all the way down the two flights to the printer before it started printing the last few pages I had reedited.

"Boo!"

Donny was standing by the door, ready to leave and I didn't see him. Years ago, I would allow that to throw me into tears and go into a pity party.

"Poor, Pamela," I would say, pouting. "I can't see, even though he was standing right there."

Now, I'm so glad that I was startled and surprised, but not upset. I still hate when he does that, but we can laugh.

𝒯hanksgiving Day 2008

My thanks is unspeakable in its depth. My mind haunts me with shouts of being unworthy for all my blessings. I fight the torment, trying to ignore its taunts. Instead, I send praise to my inner being for shining a light, a high beam, that refuses to let even a shadow of darkness into my peace. With every blink of my eye, I think of another blessing that I have received.

*F*EBRUARY 2009

It's a big star day. This morning Donny and I had eye doctor appointments in Crosby with Dr. Poland. Donny has seen him before, but I haven't. He was filled with information and gave me hope.

"You must have the x-linked gene, because you're a female and will probably never go blind," he said.

Probably never go blind? Did I hear that right? I can't believe my ears. I was as shocked as the day that I had been diagnosed. How could this be? No doctor had ever given me any signs of hope. Most just had pity for my journey.

I told him I had been told for 18 years that I would eventually lose all sight. I told him about my sister, Joan, who is in the beginning stages of RP and that two of my mother's cousins have it.

"Are they female and still have sight?" he asked.

"Yes," I said

"That is probably your case too."

He continued to tell me he believed that there would be a cure for RP within my lifetime. He believes a breakthrough would evolve probably in Italy first. "And when it does," he said, "I'm taking you there."

I felt elated. A big, thick, heavy black door has been ready to slam shut for 18 years, and now, it vanished. I cried for joy all the way home. So much could change now. Part of me was furious that I had been led to believe this lie, this hurtful emotional draining lie, for so long. I have seen so many doctors, and he was the only one to tell me this. And yes, I knew in my heart, that he was correct.

Five years ago, I decided to stop acting like I was blind. I would imagine God, taking a huge eraser and correcting the mistake of my diagnosis day. I was determined to use the sight remaining to the best of my abilities.

Oh dear, God, thank you, thank you, thank you!

It's a new life, a new way of thinking.

What do I do now?

REFLECTION, PRESENT DAY

THE VEERY THRUSH SITS within the branches of the growing bush, feeling the warmth of the sun as it sings its joy-filled refrain, encouraging the buds to prepare for their glory.

Chapter Thirty-Seven

BLESSED

MARCH 2009

SPRING SIGNS ARE ABOUNDING. There was great excitement when Gary, my goose, returned to his mate, Gladys. She has been honking a lot more than usual the past few days. He soared overhead, circled twice and glided in for a perfect landing where she anxiously awaited. Such deep love could be seen as they embraced in their gooselike fashion, honking their commitment toward another season. Gosh, it's so exciting to watch. I'm sorry I didn't get it on video.

I'm struggling with my writing lessons from Connie. The overwhelming wall of doubt, that I'm not good enough, or that my story isn't worth telling needs to crumble. I need confidence and joy through this process. The dark presence shadows me. I feel cold, as it comes and goes, and then, in a flash, I pushed the wall away.

I listened to the book, *Cockeyed: A Memoir* by Ryann Knighton. He told of his journey of blindness with retinitis pigmentosa. At first, it was very hard to listen to. Now, I'm enjoying it, thinking of my own story and the book I haven't written. I still have the desire but need to get over the fear.

April 2009

I've been going across the road to the Riverside Cemetery to walk. There, I can walk without worrying about the traffic. It's very peaceful and I don't get disturbed, kind of a dead silence (insert groan or a giggle here).

Walking four laps around the outer road within the cemetery equals a mile. I've even jogged short spurts after the first lap of picking up debris. It's emotionally charging for me as I completely forget about my RP, falling into the joy and rhythm of my steps. The tall whispering red pines and the chirp of the variety of birds lull me into a pattern where I soon find I've gone several miles.

May 2009

I just fed my ducks. All five spent the winter on the river eating the corn I tossed. Without the snow, they come to eat out of the bucket. They quack-talk to me, eat, then waddle back to the river in single file.

One night, before sunset, Donny was trying to sleep early because he had to leave for work before dawn. I was upstairs watching TV when the ducks actually tapped at the sliding glass door, quacking for food . . . Maybe I pampered them too much.

*J*UNE 2009

I WAS SITTING ON our deck when a huge flock of geese, about seventy-five, flew over, displaying a beautiful V-formation. It reminded me of Mom's favorite joke.

"When geese fly in a V-formation," she would ask, "why is one side longer than the other?"

"I don't know, Mom. Why?" I would reply, even though I knew the answer.

"Because there are more geese on that side."

*D*ECEMBER 2009

THIS PAST YEAR WAS filled with many activities. Besides running my massage business out of my home, I was chairperson for putting together a cookbook at church. I had the narrator singing part in *Joseph and the Amazing Technicolor Dreamcoat* for the church Christmas program. I sang at several funerals. I gave piano lessons, ran at the cemetery, sewed quilts, knitted socks, and found anything else I could do to keep myself busy while Donny traveled around the country to work at various job sites.

*R*EFLECTION, PRESENT DAY

WITH EACH DELICIOUS ACTIVITY I could feel uplifting positive action giving me momentum to do more. My RP was going to a new place, a place of actual joy instead of doom and despair. I didn't focus on what I couldn't do. I cherished what I could do and forgot about the rest. What a wonderful sensation that was.

The activities were my therapy to keep my mind off my

vision issues. I did not continue my writing though. I still couldn't convince myself that I was worthy enough.

*c*May 2010

AFTER OVER A YEAR of training, I decided to run the five-mile distance in the Run Around Woman Lake event in Longville. I made a comment to Donny before the race about me trying to be the winner ahead of everyone.

"You're all winners just for finishing it!" he said.

It was forty-five degrees and a light rain was falling. A crowd of about seventy-five runners gathered at the starting line. Alicia and I chose to be toward the back of the pack as it was easier for me.

"On your mark, get set—BANG!"

And off we went, adjusting to the waving ripple of runners in the front, each runner getting into their rhythm. I kept focused on what was in front of me, while Alicia ran alongside me on my left, letting me know of potholes and other objects that might affect both of us, but me especially. Each of us took turns asking the other if we were doing okay, or if we should walk a bit, which seemed to be common with many other runners.

At the halfway turn around was a refreshment stand where volunteers encouraged us on and handed out drinks. I took a few sips, thinking it was water, and discovered it was Gatorade. It was refreshing, but after three minutes of running again, my heart started racing. I would walk to get it to slow down, but it would speed up again. I couldn't breathe and Alicia tried to keep me calm.

"In through the nose, out through the mouth," she repeated.

That really helped and I kept remembering Donny saying that I would be a winner when I finished.

I pressed on.

I pushed the last sprint to the finish line and had to sit down against a wall. The crowd had swelled with people congratulating the runners. I tried to look for Donny, thinking he surely should have watched me come in, but I couldn't find him.

My heart wouldn't slow down. Bonnie, an EMT first responder came to congratulate me and noticed my condition. Alicia was next to me while Bonnie got a heart monitor for the finger. It was beating 197!

Donny finally found me. Bonnie told him of my condition and said she wanted to call the ambulance. They got me inside, laid me down, and wanted to put an IV in my arm.

"No! I hate needles," I said.

They inserted it anyway. Instantly, my heart went to normal, but regardless of my insistence that I was okay, they still wanted to check me out at the hospital in Crosby, an hour drive away.

The scariest thing for me was not being able to breathe deeply while my vision swirled in the kaleidoscope of flashing lights, as if I looked at a disco ball. Shutting my eyes during the trip helped, because it made me dizzier to look out the back window at the scenery racing away. I felt the presence of Dad in the ambulance calming me.

At the hospital, after a few tests, they said I have a very strong heart and can resume my activities in a few days. My chest felt bruised, and I slept the rest of the day. The worst part though, was I didn't get any, woo-woos; no sirens during my ambulance ride.

I'm so pleased that I found the courage to do another

activity regardless of my vision.

August 2010

I've been mowing the lawn weekly while Donny has been out of town working. He makes sure that branches are cut back so I won't run into them. Before I start, I search the yard for fallen sticks and other debris. Our yard isn't that big, and I can usually finish it in an hour. It's such an empowering simple task that makes me feel normal.

My sister, Rita, called to tell us that Mom had fallen and was having surgery. Evidently, she was standing on a chair to change a light bulb, turned to test the switch without getting down and fell. She suffered all night alone in her apartment while trying to scoot down the hall to her phone in the next room. It took her five hours to do so.

"I just wanted to fall asleep so it wouldn't hurt so bad," she said.

Mom's hip replacement surgery went well, and we visited her in Eau Claire, Wisconsin several times.

"Oh good, you're here," she said during one of our visits. "Now we can get our chores done."

I said, "Okay, what do you need?"

She said, "Donny, twist that flower vase so I can see the other side. Pamela, move the other flowers over there. I'll move the TV remote over here . . . There, chores are done. Now we can visit. That's what Ida would always do."

Ida, her mother, was in a wheelchair with MS my whole life. Her strength and joy during her trials empowered me. I never saw her upset about her situation or playing *poor me*, ever.

October 2010

I BETTER GET OUT of this mood. Useless, is the word that is repeating in my head as problems pester me. I can't lose weight and feel fat even though I work out and try to eat right daily.

My children are hurting in their relationships and life struggles in the Cities, which breaks my heart being so far from them. Being a wife, taking care of all the maintenance issues, and running a household while Donny is gone is also challenging.

I can't run my massage business successfully and have experienced a 60% drop in income the past few years. I can't do music right at church and have been replaced as contemporary music director. I'm afraid to write a book.

I can't do anything good enough. I can't see! Why bother even trying? I'm not listening to God enough and think that He doesn't want to bother with me anymore. No, I'm not suicidal, just done trying. I had my chances and didn't succeed.

Listen, a song is whispering. It's Elvis singing, *"There will be peace in the valley."* I'll rest for now.

Reflection, PRESENT DAY

OH, DEAR ONE, IT was so hard to read these words and the circumstances throughout the months that brought me to that point. I held you, my former self, with loving arms, and shared in your pain, knowing that there was a solution. When you didn't try anymore, you gave it up to the One who knows your worth and has seen your solutions in everything you asked.

It would get better.

*N*ovember 2010

I reached out to my dear friend, Ben Lindstrom, who had been a visiting summer client for years. He was a pastor in Washington and spent his summers in Minnesota at a cabin. After each session he blessed me with a prayer. I shared with him the depths of my despair over the past months. I needed help, and I knew he would be able to guide me toward a positive outcome. This response blessed me deeply.

Here was his reply:

> Wonderful Pamela,
>
> Absolutely—entirely—I am placing you in Jesus' arms and claiming that God is overwhelming every part of you and filling you so much with His presence that you're feeling great peace and great joy. Whenever I get into one of those places—where I ask of God—why am I here? God answers; you're here, not because you got it all right, you're here, because I need you to be here. In fact, your humanity is exactly what I need. I never work through perfect people, but I do great things through people to realize they're imperfect.
>
> Pray daily; "Lord, if anything good is to come out from me it will have to be not because of my adequacy, but because of your desire. And so, Lord, I claim that whether I am feeling it or not, you're doing great things through me and my presence here on this

earth is important to you. So, it's all in your hands. If you want me to do something, be something, YOU put me in that place, and put inside me awareness that whether I saw anything happen or not, yet, because I committed that moment, that relationship to you, something wonderful happened, by Your hand."

If we are here on this earth for no other reason, God has placed us here to remind each other that God is at work in our lives. I know it because I feel it, every day I am nourished, strengthened, encouraged by it.

So thank you for you, for your honesty, your openness, your willingness to be my friend and God's servant. My reciprocal prayer is that God may fill each of your moments with a deep awareness of His love and that whether you see it or not, God is at work.

Bless you—Bless you—Bless you,

Ben

There is joy sneaking into my heart again and I'm so thankful.

December 2010

WE WERE ON OUR way to Donny's company Christmas party when I slipped and fell inside a gas station, landing fully on my right thumb as I was holding my cane. Ouch, I thought it was broken.

I had bought new boots, stylish ones with heels. They looked great but were hazardous. We stopped to buy more practical, boring ones in the next town while traveling.

Chapter Thirty-Eight

I Can and I Want To

And sleep, that sometimes shuts up
sorrow's eye, steal me a while from mine own
company.

— *William Shakespeare,*
Midsummer Night's Dream

JANUARY 2011

WHILE I WAS SEWING the final seam on a quilt and focusing on the nesting of the next point, my finger got in the way. Ouch! The needle went through at the top of the nail. When I pulled quickly away, it sliced through, so it actually looked like I cut it with a knife. I replaced the needle and was glad that it still worked. Also, it's a good thing I didn't faint. I knew I should have used my pointer tool.

I was waiting for my ride to music practice at church and realized I had been forgotten and needed to ask Donny to take me. It was hard for me not to dwell on my limitation, control my impulses, and focus on what my drivers want to do.

My limited vision feels more confining lately.

February 18, 2011

Twenty years ago today, I was diagnosed with retinitis pigmentosa and told I would be totally blind in five to ten years. I now have about six degrees of central tunnel vision. Because I am female, I will probably not lose any more than that. I'm doing as much as I can with what I have left, and I cherish it. Well, mostly. I wish I could have it all back, but God has held me through this journey and led me even though I often forget He's here.

I'm overwhelmed, remembering that day's roller coaster of emotions, the numbing pain, and my disbelief. *Was this really happening?* I wondered. *It can't be me. I must be living in someone else's reality. No!* I imagine myself screaming as the daydream rewinds time. My waterfall tears flow uncontrollably. I rarely let myself do that, but I feel a need to.

I posted on Facebook about the anniversary and received many positive comments. That wasn't the reason I shared, but it helped to feel embraced.

March 2011

I finished Tim's quilt. After I laid it out on the spare bed, I cried. Not sure why. I guess because it's a gift of love that, because of my RP, I never thought I could really give. I felt the same way when I sewed Sarah's quilt last year. I can't wait to get started on Alice's. I have a challenging sunflower pattern to use for hers.

✳ ✳ ✳

I HAVE ANOTHER ANNUAL eye exam today. I'm emotional about it, which hasn't happened for several years. There's a dark, black door in the distance that is always lurking, waiting to open and suck me inside. It's called blindness and it's waiting to swallow me. It cracks open a little wider during my appointment month. I'm afraid of that door, but it was once closer and much bigger. I'll allow these emotions for a while because I will bounce back and do everything I can with the vision I have remaining.

* * *

AT THE APPOINTMENT, DR. Poland told me I had the beginnings of cataracts in both eyes. I stayed composed until later in the afternoon, when it hit me like a punch in the stomach. It felt like the day I was diagnosed. All the logical things ran through my mind: *Yes, cataracts are common. Yes, they take years to develop. Yes, there is surgery to remove them when they are further along. No, it's not going to kill me. Yes, I'm being a baby about this.* But oh God, it was so hard to hear. This would make it harder to navigate my small world.

Should I just give in and stop trying? No, I can't and won't ever do that. I'll take this moment to let all the emotions gush out, then forget about it and go on like I have.

> *Dear Lord, help me to walk this day as your confident child. Keep my heart and mind clear by your promise to be with me. Your word reminds me that, underneath, are the everlasting arms: Your love and care. Set me free from troublesome worries and anxieties about the affairs of my life. If surprises come, give me steadfast faith to cope with them. In a frightened world, let me be a living witness to the peace which passes all understanding. Amen.*

That is my go-to prayer, given to me by a friend years ago. I don't know who wrote it, but its comfort is powerful. I need it today.

May 2011

I RAN THE FIVE miles at the Run Around Woman Lake again, this time without incident. I was number 56 of the runners and came in second place in my age category. The weather was perfect, not too cold, not too hot, no rain, and cloudy. I was able to do four practice runs in the past month. My heart was fine, but toward the end, it felt heavy like it was going to start racing. It didn't though.

I'm so very proud of myself.

September 2011

WHILE WALKING THROUGH TOWN to the post office, only a couple blocks from home, I almost got run over three times. I used my white cane but that didn't help. The first incident was at the crosswalk across the street from the post office. A truck was parked on the crosswalk, so I had to go around it—a car almost got me.

Then, coming out of the post office, a car stopped for me to walk the crosswalk. Another car went around him and almost hit me.

Then, stepping off the sidewalk at the grocery store, I was about three feet into the parking lot when a car raced around the corner and almost hit me.

Yikes, tourists. I can't wait till they're gone after Labor Day Weekend. They forget all their driving skills on vacation. I was so shaken up after each event. I have to focus on so many things when Longville's population grows from 190 to over 1,000 because of the lake cabins and resorts. I hate to give up my independence, but I'll have to figure something else out.

September 17, 2011

My son, Tim, and his wife, Emily, (aka Timily, as their friends call them) were married in a beautiful ceremony. My most precious memory from the wedding day, and the time when my tears flowed, was during the mother-son dance. It was an experience I never thought I would be able to see. I remembered watching my little man while he slept at night, wondering where his journey would lead him and if I would be able to witness it. There he was, all grown up, in love, marrying the woman of his dreams, and working as an architect.

I'm so happy and proud of him.

I sewed a lavender and beige Wedding Ring quilt for them and presented it at Emily's bridal shower.

October 2011

Donny retired and we had a party in the garage. Over seventy-five friends came to celebrate with him. I'm not sure how we'll adjust with my massage business in the home and him finding enough to do to keep busy.

My vision seems more narrowed. I keep getting startled by things coming from my left side. I really have to slow down and concentrate on what I'm doing and where I'm going. It's scary at times, but I'm using all that I have left to the best of my ability. Donny loves to hide and startle me, but I think he now knows how much I hate that.

January 2012

A NEW QUILTING GROUP, Loving Hands Community Quilting, has been organized in town to help area people in need. We will meet at the fire hall every Tuesday morning in the months of January, February, and March. Tops will be sewn by ladies at their homes during the week, a simple ten-and-a-half-inch block pattern. Each quilt will have six blocks across and eight down. They'll be matched with a backing and pinned to the quilt rack with batting between. Yarn will be tied in the center of the squares before it is taken off the rack. Then they'll get trimmed, pinned, and the bindings will be sewn.

Reflection, Present day

ABOUT 300 QUILTS WERE made annually by over 40 women doing various tasks. They were then handed out into the area communities each season. They went to fire victims, homeless, police cars, food shelves, and anyone in need.

February 18, 2012

THE DAY IS FINALLY here. We leave for the Cities, then fly to Cozumel tomorrow. I can't believe I'm traveling out of the country and out of the winter season for the very first time in my life. I'm almost 55 years old. This is going to be great.

ENDLESS SENSATIONS OVERWHELMED ME, taking me on a euphoric thrill ride like I'd never experienced before. Cozumel, and the all-inclusive resort we stayed in, gave me a sensation of time warp. It felt like a world untouched by the drudgery of economic stress, a wonderland, as if desires were made real just for me.

Smells engulfed me the moment we landed on the runway. The moist air enveloped me like a comforter, its warmth reminding me it was time to don my summer attire and feel the exuberance of being away from the cold twenty-two degrees in northern Minnesota. Languages from around the world intrigued me, and I wondered what they were saying to each other.

While relaxing in my new surroundings I heard unfamiliar bird songs. They sat in branches conducting a melody just for me and sounded just as curious about me as I was about them. Their vibrant colors were mesmerizing. Other new sounds enveloped me too, water crashing to the shore at moments, while at others, it was a cool lapping, tasting the shore, inviting me to experience its beauty.

I stayed busy seeing all I could. Even though colors were not pure, I could tell the vivid pink of the flamingos, textures of the peacocks fanned tails, deep blue changing hues of the ocean, and the forest greens.

We traveled with friends, Alicia, Doug, Kent, and Ev, for a week. The four of them were frequent travelers and enticed me to try snorkeling. It was my first time ever. Alicia calmed me with simple relaxing advice, which made it easier for me to adjust to the new breathing method. Underwater, it was hard for me to see colors, but she was able to point out different fish. What a wonderful world existing below the surface, and I caught a glimpse of it. They saw more than I was able to, but it was a wonderful experience.

The sunsets were spectacular. Each evening we joined the crowd of tourists to experience a new phenomenon, the green flash. As the sun sank into the horizon, the split second of its disappearance emitted a bolt of green. In the blink of an eye, its display delighted all who experienced its beauty. I was very pleased when I was able to witness it a few evenings.

One of the employees suggested we take in a grand event in town, a celebration of Carnival, their version of Mardi Gras. It was the biggest, best, loudest parade I'd ever seen with thousands of people crowding the streets. Beautiful floats, completely lined with lights, were traveling bumper to bumper through the street, filled with children and adults cheering in the excitement and showing off their attire.

My eyes took in as much as they could as I tried to focus on each one in succession. The brightness of the lights was slightly painful, while the contrast of the night blocked out my surroundings. Donny kept close to my left, allowing me to know he was there and available if I needed his elbow.

"Look at the boys dancing on the top of that float," he pointed out.

His guidance helped, because I had been looking in a different direction.

Activities occurred each evening, blending the days into a vacation filled with memories to last a lifetime . . . or at least until next time. There was karaoke and I sang "The Lion Sleeps Tonight." I enjoyed entertaining the audience while the staff acted out the words to the song. That was fun.

While walking from our grass hut toward the beach, a boy, about eleven, stopped to ask me a question. I thought he would be curious about my cane as I was tapping along.

"Dutch?" he asked.

"No, English," I said. "Are you having a good time?"

He showed me his watch and the time then walked away. I laughed when I told my experience to the rest of the group. I never found out what that was all about.

An elegant evening at the steak house was our special treat one night. A very handsome waiter greeted us when we arrived and seated us at a white-clothed table set for our group. Each knife, fork, dish, piece of glassware was precisely placed, giving me a brief worry over using the correct one at the correct time. The waiter pulled out my chair, seated me, took my napkin, and draped it over my lap. Wow, I was impressed and felt special. I don't get this treatment too often.

During the meal, I needed to use the restroom. The room was dark with ambient lighting and hard for me to see, so Alicia went along to guide me. When we got there, we discovered the restroom was being cleaned, and by then, we both really had to go. Neither of us had a room key, so we ran, me gripping her elbow, toward the beach to use the one at the back of the beach bar. It was darker than dark to me. I totally relied on my navigator's direction. It took us a while to even find that building. We finally did, went inside and tried to find the light switch. I couldn't see a thing but knew she was reaching around on the walls to find it also. I reached out to put my hand on her shoulder like I did when we were walking because I couldn't see in the dark.

"That's not the light switch!" she exclaimed.

Mistakenly, I had my hand on her boob!

We laughed so hard I almost wet myself. I removed it and went forward to where I remembered there should be a stall.

ℛEFLECTION, PRESENT DAY

THAT VACATION EMPOWERED ME more than anything I had done regarding my RP. I felt a joy and accomplishment and was no longer afraid to try new experiences. I felt more whole and uplifted in this new facet of my kaleidoscope world. I gained new self-esteem with a can-do spirit.

March 2012

I finished Alice's quilt and was thrilled with the intricacy of it. The quilt design was called *Montana Hearth*. It had block designs resembling sunflowers surrounded by cobalt blue. I think it was my favorite quilt out of all I'd made so far because of the challenge, courage, strength, patience and peace it gave me.

Once it was finished, I realized I never would have chosen that pattern because it contained a new technique of insert sewing that needed to be exact by adding a piece to a seam toward the inside of a piece that was already attached. I made a practice block out of scraps to be sure I really understood the directions. Having finished, it was a boost to my self-confidence, because I discovered more about who I am.

"Look what you can do with your vision," I told myself.

A friend suggested a mantra: "Because I can, and I want to."

Reflection, Present day

The Veery Thrush sang to me, pulsing into my soul, vibrating a rhythm that could not be contained. Its pure joy awakened my desires with thoughts that I wanted to think, thoughts I'd previously abandoned. I soared, empowered. Nothing can keep me down. I feel unity again with who I am without thinking of the girl I left behind in 1991.

But she was not left behind.

She is with me in this journey and has grown. We are one.

Chapter Thirty-Nine

TRUSTING YOUR WINGS

MAY 4, 2012

I'M AT ABBOTT NORTHWESTERN Hospital in Minneapolis.

Donny had three stents put in his heart yesterday. He had been having some issues and his doctor decided, after finding he had an enlarged heart that he needed to have a specialist look for a solution. It was a three-hour drive from our home to here and they thought he would be fine to drive himself.

Were they crazy!? I absolutely hate my RP at times like this when I should be driving.

Thanks to texting, I was able to contact my children who live in the Cities and let them know the situation. They met us there. I couldn't say enough thanks for all three of my kids being there for us.

It's amazing what they can do to the heart through a tiny cut in the groin. Donny was awake during the whole procedure. He's doing great this morning and has a lot more energy than he has had in a long time. He'll be released today.

May 20, 2012

I GOT A CALL from my doctor's nurse telling me about my blood test results. The test showed mild to abnormal blood platelets, a condition called thrombocytosis, and could cause blood clots. The doctor referred me to a hematologist.

Really, don't I have enough going on with Donny's health? And don't tell me that God doesn't give me more than I can handle. That's crap. I feel stronger when I remember that during these times, He's the one that is by my side, comforting me.

May 24, 2012

My MORNING MEDITATION AS I recline in my Adirondack chair on my dock soothes me. The babble of the river, the flow of the waterfall, the spring songs of the birds bring me peace in my hectic world.

As I glance downstream to my left, I see an eagle perched at the top of a dead tree. It reminds me of the strength I felt from statues of eagles when I was first diagnosed with RP. The recurring dream of that year comes to my mind as I remember the flight of peace, soaring through clouds on its back, spiraling high.

"Let go, I have you," I hear a voice say from inside. "Everything is done. Everything is going to be okay."

Oh joy, the eagle screeches as if just to me.

I'm finding my strength by letting the river take away all my fears and anxieties, at least for the moment. How refreshing.

* * *

Yesterday, a hematologist called to talk to me. He's unsure of why I'm seeing him.

"The numbers are high, but not a lot," he said. "I want to take a blood test next week and send it to Mayo in Rochester, Minnesota."

He wasn't too concerned about my mildly abnormal blood platelet level, but he is researching and will talk to a doctor at Mayo. He instructed me to take a whole aspirin a day to thin the blood and reduce the chance of clotting.

"Anytime the cells clone, it's considered cancer, but this is very minimal," he said.

Seriously, did he use the C word? I wasn't sure I wanted to add that to my repertoire of health issues. It was a good time to surrender to God.

* * *

Donny's cardiologist appointment went great. He has so much more energy. Thank you, God, that the blockages were caught in time.

* * *

I have a new client who is a writer.

I shared with her my desire to write my story and the stumbling blocks I've come across with each attempt. She was very encouraging and suggested some blogs to look at.

"I think I've stopped trying because I never feel like I'm good enough at anything," I confided, speaking the unrealized words from my heart.

"Tell the story as if to a friend, each chapter at a time," she said.

She sees potential in what I have to say. I hope I can continue with her words of reassurance. I haven't tried now in almost five years.

JUNE 2012

THIS IS THE LAST year for Alicia and me to do our Turtle Town Art Fair.

We started this event eleven years ago with Kim, who decided a few years ago she couldn't continue. The art fair had been a great boost for the town, bringing tourists into our beautiful part of the world. Over the years, it grew to almost 80 vendors for this one-day event.

We're thrilled that The Longville Area Women of Today have so graciously taken on this venture and will continue to create an environment of excellence for people to show what they can do and for the community to be awed in their findings.

JULY 2012

IT'S BEEN A VERY busy summer with clients. It's difficult at times with Donny in the house now that he's retired. I think we've found a rhythm of coexisting while I work.

I always leave the conversation up to the client. If they ask questions or talk, then I will, otherwise I respect their time.

I was very touched by the ease of a new client as we got to know each other through her inquiries. She encouraged me to continue writing my book about my journey with RP.

The desire is still there and growing. Is it bigger than my fear? Bigger than the dark shadow that I'm not good enough and need help with so many things. I feel inadequate but hopeful.

AUGUST 2012

I THOROUGHLY ENJOYED MY adventure at Fair Maiden Days at Camelot. Queen Mary requested my presence for this year's Dragon Days. Thirteen maidens gathered in our finery for the progressive dinner at Battle Point on Leech Lake.

Mary's whole house was themed in Camelot, even the music played tunes from the movie. As I looked throughout her home, I saw crowns, jesters, and a real suit of armor standing in the corner. Her dining room had been stenciled in vines with the words, "And they lived happily ever after," above the arch. A stockade was displayed in the yard for those who dared defy the Queen.

King Curt presented the feast as each maiden found their new name on a placard where they were to be seated— Duchess Pamela was my name for the gala.

We spent several days doing fun activities that Queen Mary organized for her own delight. On our final day, an archery instructor came and gave lessons. I had had one archery class in high school but didn't remember a thing. I loved it. I had a great time and laughed when the alarm sounded.

"Duchess Pamela is preparing her quiver!" exclaimed the Queen. "DUCK!"

I completely felt at peace with who I was during this outing. Relaxing with friends, I was able to feel free to be me. Archery became my metaphor: Stand your stance, focus on where your target is (which is where you feel the inner peace of who you are), take in a full relaxing breath, hold it, feel the confidence soar, adjust to your spot on direction, feel your purpose, feel the momentum, feel the pride, and feel the joy.

I concentrated on the target, stood the stance, pulled up my bow, took a deep breath, held it . . . then released. Smack, into the target, most, well, almost *some* of the times.

I discovered so many lessons to explore and live by. Feel the love energy flow and stay with you in your discovery. How precious a lesson that was; it fanned the sparks of the flame beginning to burn: "Yes, you can," it said. I was able to be myself and not let the darkness even peak in my moment of triumph.

I thanketh thee, Queen Mary, for being a steppingstone in the moat toward the castle and for allowing me out of the dungeon of doom and gloom.

Or maybe, I did so well because I was frightened by the stockade? I bow to the Queen.

SEPTEMBER 2012

AFTER RESEARCHING, TALKING TO a specialist at Mayo, and another blood test, my hematologist feels that I should be put on a low dose of preventative medicine to fend off having a blood clot that could lead to a stroke. At least he never used the C word.

DECEMBER 2012

I'VE SET MYSELF TO a new task. Well, it's really one I've attempted many times, but hopefully I can see this one through (pun intended). I am going to take the journey through my journals, something I have never done before. At times, I've felt that by reading them, the RP would get worse, that it would exercise its full strength and send me into total blindness. By writing the entries, then ignoring them, I wonder how I thought it would affect my vision. I know that there is a physical and emotional manifestation when you dwell on negative thoughts.

I want to write my story. It's all there, but it needs dissecting and redoing. I will read through the years putting my RP story, with all my adventures, into a book. I will accomplish this a little at a time, from starting at my RP beginning, to the present.

FEBRUARY 2013

WE RETURNED TO COZUMEL for another winter vacation. I was once again thrilled by the splendor this world has to offer. I was so glad that I could see it but didn't have the overwhelming dread that I had to see it all before the darkness set in.

We met two lovely ladies, Michelle and Diane, traveling from Canada. Michelle has a daughter who is handicapped, mostly blind, deaf, and unable to walk. She was eight but had the intellect of an eighteen-month-old. Michelle had a stroke while pregnant and had since recovered. The doctors told Diane's mother that Diane would be a vegetable at birth because of a brain tumor, but she isn't.

They both commented about adjusting to what you have. I felt a connection that sang softly to me. It wasn't about feeling better because their burdens were worse but a song of all of us having different challenges and finding our joy. We all kept the tempo by listening to the next beat, the next note, and the next lyric to lift us up and over to the next rest. We each heard our own joyful noise in the song of life, sending us from our minor key moments into a blissful crescendo.

Majestic serenity. Lilting harmonies.

Our dance of life.

*A*pril 12, 2013

Changes are happening in my life as spring approached but refused to come. We received a blanket of snow over the evening with threats of yet another storm later in the week, but I don't want to talk about the weather here.

I moved my business out of our home and into the salon in town, Haircuts & More. Kim is the owner and Alicia's daughter-in-law.

Last week was my first week there. I hadn't realized having my business in the home had become a burden, but I felt an overwhelming sense of relief after moving. It seemed like regaining control, independence, returning to the person who left the day I was diagnosed.

I came across words from Wayne W. Dyer's *Power of Intention* that settled within me and allowed me to contemplate thoughts I never dared to have before. I understand his message to say, "suppose your thoughts of being unimportant make you realize your value."[26]

His views on intention were interesting, and I allowed myself to, not just read, but bring about emotions that I have stomped down to my deepest, darkest place.

Am I important? I matter? I'm not a lesser part of humanity because of my vision loss? I have value? Wow, where can these feelings go, and am I able to maintain them?

One of my dear friends, whom I have reached out to for assistance in writing this book, said she had a message for me

---

26   Wayne W. Dyer, *The Power of Intention: Learning to Co-create Your World Your Way.* (United States: Hay House): 2010.

after her morning meditation. She didn't understand what it meant but knew I would.

"The key is at the bottom, but it's not a key," she said.

I meditated on her words before I wrote again. Her words changed my thought process. It wasn't a key, it was a direction, a releasing, lifting me up from the depths of despair and letting go of the thoughts pulling me down. It meant going toward the light through the tunnel, toward the horizon where I was worthy, equal, whole.

I am better because of the journey.

April 22, 2013

Last Friday, I had the day off and wanted to use the tanning bed at the salon. Donny dropped me off and said he would be back to get me when I was done. I thought it was strange that he returned with the truck instead of the car but didn't think much more about it. I opened the door to get in. A nice-looking gentleman sitting behind the wheel lowered his paper and looked at me.

"You're not my husband!" I exclaimed in shock.

"Um, no, no I'm not," he replied.

I turned ten shades of red, with a nice brown glow of course after tanning, slammed the door and went back inside the salon. Kim wondered what the heck I was doing, and I'm sure she giggled on the inside.

Donny soon came pulling up with the car. You would think I had a vision problem or something (wink).

I posted that story on Facebook and got twenty-five likes and thirteen comments.

One friend replied, "That's what I would call speed

dating!"

*A*PRIL 30, 2013

IT'S MY BIRTHDAY. I'M fifty-six. I wish I would have been warm enough to journal while sitting on the dock a few minutes ago. I took a picture of my view and I will have that as my peaceful memory place to go for a long time. I'm even thinking of making it into a quilt wall hanging using a technique I learned at a quilt retreat.

The scene that embraced me was serene and tranquil. The far left of the river from my dock view was in a fog haze from the cool 32 degrees. The eagle sat majestically at the top of the white pine gazing in my direction. Two deer stood at its base, eating the little bits of fresh spring grass sprouts. A beaver, although not pictured, was sitting on a clump of last year's dead reeds while cleaning itself. My nesting pair of geese, Gary and Gladys, swam lazily in the river after their breakfast of corn. Floating along with them were my mallard ducks who had also enjoyed their corn feast.

The many sounds of spring birds singing included robins, chick-a-dees, pileated woodpeckers, and finches, many of which were gathering debris for their nests.

And above it all, while I sat in my Adirondack chair on my dock and drank my first morning coffee, to my right was the ever-present peaceful roar of my waterfall. I gave great thanks and was humbled by the many, many blessings in my life.

Why do I so frequently forget about them?

May 2013

I'M RECOVERING FROM HAVING a tooth extracted yesterday. I'm doing great. My mouth really doesn't hurt. I'm just tired from the gas that I was given. The extraction went so fast. After Novocaine and having gas, Dr. Cargill told me to concentrate on my breathing.

"You'll feel some pressure . . . Breathe. You're doing great," she repeated several times until it was out.

When I was able to speak, I asked, "Is it a boy or a girl? The way you were coaching me, I thought I was in labor."

She replied, "It's a boy, he has prongs!"

June 2013

I HAD A HORRIBLE moment while cleaning the kitchen after supper tonight. The curtains were closed and only the kitchen light was on so that the stairwell, living room, and dining room were dark. I wasn't sure where Donny was, so I scanned toward the stairs and back to the dining table several times.

"What are you looking for?" Donny said, startling me.

I stopped in shock when I suddenly saw him, three feet away, in the living room. He was right there! He was standing right there! How could I not have seen him?

I'm so confused at how this can happen. I want to be normal.

It triggered a waterfall moment that I allowed for three minutes in another room, away from Donny. He sensed that I needed alone time. He was very loving later.

RP's darkness is always here, no matter how much I

pretend I have perfect vision. It creeps up when I least expect it.

AUGUST 2013

I SAW TWO EAGLES today, which reminded me of the recurring dream from last night. The eagle dreams are back and lifting me up toward the future again. I have such an uplifting feeling, a lighting of my heart this week.

I dreamed of many eagles soaring above me. I counted ten, soaring in a circle above me, but then, I realized above those, were hundreds, maybe thousands, all gliding on their own currents but all flowing as one.

There was a peace within me, a quiet knowledge of pure love and acceptance of all. Breathing in deeply and slowly, letting out my breath, I could sense my purpose becoming stronger and growing within.

I am meant to share love with wings like eagles, uplifting others to feel and find their own love that is trying to come out of them. I am a healer, a finder of purpose, of source, of intent. I already have been given that gift and have used it, but now is the time to share its full potential so that others can find their own flight. My success depends on the positive difference that I can show in my own journey, possibly shining a light on theirs.

DECEMBER 22, 2013

TIM PRESENTED A LAVISH feast as we celebrated Christmas at Alice and Andrew's, her fiancé, apartment in Minneapolis. Tim prepared three roasts by smoking them after soaking them in brine.

While we sat to dine, before giving thanks, Tim stood and made an announcement in an emotional voice: "We're having a baby in July!"

Excitement and joy filled the room, and the news gave loving meaning to Andrew's blessing. It meant so much for me to be a part of this day with all my children together.

March 2014

It's the final week of The Loving Hands Community Quilt Club for the season. This is the third year and we have made and donated almost 900 quilts to the people in need in the community. I'm honored to be a part of such an effort.

Participating in these acts of kindness has given me a deep sense of gratitude. I find that my RP doesn't seem as bad when I am giving. The act lifts me to a higher place and fosters thankfulness for all my blessings. Each day, I am able to help others in many ways, doing things that I never dreamed of because I limited myself. I'm grateful for these opportunities. My attitude has changed since I was diagnosed in 1991.

A voice whispers, "Go help others, because it will help keep you from being so depressed."

I feel so blessed for my journey with retinitis pigmentosa and how it brought me to this part of my story. Being a massage therapist and having the ability to using my other talents to bring peace to others. I find joy in these things like nothing else, a joy that I don't think I would have reached if I didn't have this contrast in my life.

June 2014

Longville's population swells during the summer

months and so does my clientele. I had a no-show yesterday and felt the old twinge of being upset and frustrated that someone would disregard my schedule. And it was too late to call someone on my waiting list who really needed the appointment.

When there is a no-show, I have found that it's an opportunity to be creative in another way. I refocus, because there must be something else at that moment that needs my attention. I remember when I would let myself slip into the dark place where I would doubt myself and ask irrelevant questions:

"Why aren't you good enough?"

"Now what have you done wrong?"

"You'll never be a normal person again and have a fulfilling life."

Once, my inner monologue would go on and on like that, pulling me into a downward spiral and blocking out all joy and rewarding gratifications. Oh, how I used to punish myself.

I don't like remembering the girl I was then. I had so many people to please and nobody knew the agony. I was so full of pain. There were days I didn't want to go on, days I wanted the blindness to take hold and do what it was going to. Maybe then, I wouldn't have had to work so hard to continue the fight.

Oh, but how wrong I had been and somehow, I knew that.

I cherish my vision, every sight, every moment of every day. I'm so glad that RP hasn't won and that I continue to be strengthened in my challenges. There are moments when I'm aware that if I go totally blind, I will be okay, I will find joy. How can I think that? It's only possible during my positive moments.

Today, *poor me* mode is tugging, but I'm only giving it an allotted amount of time. I've found that's what works best. My dear friend, Barb, taught me that philosophy, and it has worked well from the very first try.

"Okay," she stated firmly, "that just happened. You have only two minutes for a temper tantrum."

I let it all out by screaming or stating what is at the core of my anger. When that time is up, I must forget about what it was and move on. But in moving on, I make a plan and find solutions.

Today's plan is writing. I have everything in place. My candle is burning, soft spa music is playing, all my notes and journals are before me. I have everything I need to continue writing my book.

* * *

I'VE REALIZED THAT I don't allow myself to embrace my deepest desires and joys because of my limitations and thinking about others' reactions to what I want. I'm stuck in an attitude that I can't do things because others think I can't, and that feeling is getting old.

I feel an urge, no, a sense of strength from deep within rising, wanting to erupt and experience the joys I've suppressed in my life. These joys include my family and many outdoor activities, adventure walks, kayaking, and much more. How about I try skydiving? My dear friend, Kathy, took that challenge on when she turned 60. I'm not fond of heights, and why would I jump out of a perfectly good plane? This reminds me of a joke.

Why don't blind people skydive?

It scares the dog!

I must overcome the barriers I have built around myself. I will break down those stone walls and rejoice in their

365

crumbling.

Who am I trying to kid? I'm not good enough. I can't have my desires, no matter how hard I try, how much I feel I'm worthy... I can't, I can't, I can't. RP is having its way with me, putting my feet in cement blocks. I'm unable to move toward my brighter hopes and dreams. I'm limited, surrounded by reality showing me what isn't possible anymore.

A car drives by, the driver having the freedom to go anywhere, anytime, anyplace. I don't have that.

I broke down in heavy sobs after a friend shared a day of freedom she had when she got in the car and took herself out for dinner. No explanation necessary, no reporting in, no judging, just time to be within herself. A lump forms in my throat, an aching pain in knowing that my independence is gone, gone, gone, along with the true me, lost forever.

Suppose, as Wayne W. Dyer said, my thoughts of being unimportant were making me realize my value? There is an opportunity in my set back, a flow that is surging me toward an awareness of who I am. I'm allowing it to flow by serving the needs of others through my skill with massage.

Chapter Forty

HEALING

July 2014

I HAD TO FORCE myself into coming back to writing. The pain from my last writing session sunk in deep. I didn't want to revisit the sting.

There still is no cure today for RP. I don't even keep track of the current studies because I can't keep my hope up to that level anymore. When and if it happens, I will be ready. For now, I will be ready for today. I don't know what is in tomorrow, so I will cherish what I have.

When I read back to a page in journals of the long past, I realize how far I had come. I was afraid to use my cane then because of the stigma associated with it. However, it was a stigma I allowed to sear through my hollow shell. The stares and degrading looks were unbearable as if when I looked into their faces, I could read their thoughts.

"That poor, poor girl," I imagined someone would say. "Lower class citizen."

Another saying, "I'm so much better than her."

In 1998, I wrote about needing Donny to take care of me. I don't remember that, and now I'm stronger knowing that I can and will take care of who I am and where I am going. Today, I'm so glad that Donny is a partner along with me, enjoying day to day life.

*J*ULY 15, 2014

BABY MOORE WAS BORN this morning. Emily and Tim announced yesterday that they were entering the delivery room, so Donny and I headed to the Cities for a long day of waiting. I felt helpless as I watched my son live through a range of emotions. We hadn't prepared for spending the evening so when conditions showed that it might be awhile, we said our farewells to Tim and drove the long three hours back home. That was the longest and hardest thing I have ever had to do. In the morning, without hearing any news, we ventured south again. On the drive, I received a text from Tim—

It's a boy!

I can't describe the joy that surged through me when I first saw my son standing next to his son lying in the bassinet. I've never felt a love so strong and rooted so deep. It flowed into me, into my very being with a warm weight that felt solid, strong, and forever.

Then I picked him up; pure joy filled me, and a tear flowed.

They haven't named him yet. They have a couple choices and are waiting to get to know him before they decide.

A memory flashes and I see myself walking down the runway-lit hallway years past, walking from room to room, memorizing my children's faces, wanting to hold on to their images. I was so wrapped up in holding onto those shadows that I never dreamed that I would be allowed to see this precious moment. I never imagined the moment I'd meet my first grandson.

I have conquered my RP fear, at least for today.

July 16, 2014

Baby Moore has a name: Eamon Alexander Moore.

I'm a GramE.

September 2014

For the past year, every Tuesday afternoon, Donny has taken me and my portable massage table to three of my clients' home where I give each of them a massage. It's been a delight getting to know them and assisting in their health needs.

Gary had a stroke several years ago and is the main reason for my venturing out. His wife, Barb, and his home health care assistant, Nichole, also receive sessions because my traveling policy requires three or more.

For Gary's 80th birthday, he asked if I could make him a pineapple upside down cake.

I had a recipe from scratch with a brown sugar caramelized topping that was similar to how he remembered his mother making it. I so wanted to please him, so I followed the recipe step by step, adding this, then mixing that, putting the pineapple rings on the bottom while perfectly placing the maraschino cherries in the center of each ring. I held my breath while smelling the delicious aroma during baking. My mouth watered as I slid the cake pan out of the oven just in time to take it to their home so that he would have a warm piece.

"I think it turned out perfect," I said as I beamed at Donny.

Except, I had the oven rack in crooked and it was lopsided—I'll blame this on my RP; I hadn't leveled the rack when last cleaning and replacing it.

One side of the cake was obviously smaller than the other. The trio laughed and thought it was exceptionally good.

Gary wanted the thinner piece. "It has more caramel," he said with a grin. "It's about 95% perfect. I think you should try again for practice."

OCTOBER 4, 2014

A SPECIAL MEMORY WAS made today when I watched my darling daughter glowing before my eyes as she tried on wedding dresses. How precious to see this beautiful moment that I believed my vision wouldn't allow.

Alice's first dress choice was stunning. She elegantly displayed it for the ladies gathered. As she came out wearing her fourth choice, she was choked up in tears and so was I. That was it, the dress for her wedding.

Sarah said, "She was stunning in all the dresses, but this one said it was made especially for Alice."

Another important memory on this day happened when Donny and I stopped to see Emily and Eamon. Tim was gone on a fishing trip. I held Eamon, who was only a few months old. He cooed, smiled, and looked at me for the first time.

Oh, I love this GramE thing.

November, 2014

I HAD A BONE scan, and the results indicated I have osteopenia in my L3, L4 and L5 vertebrae and osteoporosis in L2. I'll meet with my doctor to discuss if and when I should do anything about it. I've wanted to have the scan for several years due to the family history. My sister, Joan, has osteopenia and gets a Beneva infusion every three months to stop the progress. My other sister, Rita, has osteoporosis like Mom and has another type of infusion once a year. Mom stopped taking anything because of the side effects and said it wasn't doing any good.

Crap! I don't want to have anything else going on. How can I endure and make this the best moment that now has to offer? Find something positive to focus on, a distraction like Mom used to say . . . I'll think about my precious grandson, Eamon.

May 2015

I HAD MY ANNUAL eye appointment today. It was emotional to have a new doctor because Dr. Poland was killed in a car accident last fall. Losing him was such tragedy, partly because he was so involved in the progression of cures and operations to correct eye disease. I was truly blessed to have known him and aware of the hope he invested toward a cure.

June 13, 2015

SIX THIRTY-ONE IN THE morning. It's fifty-five degrees and sunny. I'm sitting on my dock feeling refreshed after a 7.38-mile bike ride along Highway 5, which is designated as a bike route with a wider shoulder.

The air whispers a promise of another beautiful summer-soaked day. Deep breaths in and slowly out, I listen to the birds singing their morning praises. My river flows as my ducks and geese gather around me for our morning ritual. I spray a bucket of corn for them and savor my first sips of delicious dark-roast coffee.

I'm drawn to look to my right, toward my waterfall about 150 feet away, to the sound of a fish splashing at the surface. I see ever-enlarging circles, evidence of a bird's strike. Shifting my gaze, I am blessed by the site of a blue heron patiently waiting at the base of the falls for its morning feast.

An epiphany flashes. Looking at the falls and the bridge that goes over it, about the length of one vehicle, I realize the bridge makes a tunnel over the water. A tunnel! Its dimensions are equivalent to what I see or rather, what I don't see. I've already scanned my view taking into my scope, a six-degree circle at a time, from my winged water guests up the river, to the tunnel. When looking through that tunnel, I don't see anything surrounding that gap. It's as if I'm looking into a kaleidoscope.

Last year, I decided to get my bike out of storage and get it tuned up. I have a limited amount of early morning time for about eight weeks in the summer. When it's light enough and there isn't traffic in town, I can make my way two blocks through the one intersection in town and safely across to the bike route. With a helmet and safety vest, I embrace the freedom of traveling on my own or with a friend. I long for the day when I live where I no longer have such concerns and can bike my own paths and trails on my own land at a home on a lake.

JUNE 16, 2015

I HAD ANOTHER EPIPHANY when I was riding back into town this morning and I could see through the tunnel, glimpsing my chair. I adore my time on the dock, but on the other side, I had the freedom to ride as I pleased and forget about the tunnel.

Now, I'm at my dock after a seven-mile bike ride. My smile spreads, my soul full with strength and energy as I look forward to what the day will offer. Then, on the other side of the tunnel, I see something familiar. I see me riding my bike as I fly past. I know it's me. I take another sip of my morning coffee and focus directly toward the falls and once again, through the tunnel. There, on the opposite bank of the river, I see me, standing.

"What?" I ask. "What are you telling me?

The me on the other side motions *come here* to me on the dock.

This is crazy! How can I be there and here at the same time? I want to be free. I want to live a normal life again without these stupid limits that I've given myself. Just for one day, could I have that precious gift back again? The one that I took for granted and didn't utilize to reach my full potential? What if I didn't have RP? What if?

One more time, I hear myself calling—

"Come on." The free me motions excitedly. "Let's go!"

Before I can think another thought, I'm transported through time to a new space. I'm me, but I can see! I can fully see! The world is all there and the colors, oh the colors are so vibrant and stunning!

This me has no limits. This me can drive anywhere, anytime, anyplace and do so alone. I don't have to be a burden or take the chance in asking for help. I don't have to worry that I'll be turned down again.

Oh my, I can walk down the street without a cane, without people staring and whispering about the blind woman that just said hello. I can walk into a dark restaurant first before others with my eyes instantly adjusting to the ambiance. I can easily find the public restroom, walk into it, and see where the stalls, sink, soap, and paper towels are. I can see those hazardous yellow picket signs warning of wet floors. I don't have to remember if there was or wasn't a curb outside of that place of business that I just came out of. I don't have to spend five minutes searching for what I just dropped only to find it right next to my foot.

Yes, I saw you wave in my make-believe world and I wave back. See, I'm not stuck up or ignoring you. How beautiful the world is and how precious my eyesight is. One of my biggest thrills is that I can now see the stars, not just the brighter planets, but the millions and millions of stars in the night sky. Oh, how I've missed the big dipper, the shooting stars, and the fireflies.

I'm happy, not just on the outside but within. That deep, dark, dreadful fear is gone. The one where I'm enveloped by the grips of being paralyzed in a cloud that I cannot break away from, and its small opening has closed completely without ever, ever, ever releasing me.

And, in the blink of an eye, I'm back.

My coffee is cold, and I hesitate when the happiness slowly escapes with every breath. But as I inhale, I'm strengthened again by knowing it's okay. It is okay, and I reaffirm my mantra: "I, Pamela, commit to creating a magnificent life, measured by my own chosen standards."

*R*EFLECTION, PRESENT DAY

THE VEERY THRUSH SANG, surrounded by the plethora of swollen buds. One by one, the blooms stretched, enlivened by the tune and readied themselves to expose their hue.

Chapter Forty-One

RECLAIMING THE JOY

The strength of a woman is not measured by the impact that all her hardships in life have had on her; but the strength of a woman is measured by the extent of her refusal to allow those hardships to dictate her and who she becomes.[27]

—C. Joybell C.

JUNE 18, 2015

THE STARS HAVE DISAPPEARED. It makes me so sad, but I am even sadder when the people around me feel bad and stop telling me about the sparkling night sky. I don't want them to stop. It's my way of remembering their glitter.

Saturday night was clear, full of stars, and we were enjoying the campfire with friends. I asked them to describe

---

27   Peta Gayle Oats, *Every Woman Devotional: The Journey to Becoming a Woman of Purpose*, (Jamaica: AuthorHouse, 2014) 76.

it to me, so I didn't forget the sight. One person described a shooting star, and then another laughed at a firefly above my head.

Bring back that joy, I plead with my inner being, the one whom I sometimes believe took my vision away.

It has always been such a calming feeling to be surrounded by this huge universe. I did see two planets on my own, and Donny used the clock directions to show me the big dipper.

"Look straight out from my arm," Donny said, "at about two o'clock."

He extended his arm and I found his shoulder, guiding my hand down his outstretched arm. I looked and looked. I tried so very hard to make my eyes work, but I couldn't see it. I felt his disappointment.

"It's always in my memory," I reassured him.

Now, I live to see the joy and peace in others during those moments. Even though it was dark, the blaze of the campfire glowed on their faces, lighting up my night. My eyes were sensitive to the fire light, so I looked at the tops of the licking flames or found a burning log wrapped in softer tones.

RP hasn't taken that joy away yet.

My mind drifted back into my childhood. I was seven, sitting on the bank of a hill behind Grandpa Lee's farmhouse. The barn stood in the distance and we could hear the peaceful occasional moo of a cow. Not another building was in sight as we enjoyed the warm summer evening, hearing the crickets pipe their mesmerizing evening chirp. My cousins and I stared at the night sky, so bright with sparkling stars that there was barely any darkness. Grandpa focused with joy as he pointed out the different constellations far above us. A million stars flickered and then, there it was. A shooting star!

In his confidence, Grandpa shared about the glory we

had just witnessed in the journey of that star. "It will be a cherished memory for the rest of our lives," he said.

There were several more to follow that night as we watched the sky, but I only remember the first shooting star that came out of the blackness and continued on its path.

It still travels today I'm sure, voyaging through the darkness and creating light. Without the darkness it will not shine. During the daylight, it can't be seen, but it still has a purpose, a powerful energy that continues to burn. The black doesn't matter and on cloudy nights, it persists. It has confidence to continue without being noticed.

Can I learn a lesson from its freedom? Can I find freedom in every moment by thinking a more positive thought? Is there forbearance in realizing that I too can claim joy in my journey? Can I open the door for this caged bird who can't sing and allow my heart to explore its destined path? I have the choice; I am the chooser. Joy is mine when I let go and focus my intentions of being happy.

As I write, I feel the darkness lightening. As I share thoughts and explore depths of my courage, I discover something. I can sing again, because the bars on my self-imposed cage are weakening. And . . .

I can see without sight.

June 21, 2015

While camping, I don't use my cane, several reasons why, mostly, I don't want to explain or talk about it.

"You don't seem blind," is something that I hear too often.

I just want to be normal. Normal! Bring it back.

Bring all my vision back!

At the end of our weekend, I was helping pack up the camper by putting the wheel blocks away. I slammed the bridge of my nose with the storage compartment door that was latched open at a forty-five-degree angle.

Bam, there it was again. RP crashed me back into reality. Was I okay? Yes. Did I break anything? No, somehow the door didn't break my nose or scratch my glasses. Dazed, I felt for blood, but there wasn't any. Donny showed up at my side and another lady, a retired nurse it turned out, gave me a cloth with ice. When I caught my breath from the shock, I was embarrassed and felt guilty for acting normal.

It's better this morning than I thought it would be.

The beams of light are fusing through my periphery, dancing their dance, circling in the darkness. I'm always stumped at why I can see them, but the doctors have told me that it's the retinal reaction of light entering through the tunnel and the brain not knowing how or where it should go. It comforts me slightly.

I declare a new rule. I am no longer responsible for the outside camper duties, setting up or tearing down. I'm safer organizing inside, but once again, I feel RP reprimanding me, telling me to take it slow and be aware, or else.

June 15, 2015

I DO MONTHLY MASSAGE exchanges with Vicki, my friend who originally planted the seed of me becoming a massage therapist. On the way to my massage session north of Walker, Donny stopped the car for me to look at a swamp area filled with hundreds of wild purple Irises. I couldn't see them no matter how hard I tried. My retina cone cells are dying, so I can't tell purple/green. I couldn't even make out their shapes, but Donny stopped, knowing they were my favorite flower.

After searching and trying so hard to see their beauty, and sensing my despair, he calmly described each detail of this precious scene to me. Gradually, my visual mind glimpsed a thought of it. I couldn't see it, but it didn't matter now that he shared the moment. That was so wonderful.

REFLECTION, PRESENT DAY

I've mentioned before that the retina consists of two kinds of cells, rod and cone cells. The rod cells adjust to the light enabling the eyes to see from bright to the dark. My eyes can no longer adjust with the few remaining cells. It's called photophobia or extreme light sensitivity. In glaring light, such as car headlights, I feel pain and there is a halo encircling the light. I must look away to avoid the glare. I've discovered wearing my sunglasses at night helps.

Cone cells are responsible for colors. As my vision deteriorates, I can no longer make the distinction between colors. I think I'm seeing green, but it's probably blue. I think I'm seeing brown, but it's lavender.

After reading the entry for June 15, 2015, I went there again, my eyes weeping and my heart aching as I tried to understand my journey. How could I come to love retinitis pigmentosa?

I've learned to find more comfort in RP being a part of who I am. I am not ashamed of it. I walk proudly with my cane and declare my independence. I've learned to stop, scan, feel security, then move forward.

RP is a part of me, but it's not the whole of who I am.

June 19, 2015

Tim called to tell me he got a job with Nelson Design in Minneapolis. He would have a forty-hour work week as an architectural job captain. I remembered him designing a kitchen in high school, and now, he accomplished his dream.

I'm so very, very proud of him. He's such a wonderful son, husband to Emily, and father to one-year-old Eamon.

July 18, 2015

Alice married her love, Andrew, making for magical memories. The cake topper explained their dream wedding: *Make It So*, a phrase frequently used in Star Trek. The simple yet elegant ceremony was at a park in St. Paul with a backdrop of hydrangea flowers in perfect bloom.

My favorite photo was of all the guests standing on the entrance stairs to the park and cheering. Andrew had dipped Alice back, her bouquet reached toward the ground, and he gave her a prince-charming-type kiss.

The reception was held several blocks away at the Science Museum, where dinosaurs were on display. It made for another fond photo: the wedding party pretending to run away from the giant skeleton of the stegosaurus.

All were seated as the bride and groom glided onto the dance floor and performed an exquisite dance. As honored guests offered their toasts, I prepared to honor the couple with mine.

"Would all the parents, please stand and raise your glasses?" I requested. "Stay standing while the grandparents stand."—I waited—"The wedding party next."

I continued until all were standing except the bride and

groom, glasses raised and looking at them.

"Alice, Andrew," I said, "look around the room. You have gathered together all the ones who love you. We will be lifting you up in positive thoughts throughout your marriage."

REFLECTION, PRESENT DAY

WITH THIS ENTRY, I reclaimed my joy through fond memories that chase away the fear. I felt confidence growing as I continued listening to my Veery Thrush . . . trill, trill, trill, trill.

Chapter Forty-Three

LEARNING TO MAKE A DIFFERENCE

JULY 30, 2015

I JUST GOT OFF the phone from another cherished conversation with Alice, now twenty-nine and a new bride. I shared with her my writing journey and the memory of her diving. She told me how scared she had been to do her first back dive and how she stood at the edge of the board for a long time, composing herself. At the right moment, she had performed the dive and heard the roar of support from her teammates before she had surfaced.

She called to tell me about a show she had just watched about a woman with RP. The lady was given a pair of night goggles and saw the big dipper for the first time in years. My heart just felt a flicker of joy hearing this ray of hope.

Oh, how I miss seeing the stars. I hope to try that someday.

AUGUST 2015

OUR CAMPER IS IN Duluth. I needed some girlfriend time, so I invited Kathy and LuAnn, my high school tripod sisters, as we called ourselves, to join me in a few days of forgetting about the rest of the world.

For two nights, we laughed, drank, shared life, and laughed even more. We played spades until 4:00 A.M., because damn it, LuAnn hated that game and wanted to play more—that's the softer version of what she said.

I need those times with close friends.

I deserve to be happy.

After they left, I wanted more alone time to write my RP story and I told Donny. I felt brave revealing what I needed to accomplish without cowering, stating my desires and not letting judgement enter into my decision.

Out the window, as I sat at the table where I was writing, a windmill spun clockwise, facing into the wind and taking gusts head-on. It harnessed energy, recharging with every pause that the wind allowed. They worked together in their dance toward a shared goal of the moment. Each one knew the other's needs and directed their focus.

There lies my energy for today. I shall embrace it with confidence, joy, and self-promotion.

AUGUST 24, 2015

IT'S A BLUSTERY FORTY-FIVE degrees, and I'm huddled in my camper. It's been almost eighteen months since I wrote in my book. All summer I felt urges and nudges to start again. I made notes on thoughts that occurred to me. Now that I'm spending alone time, I can focus my energy toward that goal.

Words have easily flowed the past few days. I feel at peace being in my writing rhythm.

And then, after I finish writing those meaningful thoughts and positive inspirations, I take up the journal from 1998 and read where I left off.

It sucker punched me once again, and I couldn't breathe when I read details from that year. I spiral down into the depths of the darkness where my RP kept me captive, but I never hit the bottom.

Help me forgive the girl I was.

Keep looking. It's there. Keep going. Don't give up.

Your goal of sharing your story, the RP part of your story, is there.

Don't let the bastard win!

Reflection, Present day

Listen, listen, listen . . . hold on.

September 2015

Six degrees of central vision is not a lot. From where I sit, typing at my computer and looking at the first word of a paragraph, I cannot see the whole paragraph. Down three lines is the range of words. I do not see the whole screen, or my hands perched on the keys, or other items on my desk. My brain tricks me into thinking I can see them all because it has already scanned and entered the data into my brain.

Facebook offers many opportunities to share a sense

of what I see. I found a diagram and posted the version of sight with RP. Many friends were thankful for the insight and commented how they had often wondered. Now, hopefully, they better understand. My heart was greatly touched by the comments and shares by my daughters.

Alice added to her post, "It still never ceases to amaze me just how much you truly can see. Whether it be things you see in other people, things you see in life, or that you can see that eagle flying crazy high in the sky when no one else can. Love you so much! You are so inspiring in what you've done with your life considering this *different ability*."

Sarah said, "For those who ask what my mother's blindness functions like. She has between 4-6 degrees of vision depending on the day. She still runs her own business and functions as a normal person within her environment. I take strength knowing she continues on even on the more challenging days.

When someone asks about my lack of vision, I usually have that person look at me while I bring my hands straight out from my sides, palms pointed toward each other. Slowly I bring them together into the range of where I can see my fingers. It shocks them to see that my hands are merely six inches apart. I see the sympathy enter their eyes. And like always, I share a smile and act as if it's all okay, reaffirming my appreciation for what I can still see.

As I recall the moment later in the day, I will allow my heart to be sad again. I've learned that nobody wants to see my sadness. Nobody wants to hear of my challenges and daily obstacles, so, once again, I smile, brush it off, and change the subject to something of interest to them. Make them happy because in doing so it chases away my emotional darkness, at least the current shadow.

I've joined a writers' group in town. We meet at Common Grounds, a local coffee shop, once a month. Typically, there is a prompt to writing something for our next gathering. This month's prompt is: *And this is the room where it happened—school days.*

I instantly knew I wanted to write a story about Mom's memories teaching in a one room schoolhouse in rural Wisconsin and asked her to jot down some of her favorite memories. I was delighted with the details she shared and more excited when I felt a surge to compose her reminiscences into an amusing story.

"I felt like I was there as a student," one fellow writer encouraged me.

My story was well received by the group, and that gave me a sense of belonging. I realized I can be a writer, an author, and continue my RP journey with confidence.

*S*EPTEMBER 12, 2015

IT WAS MY FORTY-YEAR high school class reunion, and the small town celebrated an "All School Reunion." I couldn't believe that many years had flown by. An incident occurred during the gathering, and I'm surprised I didn't write it in my journal then. But almost a week later, the emotions surfaced, and I found myself wanting to share it.

My class graduated with eighty-two students, and since then, ten have passed away. Twenty came to reminisce and connect again. It seemed as though we had never been away from each other, picking up from where we left off five years before at the last reunion.

We met at the Pump House Bar/Grill in Downing, Wisconsin, a very dark place for me, but I've been there before and kept in mind the layout. While in my "act as if" mode, I negotiated around tables and chairs being assisted by Donny's right elbow. He is so aware of how long it takes for my eyes to adjust to the darker atmosphere, always there at a reach out distance if I need him.

Friends started gathering, hugs and chatter became the event for the evening. Our group relocated to a newly added, very nice outdoor patio area and once again, I needed to adjust as there were multi-levels and steps everywhere. The lightness of the outdoors also burned my eyes while I adjusted to it.

When I felt comfortable, Donny went off to chat with others. Of course, I had my cane, it's a part of me and I sometimes forget that I have it stretched out in front of me. It's so automatic for me to use it to navigate my surroundings. I found myself mostly staying in one area once I got comfortable with it, but there were people I wanted to chat with, and I also had to use the restroom.

I maneuvered inside and toward the darkest part of the bar where the restrooms were. I paused as my eyes took their time to adjust. I needed to wait, which seemed like forever, for the slow transition of the remaining central rod cells in my retina to adjust. Once confident in my direction and path, I proceeded. Into the women's I went, where once again, with the change in lighting, I was thrown into night. I knew from before there were two stalls. Hopefully they hadn't remodeled there also. I now needed to decide if any were empty.

Suddenly, the bathroom door slammed open and a classmate yelled, "Pam, you're in the wrong bathroom!" and laughed hysterically with a small crowd she'd gathered to watch the performance.

Shocked and ashamed over being different and not good enough, I tell myself, *Shrug it off. Don't let them see your pain. Be tough and smile.*

As I returned, they told me how wonderfully I could take a joke. Could I? Did they see the inside of me crumbled? In a flash, I was back in high school days, being treated the same rude way. And then, I was neither blind nor did I know about RP. I had never been accepted as part of the group.

Pick yourself back up, I told myself. *Keep your smile.*

I walked to where I had been, trying to remember where the door was. Still smiling, I reached it and went outside into bright blindness rather than dark. ARGH!

As the evening progressed, I had great conversations until I needed to use the restroom again. I shouldn't have had so many beers, but anyway, off I went. And did I even think to look for the crowd I wanted to avoid? No! I approach the women's restroom.

One called out, "Pam, I want a picture of you going into the men's bathroom!"

OMG, are you serious? Okay, smile, show them what they want. They can't see the pain, the hurt, or the collapsing of my spirit. Be a part of their so wonderful crowd.

So, I did, but that wasn't enough. Through the mocking and laughter, another shouted, "Push the door open!"

Did I have a choice? Part of me wanted to tell them how horrible they made me feel, to show them how degraded and rejected they made me feel. Just like in high school. But, no. *Don't hurt anyone else. Take the pain. Take the humiliation. Let them have their fun.* I opened the door and the cackling got louder as they saw another surprised classmate using the facility.

I felt numb and wandered. I was crushed and found myself looking for Donny. I found him and put on the 'everything's okay' face. Yup, everything was just fine.

As the evening progressed, several people decided to take the party out to the street. It was still an early evening. The streets would have selective lighting with many, many overwhelming dark areas. I wouldn't be able to see faces or obstacles. They would be there, and I knew Donny would be on my left. Didn't he get tired of being my constant guide, of always watching for harm's way?

I was tired, tired of the abuse and tired of acting normal. There were still classmates going who I would have loved to be with, ones who haven't seen my humiliation.

RP won, once again, and I told Donny I wanted to leave. We said our goodbyes. A few of the pranksters said again what a good sport I was. *Am I?* Evidently, I hid my pain well, once again . . . once again . . . once again . . .

Chapter Forty-Three

HEALING WATERS

SEPTEMBER 2015

WE BOUGHT TWO KAYAKS and took our maiden voyage on Mabel Lake. It was so peaceful being surrounded by nothing but nature, listening to the ripples in the water as the paddles pushed us along. Two loons kept their distance, but occasionally came closer. An eagle soared overhead, adding to our excitement.

It didn't take long for us to find an easy and comforting rhythm. Donny was concerned over keeping me safe, but he also worried about himself seeing that this was his first experience.

I was comfortable because of my experience in high school. I'd learned in a kayak my dad and brother made. The sensations returned to my mind from those adventures, and I'm looking forward to having more throughout the coming years.

OCTOBER 2015

WE TOOK A FOUR-DAY no-destination vacation early in the month. The only reason we returned so early was because we ran out of our medications. We giggled about realizing we must be old.

Earlier in the year, Donny had read an article about a sixty-foot underground waterfall in Harmony, Minnesota near the southern border. That was our first stop.

Going down into a cave with slippery steps, turns, twists, and new directions, I felt like I was physically climbing into my cavern of utter despair and darkness thoughts about my blindness.

"I've got you," Donny reassured me. "You won't need your cane."

I trusted him completely. He would be there for me, being my eyes.

Our small group followed the well-informed guide through many paths and stairways pointing out the intricate displays of interest along the way. Very early in our tour, he pointed up a small stairwell.

"If any of you have decided that you don't want to go further," he said, "now is your chance to go back to the top."

I tugged at Donny giving the signal that I preferred to do that. The darkness was overwhelming and claustrophobic. He looked deeply into my eyes in the dim light and without a word my fears melted away. I could do this. I was going to do this. And off we went.

Throughout, the caves had strung lights assisting us. As we went further down into the cave, we could hear a dull rumble, a familiar sound of a distant waterfall. Enchanted, we were filled with anticipation of seeing this natural phenomenon.

"While trying to find a lost pig," informed our guide, "a young boy could hear its squealing underground."

The story went on about how he went into the cave to retrieve his pig and discovered the underground waterfall, which flowed below the surface all the way to Iowa.

Surprisingly, my eyes seemed to adjust as we went even deeper into the cave. At one point our guide made sure everyone was secure in their positions and shut off the lights putting our scenery into total darkness. The small group oohed and aahed, but for me it was an everyday occurrence.

I found great strength in that adventure and a deeper love and appreciation for Donny.

October 15, 2015

I was reading through some of the entries on the Facebook retinitis pigmentosa support group and came across a posting talking about photopsia. My personal fireworks display, as I called it, had a name. I've asked eye doctors about the lights and have never received an answer.

Reflection, Present day

According to a web search, the definition of photopsia is: "Hallucinatory perceptions such as sparks, lights or colours arising in the absence of light stimuli and observed when the eyes are closed. They occur often as a result of diseases of the optic nerve, retina (e.g., retinal and vitreous detachment) or the brain, migraine, or they can also occur with pressure upon the closed eye."[28]

October 15, 2015, continued

I have photopsias now, constantly. It reminds me of a pebble hitting the water and the rings ever growing and expanding. At other times, the beams of bright light swirl in paisley or yin/yang shapes, spiraling around my central vision. Whenever I move my focus and the light changes the ripples are stronger for a moment until my eyes adjust. This happens, for instance, when I look around the room and the sun shines through the window.

My pulsing kaleidoscope flecks are also in constant view, surrounding my central focus. It makes life a dizzy swirl that I constantly adjust to. I don't know when they appeared more frequently, but 20 years ago, it was only a few beams at a time and nothing noticeable as far as pulsating light. Now, I have my very own fireworks show all the time, but I still can't see the stars.

Another phenomenon with vision loss is Charles Bonnet Syndrome:

> "The experience of complex visual hallucinations in a person with partial or severe blindness. First described in 1760, it was first introduced into English-speaking psychiatry in 1982. Visual release hallucinations as seeing people and objects that aren't there, but the brain makes them

---

28 Millodot: Dictionary of Optometry, "photopsia," https://medical-dictionary.thefreedictionary.com/photopsia.

occur."[29]

I've had this for years but couldn't explain what was happening. I also had a fear of people thinking I was crazy. I'll see a quick scene, less than a split second, of a person, object, something out of context that I know is not there. I've seen a boy in a red wagon, people walking past, someone sitting in a chair—

I blink, and it's gone.

These two side effects of RP have greatly increased these past few years and are mostly just annoying. I'm blessed to have as much central vision left as I do.

"Focus on the central; focus on now," I whisper to myself. "Don't fret about what you don't have and where you want to be."

An RP friend on Facebook, Dave Steele, The Blind Poet from the United Kingdom, has given me permission to share one of his many beautiful poems.[30] Every sentence tells of how and what I'm feeling. Here is a part of one that I would like to share.

If My Eyes Could See Nothing

by Dave Steele

If my eyes could see nothing, they wouldn't hurt from glare.
I wouldn't be affected by the way that people stare.
If my eyes could see nothing, wouldn't feel misunderstood, cause in their eyes I'd look just like they think a blind

---

29   Better Health Channel, "Eyes – Charles Bonnet syndrome," Reviewed on November 26, 2012, https://www.betterhealth.vic.gov.au/health/conditionsandtreatments/ eyes-charles-bonnet-syndrome.

30   Dave Steel's website: https://theblindpoet.net

man should.

If my eyes could see nothing, at night time I could sleep. Not lay here on my pillow thinking future thoughts so deep.

If my eyes could see nothing, there's so much I would miss. Reactions on my children's face each time I hug and kiss.

If my eyes could see nothing, I know I'd be alright. My journey through this tunnel taught me to always keep the fight.

If my eyes could see nothing, same person I would be. I know now that I'm so much more, than what I'm blind to see.

November 2015

MY FRIEND, KIM, WAS on my mind one day, and I woke remembering a dream that seemed meant for her. I couldn't wait to let her know about it and sent her an email—

Hello dear Soul Sister, Kim.

Once again you are topmost in my mind. I feel that your healing is steady but needs a boost. So, on my knees I go and talk to the powers above to surge another dose of great nutrition and healing so that you physically feel its instantaneous power.

As I meditated this morning on my prayer chain, I saw a vision of fish swimming up my river toward the waterfall. The waters were shimmering with their healing powers. The fish were sluggish and very, very dark, black even. As they ventured and moved the little they could, the darkness lightened and seemed to slither off their bodies in big sheets. This change created more strength, more energy, and more passion for their desire to pursue their greatest wish, to be rid of the heaviness that enshrouded them.

The closer they moved toward the falls, the more they splashed. The fish felt great excitement as they continued their upstream venture. Seeing the effects of their movement, the fish dodged the shed scales, creating more energy, excitement, and great joy. Toward the top of the falls, beams of shimmering light reach toward those seeking healing power.

There, my friend, I found you, wrapped in the healing arms of love that flow for us all. Be well dear one and feel the warmth of love surrounding you as you heal.

Blessings,

Pamela

This visual revelation toward healing, sent in email to my friend, is one that I also need. Physically it would be wonderful, but emotionally and spiritually it is also as important to help me feel the day's journey.

Chapter Forty-Four

FIND YOUR CENTER

Have no anxiety about anything, but in everything by prayer and supplication with thanksgiving let your requests be made known to God.

—Philippians 4:6[31]

JANUARY 1, 2016

EVEN THOUGH IT IS only sixteen degrees and still dark, I trudge through yesterday's deep steps in the snow toward my dock, guided by my flashlight. The crunch of the snow, the crispness of the air, the lull of the waterfall as the river flows, all give me a sense of peace, a quiet calm. I'm truly blessed to be where I am in this moment surrounded by nature's loving embrace.

A few inches of snow rest on my Adirondack chair. I brush the accumulation into the flow as clumps, as mini icebergs,

---

31 Nelson, *The Holy Bible*

gently follow the direction of the stream. My flashlight beacon shines like a lighthouse. I watch and settle into the chair, thankful for the morning's quietness as the town has not yet awakened.

My first sips of coffee warm me from the inside out as I cup the mug in my mitten-covered hands. I breathe in the aroma and welcome the warm steam filling my nostrils. I take a few more sips, relishing this "me moment," where the world's events are far away.

Afterward, I venture up the slight embankment toward the house and can't resist flopping myself backward, arms outstretched, into the nine inches of fresh snow.

Whoomp!

My bottom is much heavier than the rest of me and it sinks into a hole trapping my arms and legs straight up. Boots and mittens are all that appear. Oh my, what a sight I must be as I wiggle them, trying to escape. I'm glad no one else is watching as I force the rest of my body into the depths of the snow. I'm delighted as I first notice the crescent moon, gazing at me, winking in glee at me.

As I outstretch my arms and legs, while sinking them deeper, they fall into rhythm, pushing against the snow as if doing jumping jacks. A snow angel, one of my favorite winter activities. This is the first of the season. A few more strokes and trying not to wreck the creation, I realize my head is downhill, and I struggle to find the momentum to stand. I try to get up once, twice, still no success.

Help, I've fallen, and I can't get up, I want to shout, but I'm alone.

Giggling to myself and the moon, I roll onto my side, which takes several attempts, ruin my desired creation, brush myself off, and give thanks for the beginnings of a bright new year.

400

✳ ✳ ✳

DURING MY JOURNALING, I venture back to recollect the past year, 2015. Emotions are swirling as I ride the ups and downs like a roller coaster of highlighted entries. I had so much hope, so much focus, and so much clarity in my destination for last year, yet none of my goals came to fruition. But they are still my heart's desires.

What do I focus on now? Do I continue toward those goals? Do I surrender?

No, I can't, although I am open to where and what I hear as my calling. Today is going to be a great day, and, as Alice and Andrew's wedding cake topper stated, *Make It So.*

✳ ✳ ✳

EAMON IS SEVENTEEN MONTHS old and loves to turn in circles.

If he's too close to bumping into something, Emily gently says, "Find your center."

He pauses, looks for where he started, moves toward that point, then continues spinning until he gets dizzy and falls.

I'm discovering this phrase is a great motivation when I'm frustrated with my RP, not seeing something, losing something, or adjusting to the light changes. Stop, find your center, then carry on. But maybe I'll avoid the spinning till I'm dizzy part.

FEBRUARY 2, 2016

TIM'S ICE SCULPTING TEAM won first place with their magnificent display of a huge Ferris wheel at this year's competition during the Saint Paul Winter Carnival. His team of four has competed for seven years, and they've won third place and second place. This year was the first win for the team.

I'm very proud of his dedication and determination at accomplishing such a feat with limited time and blocks of ice.

My sewing machine tension has been acting up, and I need to take it in for adjusting. The place I usually take it, takes two weeks. A friend at Loving Hands Community Quilting told me of a place in Bemidji that will repair it the same day if they can. I'm busy sewing a quilt for a friend and would like to finish it.

I so (tempted to spell it sew) enjoy sewing and the sense of accomplishment after seeing what I can do. My tunnel focus and techniques learned thrill me. I'm electrified by everything I have created in the past several years from queen size quilts, baby quilts, t-shirt quilts, blue jean quilts, flannel pajamas, lap quilts, q-willows, and more. The list is unbelievable when I look through my three-ring binder that has details of each item.

My vision and RP are compatible with this discovery. A deep sense of joy and eagerness enfold me throughout each item. My current project is room-darkening curtains for Eamon's bedroom. It's a bit tricky, but I have most of the four panels finished. I was so honored to be asked to make them.

February 16, 2016

My morning coffee at the dock in twenty-five-degree weather was inspirational. I could see one planet shining brilliantly and watching over me. I think it might have been Venus. The thousands of stars are there also, but I cannot see them anymore. But I don't want to dwell on how that loss feels to my heart. I must go on, listen . . . I can listen to the darkness of the morning, its calming comfort, and the promise of a joy filled full-of-opportunities day.

The low water in the river babbles, caressing every stone. I remember my Aunt Connie sharing the joy she had at the babbling brook on the Allram farm.

"Listen," she whispered, "Listen to it's reassuring calmness."

There's a gentle breeze this morning rustling the stiff brittle stalks of last year's tall grass along the bank. As the yard light shines, I can see the path of the mink's tracks through the snow along the shore.

Life can be full of sadness, but joy and blessings are everywhere. God's gifts abound. I will open my heart and focus on them today. Heart is my gratitude word for today. I remember a client showed me his favorite way to hug dear friends. Instead of leaning toward the left, you lean toward the right so that your hearts are touching during the embrace. *Heart Hugs* is what he called it. I plan to pass them on.

MARCH 2016

I DELIGHTED IN THE thirty degrees this beautiful morning on the dock, and I could see the planets Jupiter, Saturn, and Mars. At 5:54 A.M., the space station passed over from the west to the northeast for five minutes. Its course, from my position, took it behind the big white pine on the opposite side of the river. Simultaneously, a pair of geese circled three times honking their morning praise. Priceless.

I miss my pair of geese, Gary and Gladys. They didn't spend the summer with me last year. I expected Gladys to make her way here to the security of the river before the lake froze, but she never came. My ducks are also gone, leaving me alone throughout the winter months. A few fowl have landed for a while, but they don't stay.

I have my mind on too many things and need to remind myself to concentrate, focus. I have tripped going up the stairs and also missed the last step going down this past week. I have to remember to count them, always, to stop before I climb and look at each one, because I do not use my cane in the house. I should purchase rope lighting and line the stairs with them. That would help.

* * *

Yesterday, I was having a delightful phone conversation with a friend when she asked what I was doing. She heard rustling in the background—me going up and down the stairs.

"I'm looking for my phone," I said in despair.

She laughed loudly and said, "You're talking to me on it!"

At first, I blamed my RP for placing my phone in an unusual spot. I'm normally disciplined at organizing and keeping items in their homes to make my search easier.

April 2016

Spring biking has once again been a wonderful freeing experience. My neighbor, Kathy, has joined me several times this year as we prepare to attend the Run Around Woman Lake in the bike category and ride eighteen miles. She wears padded bicycle pants helping her endure the longer distances. That sounds like a great idea.

While shopping at a bike shop, I thought I would try on a pair of padded bike pants. Donny watched me as I navigated the dimly lit hall with obstructions toward the changing room using my cane. As I entered the room, my cane caught on the 2x4 door frame on the floor.. I tried to stop, but my momentum kept me going forward. As I fell into the dark unknown, my metal cane snapped. I twisted my knee on the fall.

Shocked, embarrassed, and blaming my stupid RP, I found that Donny was right there to help me up. The store employee dashed away to help other customers. Anyway, my knee turned out to be fine and Donny taped my cane until I could order a new one.

May 8, 2016

I DID IT! I biked 18.87 miles in 1:37:38 in 54 degrees. Kathy and I were toward the front of the biking group at the beginning, although we were both hoping to be in the back.

The first miles were hills on Highway 84. Each of us encouraged the other as we watched faster bikers pass us, but the slower ones were far behind. Highway 11 was a smoother route, then we connected with our familiar highway 5. I felt exhilaration as we approached the finish line, watching the gathered crowd cheer us on.

My daughter, Alice, along with two of her friends had come to enter the five-mile race while spending the weekend. This was Alice's first race ever, and she ran without ever practicing. She came in fifth place in her age category, a feat that she was thrilled with. Her friend, Kristin, came in fourth place, and Melissa chose to enter in the five-mile walk.

June 13, 2016

IT's OUR FIRST ADVENTURE with the camper for the season. While setting up and getting things in their place, I discovered the shampoo and conditioner bottles had tipped over in the bathroom cabinet and spilled into the sink, over the counter, and onto the floor. What a mess. Bubbles were everywhere as I wiped.

I cleaned it up, but as I wiped my final dry pass with a paper towel, I accidentally turned on the water. I didn't notice it and went outside to visit with friends.

Much later, after we got back from eating supper in town, I entered the camper to a flooded bathroom. The holding tank, which holds 60 gallons, had filled, along with the shower bottom. Water overflowed into the bedroom carpet and underneath to the storage compartment. It was just making progress toward the steps near the front door when we returned.

Donny opened up the grey water tank to drain while I found towels to mop up. A friend gave us her fan to use after offering more towels to mop up. No major damage was done.

"I have the cleanest camper of all!" I declared afterward as I pushed away any thoughts of blaming RP.

JULY 11, 2016

LAUGHTER IS THE BEST medicine for chasing away blues. I just spent last weekend with my favorite friends, Kathy and LuAnn. My sides are sore from all the antics we find in the silliest things.

Kathy's new cabin was on a lake in Wisconsin. She had two huge floats, as big as the raft, shaped like swans for us to ride on. We were quite the unexpected sight to the others who, enjoying their pontoons on the lake, drifted by. They enjoyed our entertainment.

Kathy and I went on a three-hour kayak ride early Saturday morning. The lake was calm before the sunrise in the east, and we glided on silk, breathing in the freshness of the new day. We ventured through lily pads and watched an eagle observing us from his perch in an old dead white pine.

As we maneuvered our kayaks along the shoreline, she traveled to one of her favorite hiding places on the lake. Ahead were several aged weeping willows cascading their branches down to the water. We easily slid through their gated streams and rested in their embrace. This was her favorite reading spot, an escape from all, where the quiet of the morning seemed most vibrant.

On our return trek, a pair of loons guarded their two offspring from us. The dad danced his dance upon the water, displaying his elegant winged outreach. His call distracted us from the mom who was guiding the young in the opposite direction.

For the remainder of the day, we delighted in pontoon rides, swam, enjoyed the blaze of campfire, grilled delicious meals, drank, laughed, and walked, but mostly we reunited in our strong abiding friendship.

July 12, 2016

Donny is seventy today. He didn't want any big plans, so I am just arranging for supper out with a few friends.

This morning while I was on my dock, I saved a baby duck entangled in a fishing line. The mom was going crazy until I noticed it. Oh my. I stepped into the water and was able to gently reach it. The soft yellow down felt wonderful in the palm of my hand. It surrendered, somehow knowing I was only there to help. While I worked to free it, the mother flew at me several times, once hitting me in the head. With ease, I released its wing and leg from the lines and freed it back into the river, where it skidded off to the comfort of its mother's wings.

July 26, 2016

I'm retiring on October 1. I'm so very excited I've made this decision. During this summer, I have been thinking a lot about spending more time with Donny and how we can do the things I want to do. With him turning seventy, I realize life is short and there are adventures I want to experience while our health is still good. I'm already receiving Social Security disability, so financially, it won't be so bad.

July 30, 2016

Sarah is visiting and I'm elated. I love when my children visit, knowing their hectic lives make the opportunities few and far between. I'll cherish our joyous time together.

Yesterday, we loaded both kayaks into the truck and Donny drove us to the boat landing on Little Boy Lake. Sarah and I savored gliding through the channel and escaping into Lake Wabedo, the lake where she and I spent much of her younger life.

We paddled, smelled, and relished the abundance of nature, and Sarah wanted to show me a sheltered area that she had been told about by a neighbor when we lived there. A lagoon, secluded from the world by a secret very narrow passage, led us to a new world that we hadn't experienced before. We were in the midst of a large circle, outlined with tall cattails giving warmth to the embankment of the shore. Birds twittered, continuing on in their song as if we had always been a part of this scene.

"Listen... listen... listen..." the Veery Thrush welcomes us to where she lives, from where I heard it calling those many years before, singing a song of hope, of believing, of strength. I hear it. I embrace it. I'm filled with it once again.

While living on Lake Wabedo in the 1980's, we never had a boat, canoe, or kayak, nothing that allowed us the experience of the water, not like this. Tears came to my eyes, tears of joy outpouring as I felt nature engulf us and invite us to live this precious moment.

*A*UGUST 2016

WITH A GRATEFUL HEART, I was honored to be requested to sing at my brother-in-law, Doug Audette's, funeral. Donny's sister, Nancy, told me that he loved my voice and had always commented at other funerals that he would love to have me sing at his. I wish I would have known that this summer when his health was failing. I would have sung for him anytime.

One of the songs requested by the family was *Grandpa* by the Judds, *Precious Lord, Take My Hand,* and *It is Well with My Soul.* It was a little difficult singing as I looked into the congregation and saw tears from several grandchildren. I humbly say that my singing was filled with emotion emphasizing each word. It was like an out of body experience. I'm so honored to be blessed with God's gifts as I thoroughly enjoy singing.

This month, we also attended a funeral of one of Donny's classmates, which made my retirement seem that much more crucial. As the date gets closer, I'm more excited. I've realized something very important in my RP vision journey. Throughout the many, many years, I've lived with RP by taking care of others through massage. Now for the first time since 1991, I will be able to take care of myself. I'll be able to relax into it and discover me, who I really am.

I've been asked to play flute for one of the pieces for the Longville Area Community Choir Christmas concert that I sing with. Our annual concert is the first Sunday in December with weekly practices resuming in September. It'll feel good to limber up my lip and play again.

Earlier in the month, Queen Mary gathered her Fair Maidens for another frolic at Camelot where she lives on Leech Lake. Throughout the year, I secretly requested each Fair Maiden to create a design on a quilt block that I gave them. During the winter, I quilted these together and we presented it to the Queen.

October 2016

LOVE'S ENERGY SURROUNDED ME yesterday as I celebrated my retirement. I'm overwhelmed by the close to ninety people who came to congratulate me. I cried when my brother Steve walked in, traveling five hours. Mom was too weak to make the trip. So many moments are etched into my memory that I will always cherish. Donny was extraordinary with every detail and even signed my guest book.

"Pamela, the love of my life, may we enjoy these times together always. You worked hard to get here. Love you, Don."

Alice wrote, "You are my role model. I'm so incredibly proud of you!"

It Felt Love

by Hafiz

How
Did the rose
Ever open its heart

And give to this world
All its
Beauty?

It felt the encouragement of light
Against its
Being,

Otherwise,
We all remain

Too

Frightened."[32]

---

32 Ladinsky, *The Gift*, 121

Chapter Forty-Five

AT PEACE

And then it happens . . . One day you wake up and you're in this place. You're in this place where everything feels right. Your heart is calm. Your soul is lit. Your thoughts are positive. Your vision is clear. You're at peace, at peace with where you've been, at peace with what you've been through and at peace with where you're headed.[33]

—*The Mind Journal*

*D*ECEMBER 2016

MY MOTHER MADE HER transition to be with Dad. It was such a painful process to watch her osteoporosis crumble her physical body. She never lost her sense of joy and enthusiasm for every person who entered her room during those final

---

33   Megan Margery, "And Then it Happens. . . One Day You Wake Up And You're In This Place," The Mind Journal (website), Accessed May 19, 2021, https://themindsjournal.com/and-then-it-happens-one-day-you-wake-up-and-youre-in-this-place/.

weeks. She praised and showed her appreciation for each visitor she greeted. Never did I hear her complain of pain or of her circumstance.

"What's your pain level?" the nurse would ask.

"Oh, what was it last time, a 7?" She smiled and replied, "Let's go with that again."

During my final moments with her before she lapsed into a coma, I had Donny take a picture of our hands clasped in love. My tears flowed.

"God is with us," she said.

A few hours later, my niece Jennifer gave her a taste of maple nut ice cream, her favorite.

"Yum" was her final word.

I was gently inspired to speak at her funeral. I spoke of her whole life's message. She loved life, loved playing games, and loved supporting and appreciating everyone she knew. I never heard a curse word or anger from her.

While going through her items, my brother, sisters, and I were surprised to find eight watches. Each one was gold with a dead battery. I shared that each one was a precious chapter in her life that she cherished, and instead of changing the battery, she got a new one. Each watch captured a moment in her time. What wonderful stories and memories each one holds.

I miss her deeply but feel her presence often. Her lessons of love and kindness to all remind me to enjoy every moment and every breath. God is with us.

Yum!

*A*PRIL 2017

ALICE DISCOVERED A WEBSITE that sells enchroma glasses for color blindness. Although, after taking the test for color vision, I discovered they are only for red/green color blindness. This test showed I have blue/yellow color blindness. I guess that's nice to know, proof that I'm really not seeing normal. I was tested as having tritan-type color blindness or tritanomaly/tritanopia.[34] Hmmm, interesting.

At my mammogram, the attendant called my name and with a startled, shocked look at my cane replied, "I promise I'll be good!"

Time stood still as I recalled how hurtful those reactions had once been. I'd be upset for days, letting darkness enter again. Not this time. I gave her a half smile relaying that I didn't appreciate the comment, and then followed her for the procedure.

My tender inner being from the past glows as I realize the achievement I've made.

I am no longer in the depths of darkness that tormented me. It's none of my business what others think of me, what is my business, is what I think of myself. I am worthy. I've found great delight in each moment of my many paths, I delight in being happy with myself and expect to revel in each new segment of the day. I've found great joy and can now see the lightening of my burdens—so many years of a heavy heart,

---

34 "Types of Color Blindness," National Eye Institute, updated June 26, 2019, https://www.nei.nih.gov/learn-about-eye-health/eye-conditions-and-diseases/color-blindness/types-color-blindness. According to the National Eye Institute, this blue-yellow type of color blindness is less common type that makes it hard to discern between blue and green (tritanomaly) and between yellow and red. Tritanopia makes colors look less bright and the affected person will be unable to differentiate between blue and green, purple and red, and yellow and pink.

dark feelings, and negativity.

The once hurt girl is smiling. I am valuable. I am loved. I enjoy every moment. I know and allow my desires. I attract only positive well-being. My resistance to feeling happy has been released. For the first time, I am at peace with me.

Chapter Forty-Six

HEART AND SOUL

HOPE IS A THING WITH FEATHERS

by Emily Dickinson

Hope is the thing with feathers
That perches in the soul,
And sings the tune without the words,
And never stops at all,

And sweetest in the gale is heard;
And sore must be the storm
That could abash the little bird
That kept so many warm.

I've heard it in the chilliest land,
And on the strangest sea;
Yet, never, in extremity,
It asked a crumb of me.[35]

---

[35] Publisher's note: "Hope is the thing with feathers" by Emily Dickinson is in the public domain.

*J*UNE 2017

THE EVENING SETTLES INTO its gentle sway, remembering all the events of the day while allowing them to flow gently with the stream. They bob from one joy to the next, one moment to the next. Each scene is a picturesque part of my being.

The Veery Thrush's evening whisper tells of appreciation for the day. It's there now, I hear it. Every cell of my body dances in its song spreading goosebumps of joy. Sing to me again. Sing your song of love, of manifestation, of desires.

And there, with the last beacons of light from the setting sun, I see her sitting within the branches of my bush, and I glimpse my first bud now open, full in its splendor, just for me. More blossoms of beautiful pink roses release a mesmerizing aroma, transporting me into grateful bliss. At the soul of each flower is the shape of a heart and my heart explodes with joy. I feel as if I'm embraced by a heart hug.

Be well in your well-being with love energy. "The more love you receive, the more love you have to give," my Veery Thrush sings. Therein is my joy.

*J*ULY 2017

WHILE ON MY DOCK, I felt a gentle nudge to glance over my left shoulder into the building next door that used to be my church. I saw a shadow of me, years ago, sitting in the pews of the church staring out the window at this waterfall. I was about to go homeless and probably have to give up custody of my children in 1989 before my diagnosis.

As I gave up total control to God, I had a view of this very same waterfall that is now in my backyard. God knew then that this would be my home. The gentle thought this morning gave me such deep strength, courage, clarity, joy, and uplifting. My desires are worthy. I can enjoy the journey of my guided path in every moment with appreciation and satisfaction.

This is going to be fun. I can enjoy the best idea I ever had about me. I can allow myself to be and do who I am. I've enjoyed delicious moments at my piano and also playing my native flute. I'm going to play my other flute, my keyboard, and even my mandolin that hasn't seen light in years. It's time for my music to flow again, for me to open up the blockage, and maybe I'll be inspired to write songs again.

I can allow me to be who I am in every facet of my kaleidoscope life. This is not the end; this is just the beginning of the real me.

I remember the scene in *A Muppet Christmas Carol*, which I play every time I make lefse. Scrooge realizes, after the three spirits visit, that he has awakened, and he didn't miss Christmas morning.

I feel just like that, giddy with excitement in my new day, my new now. I'm listening to the radio and it is appropriately playing *I Can See Clearly Now*. And yes, it is going to be a bright, sunshiny day.

Something opened in my being, letting go, and I want to share this joy with the world. My emotions are overflowing with so many thoughts and desires. I have so much to share in my joy. Nothing has happened, yet everything has happened. My soul feels lighter, floating in love. All doubt and worry have been let go with love energy.

I feel I am finally the me who has come through a journey, who has trodden a path of stepping-stones guiding me, if I only listen, listen, listen to a powerful inner being who loves me so much, always has, and always will. I'm eager, exhilarated, excited, and filled with joy for my future travels. I'm ready, and I welcome my whispering path.

Joy is my word for this journey, for every breath I take will be a thank you for the appreciation of deep love growing and radiating from within me. It's me, without the fear, the doubt, or the challenges. It's me in my freedom who makes choices for my joy and who expects a belly laugh every day.

I am enjoying daily miracles and know that I am never alone. I am loved unconditionally for just being me. Even better than seeing it is feeling this love from the source that surrounds me, keeping me satisfied with where I am and eager for more.

I saw stars yesterday for the first time in over ten years. At first, I noticed two planets, which I never lost sight of, but they didn't seem big enough, then, ever so slowly, as if time stopped, I saw five stars come into focus. I was afraid to blink or look away. Was I really seeing them? Joy filled me and the knowledge that, yes, I was.

Chapter Forty-Seven

THIS IS A NEW DAY

AUGUST 2017

I BOB AND DRIFT along in my kayak, feeling the freedom, ease, and joy my morning activity brings to a life filled with wonderment. The clouds open and mesmerize me as I drift in the middle of the lake, feeling like I could soar into the sky. An eagle also soared high, circling on the gusts of wind, expanding its flight, gliding a figure eight, and going higher and higher until it vanished within a peak of a billowing white cloud.

While sitting quietly and enjoying the shoreline reeds, I watched two small birds looking for bugs. One of the birds was as small as a child's fist, fluffy with hints of yellow. Two pileated woodpeckers traveled from tree to tree pecking their rhythms. A pair of loons sang their song as if kissing the morning with heart love.

The next morning while in my kayak, I was surrounded by fog. I was in a cloud, no shore in sight and not worried, only experiencing total joy. The shore would come eventually as I let myself be engulfed, letting go, as I had in my dream of soaring on an eagle. I was thankful for the moment of now and the now to come, feeling thoroughly satisfied.

Traveling through so many facets of my life, through its contentment, discovery, pushing onward, stepping back, trials, hurting, and finding my joy is a journey in which I wouldn't change a single thing. Through each contrast, I now know and can clearly see the growth that I needed to discover for myself, to continue on, to find my inner peace and who I was. Who I *am*. I've found that, and I have a deep desire to allow it to blossom. My path is forward, toward, well, who knows? I do know that it will be a great adventure with many delights.

The future horizon is ahead, and I travel toward the light that illuminates joy. Facets of my kaleidoscope shine brightly, encourage me, fill me with deep joy and satisfaction. My journey thus far sparkles and enlightens every blessed moment within each facet.

Retinitis pigmentosa is a condition I have. Someday, as Dr. Poland said, there will be a cure. Until then, I have gathered my tools to adjust to each challenge that comes, find a solution—there's always a solution; a perfect soul-ution—and embrace the next segment. I don't have a disability, but rather, possibilities . . . possABILITIES. Look at what I can do!

Looking through a kaleidoscope that has flashing frequent fireworks is how my world shines. I pause and give thanks for this delightful journey, embracing me forever with . . .

HEART HUGS!

About the Author

PAMELA EDWARDS HAS WRITTEN this poignant book about her life's journey with retinitis pigmentosa. In sharing her story, she hopes to help anyone who has been diagnosed with RP to know there is light at the end of a long, sometimes scary, yet rewarding tunnel. This book is to also help their loved ones understand the journey the person is on. Throughout the book Pamela shows that she is a strong and resilient woman.

Her family is very important to her. They have been supportive during her journey, upholding her when she needed it and celebrating her successes. She has learned through her journey she can do more than she originally believed possible: composing music, quilting, kayaking, and much more.

Pamela lives in Longville with her husband and enjoys all the wonders of nature in northern Minnesota. She enjoys friends and quiet times beside the river in her backyard.

You may reach her at pamelaedwardsauthor@gmail.com.

Bibliography

Berry, Wendell. *New and Collected Poems*. (Berkeley: Counter Point): 2012.

Better Health Channel (website). "Eyes – Charles Bonnet syndrome." Reviewed November 26, 2012. Accessed May 19, 2021. https://www.betterhealth.vic.gov.au/health/conditionsandtreatments/eyes-charles-bonnet-syndrome.

Driscoll, Michael. *A Child's Introduction to Poetry (Revised and Updated): Listen While You Learn About the Magic Words That Have Moved Mountains, Won Battles, and Made Us Laugh and Cry*. (United States: Running Press): 2020.

Dyer, Wayne W. *The Power of Intention: Learning to Co-create Your World Your Way*. (United States: Hay House): 2010.

Hay, Louise L. *You Can Heal Your Life*. (California: Hay House): 2006.

Hirschenberg, "Solid Goldie," Vanity Fair (March 1992): 220, Accessed May 13, 2021. https://archive.vanityfair.com/article/1992/3/solid-goldie.

Klein, Traci. "Slipping away, Disease slowly takes woman's sight." *Leader-Telegram*, November 24, 1993, https://newspaperarchive.com/eau-claire-leader-telegram-nov-24-1993-p-14/.

Hafiz. *I Heard God Laughing: Poems of Hope and Joy*, trans. David Ladinsky. (United States: Penguin Publishing Group): 2006.

———. *The Gift: Poems by Hafiz the Great Sufi Master,* trans. David Ladinsky. New York: Penguin Compass, 2014.

Hirschenberg, Lynn. "Solid Goldie." Vanity Fair (March 1992). Retrieved May 19, 2021 from https://archive. vanityfair.com/article/1992/3/solid-goldie.

Longfellow, Henry Wadsworth. "The Rainy Day" Henry Wadsworth Longfellow, Maine Historical Society, Accessed May 19, 2021. http://www.hwlongfellow.org.

Majethia, Niti. *The Battle Cry: A Little Book of Comfort and Strength*. United States: Partridge Publishing India, 2020.

Mafi, Maryam and Kolpin, Azima Melita. *Rumi's Little Book of the Heart*. United States: Hampton Roads, 2016.

Margery, Megan. "And Then it Happens. . . One Day You Wake Up And You're In This Place," *The Mind Journal* (website), Accessed May 19, 2021, https:// themindsjournal.com/and-then-it-happens-one-day- you-wake-up-and-youre-in-this-place/.

Millman, Dan. *Way of the Peaceful Warrior: A Book That Changes Lives*. N.p.: Peaceful Warrior ePublishing, 2000.

Millodot: Dictionary of Optometry and Visual Science, 7th edition. S.v. "photopsia." Retrieved May 19 2021 from https://medical-dictionary.thefreedictionary.com/ photopsia.

Oates, Peta Gayle. *Every Woman Devotional: The Journey to Becoming a Woman of Purpose*. Jamaica: AuthorHouse, 2014.

Quote Investigator. "Keep Your Face Always Towards the Sunshine, and the Shadows Will Fall Behind You," Updated March 5, 2009, Accessed May 13, 2021, https://quoteinvestigator.com/2019/03/05/sunshine/#note-21912-21.

———. "Writing Is Easy; You Just Open a Vein and Bleed." Updated September 14, 2011. Retrieved on May 19, 2021 from https://quoteinvestigator.com/2011/09/14/writing-bleed/.

Rumi, Jalal al-Din. *The Mesnevi: Trübner's oriental series*, trans. James W. Redhouse, Release Date March 31, 2020: 667–669, https://www.gutenberg.org/files/61724/61724-h/61724-h.htm.

Stiefel, Dorothy H. *Retinitis Pigmentosa: Dealing with the Threat of Loss*. United States: Business of Living Publications, 1988.

Thomas Nelson, Inc. *The Holy Bible: Revised Standard Version*. New York: Thomas Nelson, Inc., 1972.

Underwood, Corinna. "Electroretinography." Healthline. com. Updated April 20, 2020. Accessed May 19, 2021 from https://www.healthline.com/health/electroretinography.

WayBack Machine (website) and AiSquared (company website). "Company History." Updated April 7, 2010. Accessed May 19, 2021. https://web.archive.org/web/20100407090547/http://www.aisquared.com/about_us/categories/category/company_history.

Zientara, Peggy. "DECtalk lets micros read messages over phones." *InfoWorld* 6, nos.2-3 (January 9-16, 1984). Accessed May 19, 2021. https://books.google.com/.

CPSIA information can be obtained
at www.ICGtesting.com
Printed in the USA
LVHW080202211121
703923LV00004B/10